I have known the author for over thirty years and her late husband for nearly as many. This journal is truly a reflection of all the incredible conversations Mandy and I have had since the passing of Max…. In the end, she will have to admit her husband is still hanging around. It's like Topper in real life. *Tom Panholzer, Author/Historian*

Death Is Not "The End" resonates with all that is true! After the death of Mandy's husband, Max, she started to have many spiritual experiences very similar to the spiritual experiences I encountered after the death of my father, Ralph Neil. For example, Mandy became aware of her husband's loving sentiments through the song "You've Got a Friend" by Carole King. These awesome lyrics (obtained by permission) are at the end of Mandy's first chapter. I too received the same type of message from my dad, which I share in my newly published book, **Secrets Of My Soul**. During one of my father's visits, he said to me, "Dad is going now. Always remember, just call out to me and I will hear you and come. I will be back later. Bye for now, my doll." *Olive Neil Noseworthy, Psychic Medium, Author of* **Secrets Of My Soul**

I know that Mandy's work will benefit so many others who doubt the spirit world. After meeting her and knowing how very genuine she is, it is a joy to see her work come to fruition. She shares her story from the heart. *Blessings, Teresa Brown, Psychic Medium, Author of* **Discovering The Power Of Ceremony: How Ceremony Can Change Your Life**

Psychologist Dean Radin comments on the analysis of a book that "flew" off Mandy's bookcase after Max died: a t score of over 800 has a p value that is so close to zero that it is not calculable. E.g., a z score (standard normal deviate) of 30 is associated with $p = 10e\text{-}198$, so the results of your test are much, much smaller than 5 in 10,000. More likely greater than 1 in a trillion trillion trillion trillion ... etc. i.e., this wasn't chance. Something threw that book. *Dean Radin, PhD, Senior Scientist, Institute of Noetic Sciences, Author of* **The Conscious Universe, Entangled Minds,** *and* **Supernormal: Science, Yoga, and the Evidence for Extraordinary Psychic Abilities**

Rich and utterly poignant. Mandy's real life encounters with her Beloved Max have touched the depths and far reaching corners of my soul. In her precious sharing of these most intimate and at times humorous encounters with the 'afterlife', Mandy offers us all a doorway into the infinite nature of true love. My heart stirs and sings after reading each magical page. I feel Mandy's tender, caring heart in each word. I have a delightful recognition and a new found friendship with her Max! His love for her is palpable and has given me so much peace and faith in Spirit and Life after Death. Thank you Mandy and Max! *Sincerely, Mahalia Michael, Author of* **Sensual YOU** *and Creator of ALLUMINA Dance Alchemy; www.lummunocity.com*

DEATH IS NOT "THE END"

One Agnostic's Journey
on the Bumpy Road to Belief

Ψ

MANDY BERLIN

abbott press

Abbott Press books may be ordered through booksellers or by contacting:

Abbott Press
1663 Liberty Drive
Bloomington, IN 47403
www.abbottpress.com
Phone: 1-866-697-5310

ISBN: 978-1-4582-1710-3 (sc)
ISBN: 978-1-4582-1709-7 (hc)
ISBN: 978-1-4582-1708-0 (e)

Library of Congress Control Number: 2014918655

Print information available on the last page.

Abbott Press rev. date: 05/06/2015

CONTENTS

Acknowledgments ix

Dedication and Summary xi

Copyright Acknowledgments xii

Introduction xix

Preface xxix

Foreword...xxxi

PART I. THE HOPE

Journal Entry 1 - The Night Max Left 3

Journal Entry 2 - Christmas Eve Thunderstorm 9

Journal Entry 3 - Fritz and Baby Steps 11

Journal Entry 4 - Visitation On New Year's Day 14

Journal Entry 5 - Dead Butterfly in Max's Truck 29

Journal Entry 6 - Apparition and the Movie *Ghost* 39

Journal Entry 7 - My Dream and *The Evolution Angel*..................44

Journal Entry 8 - Another Amoeba Formation 48

Journal Entry 9 - Commotion in the Kitchen............................49

Journal Entry 10 - The Toaster Trick 51

Journal Entry 11 - More Deaths in the Family 53

Journal Entry 12 - Max Curls Up with Me 56

Journal Entry 13 - Max's Last Day and Ring Movement.................59

Journal Entry 14 - Max Appears to Tessie..................................71

Journal Entry 15 - Max's Friend Passes On 74

Journal Entry 16 - Candy for the Oncology Staff...........................76

Journal Entry 17 - Valentines for Max - Lunch with Mel 78

Journal Entry 18 - Prayer to Hear Max Again 81

Journal Entry 19 - My Prayer is Answered................................82

Journal Entry 20 - The Eye and the Untangled Necklace..............87

Journal Entry 21 - An Unexpected Gift..................................89

PART II. A LIFE FOREVER CHANGED

Journal Entry 22 - Max's Notes and an Extraordinary Find 92

Journal Entry 23 - The Death of Another Loved One 98

Journal Entry 24 - Max's Fifty-first Birthday.............................100

Journal Entry 25 - No More Tangles 101

Journal Entry 26 - A Spirit Guide Speaks................................104

Journal Entry 27 - Max's Churning Computer...........................106

Journal Entry 28 - Book Flies Off the Shelf.............................109

Journal Entry 29 - A Friend and Neighbor Dies Unexpectedly......124

Journal Entry 30 - Holiday Weekend in Las Vegas......................126

Journal Entry 31 - Max and The Ethereal Eye...........................136

Journal Entry 32 - Sudden Death of My Girlfriend's Husband......138

Journal Entry 33 - Meditation – Charlemagne and Max 142

Journal Entry 34 - Independence Day and the Theory of
Everything.....................................148

Journal Entry 35 - The Hair Dryer Affair 165

Journal Entry 36 - Max's Guardian Suffers a Stroke.....................169

Journal Entry 37 - The Crazy Treadmill 170

Journal Entry 38 - Survivor Max...174

Journal Entry 39 - The Director Blows....................................176

Journal Entry 40 - Solid State..177

Journal Entry 41 - Awe-Inspiring Winged Creature......................178

Journal Entry 42 - Max the Astronaut...180

Journal Entry 43 - Baffling Warning at the Gym..........................181

Journal Entry 44 - Elisabeth Kübler-Ross Passes On 183

Journal Entry 45 - Toe Mishap On a Sunny Day..........................184

PART III. THE KNOWING

Journal Entry 46 - A Shining Piece of Silver................................187

Journal Entry 47 - Char in London...195

Journal Entry 48 - Oxford and the Hedgehog.............................199

Journal Entry 49 - The Horses and On to Surrey.........................201

Journal Entry 50 - Wellington School and The Willows...............205

Journal Entry 51 - Max's School Chum.......................................208

Journal Entry 52 - The Taillights Are On.....................................221

Journal Entry 53 - Earring and Post-Holder Travel into Ear.........224

Journal Entry 54 - Blown Down Bulb...227

Journal Entry 55 - Stan's Taillights Are On 228

Journal Entry 56 - Electric Light Show..229

Journal Entry 57 - Vision of Max 231

Journal Entry 58 - Blinking Ethereal Eye 234

Journal Entry 59 - Third Eye Definitions and Commentary 239

Journal Entry 60 - Max's Healing Spirit......................................241

Journal Entry 61 - "B" is for Bouquet on Veteran's Day................246

Journal Entry 62 - That Buzzing Sound and Boppin' Sheep.........247

Journal Entry 63 - Inspiring Words from Max 249

Journal Entry 64 - Toady and the Muppets 251

Journal Entry 65 - Nativity Scene by the Gift Shop.....................254

Journal Entry 66 - Thought Forms and Automatic Writing 257

Journal Entry 67 - The Metaman Tune...262

Journal Entry 68 - The Day Before Pearl Harbor Day...................265

Journal Entry 69 - Max Wakes Up!...267

Journal Entry 70 - Church and *The Man with Two Brains*.............269

Journal Entry 71 - The Silver Star and Other

                Christmas Mysteries...272

Epilogue...281

About the Author...285

Index...287

ACKNOWLEDGMENTS

For their scientific and technical reviews of key journal entries, I would sincerely like to thank Eric Culberson, BS; Steve Elliott, PhD; Ashley Graybeal, BS; Tom Panholzer, MA, journalist, editor & author of books on place names; Dean Radin, PhD, senior scientist with Institute of Noetic Sciences, and author of *The Conscious Universe, Entangled Minds,* and *Supernormal: Science, Yoga, and the Evidence for Extraordinary Psychic Abilities.*

Special thoughts of appreciation go out to Tracy Sieglaff, MA, for the editing of my book. For their general or substantive reviews of journal entries, I also appreciate the suggestions made by Judith (Judy) Arthur, now deceased; Grace Riordan Caporale; Nikki Stamatin Dodson; Nancy Krauter; Mahalia Michael, author of *Sensual You*; Olive Neil Noseworthy, Psychic Medium; Tom Panholzer; Alan and Sheila Rogers; Theresa Roth; SAM at www.lightworkerslog.com; Denise R. VanZante-Tift, MA, LSW; Charlotte Young, BSc; and Paula Young.

For their technical commentary, technical video support, or blog reviews, I would like to thank Judith (Judy) Arthur; Teresa Brown, Intuitive/Medium & Artist; Roxanne DeWinter; Robert Evans and Matt Thomas of The Messenger Studio; Carlos Gallardo; Robert Madej; Amy Richmond; and D.R. Wilke of Wide Range Productions.

For their computer IT or website/blog support, I would like to thank Paula (Cami) Cowan, Expert IT Solutions; John Krawczyk of SEO Management Consultants; and Jason Neff.

For their book cover suggestions, I appreciate the clever ideas of Paula (Cami) Cowan, Artist Tyler Lowe, and Artist Lynn Svetic, RN, now deceased.

For the beautiful piece on the cover of my book, I am indebted to Artist Tawny Gamboa, BA. For the image on the last page and on the back of the book, I am so appreciative of the fine artwork of Artist Instructor Amy Whitehouse, BA, MA.

For my Bio picture, I am grateful for the fine photographic vision of Edward Buchmann of Edification Studios. For the lovely photograph of my mounted Sulphur butterfly (displayed on the spine of this book and in Journal Entry 5), I am delighted with the work of Cami Cowan.

For their encouragement and support of my book endeavors, I am thankful for Grace Riordan Caporale; Choneye; Kay Johnson; Sunny Dawn Johnston, Psychic Medium; Nancy Krauter; Nancy Madison; Patricia Madison; Elaine McCauslin; Sharon Ozer, Ph.D.; James Arthur Ray, author and motivational speaker; and Kris Robinson.

For their clerical and technical office support, I am grateful for all the work, extra hours, and reliable assistance of Kristen N. Adams, LPN; Cami Cowan, AA; Virginia (Simone) Donaghey; Jozet Foster, Accounting Assistant; Ashley Graybeal; Adrianna Gutierrez; Glenda Ignacio; Maria Jimenez; Lorraine Lowry; Barbara Shaharier; Tracy Sieglaff; Barbara Snyder; and Denise R. VanZante-Tift.

This book would not be possible without you. ~MB

Dedicated to My Earthly Angel, Grace

The events chronicled in **Death Is Not "The End"** are true. All of the incidents, accidents, and supernatural phenomena described herein happened. I have endeavored to describe the unbelievable events I experienced in the year 2004. Additionally, I am honored to announce that several of our friends and loved ones released their amazingly connected stories to me, for inclusion in this book.

I have made every effort possible to shed light on the awesome happenings. I take full credit and full responsibility for the interpretations set forth in my journal. However, alternative explanations abound. I encourage you to formulate your own interpretations as well. It is interesting to note the sheer number of phenomenological events we encountered in the course of one year. Simply coincidences? Let the reader be the judge.

In the last analysis, perhaps what I seek most is to impart a sense of Hope – just as Hope arrived at my door on January 1, 2004.

~**Mandy Berlin**

COPYRIGHT ACKNOWLEDGMENTS

Song Lyric Reprint Permissions*

You've Got A Friend
Words and Music by Carole King
(c) 1971 (Renewed 1999) COLGEMS-EMI MUSIC INC.
All Rights Reserved International Copyright Secured Used by Permission
Reprinted with Permission of Hal Leonard Corporation

Paralyzer
Music and Lyrics by SCOTT ANDERSON, SEAN ANDERSON, RICH BEDDOE, JAMES BLACK and RICK JACKETT
© 2007 BMG RIGHTS MANAGEMENT (IRELAND) LTD. (IMRO) and FINGER ELEVEN PUBLISHING (ASCAP).
All Rights Administered by CHRYSALIS ONE MUSIC (ASCAP).
All Rights Reserved.
Used by Permission of ALFRED MUSIC.

The Voice
Written by Justin Hayward.
Published by Nightswood Limited.
Sub-Published by Fintage Publishing B.V.

Unchained Melody
by Hy Zaret & Alex North
© 1955 (renewed) North Ohana Publishing (ASCAP) and HZUM Publishing (ASCAP) c/o Unchained Melody Publishing, LLC
All Rights Reserved. Used By Permission.

(continuted on next page)

Forever (continued)

Used by Permission of I Make Dumb Music, Dave Buckner

Words and Music by Simon Katz and Samuel Martin

My Prayer
Music by Georges Boulanger
Lyric and Musical Adaptation by Jimmy Kennedy

I Got a Name
Words by NORMAN GIMBEL, Music by CHARLES FOX

Love Letters
Written by: Edward Heyman & Victor Young

My Father's Eyes
Composed by Eric Clapton

Mr. Tambourine Man
Performed by Bob Dylan
Bringing It All Back Home.

Is it a Crime

Written by: Hellen Adu, Andrew Hale & Stuart Matthewman
© 1985 Angel Music Ltd. All rights on behalf of Angel Music Ltd. Administered by Sony/ATV Music Publishing LLC, 8 Music Square West, Nashville, TN 37203. All rights reserved. Used by permission.

TWILIGHT TIME

Lyric by Buck Ram; Music by Morty Nevins and Al Nevins
TRO - © Copyright 1944 (Renewed) Devon Music, Inc., New York, NY
International Copyright Secured Made in U.S.A.
All Rights Reserved including Public Performance for Profit
Used by Permission

All Rights Reserved.
Used by Permission of Acorn Publishing.

Hello It's Me

Words and Music by Todd Rundgren
© 1968, 1969 (Renewed 1996, 1997) SCREEN GEMS-EMI MUSIC INC.
All Rights Reserved International Copyright Secured Used by Permission
Reprinted with Permission of Hal Leonard Corporation

Every Breath You Take

Music and Lyrics by Sting
© 1983 G.M. Sumner
Administered by EMI MUSIC PUBLISHING LIMITED
All Rights Reserved International Copyright Secured Used by Permission
Reprinted with Permission of Hal Leonard Corporation

Your Wildest Dreams

Written by Justin Hayward
Published by Nightswood Limited
Sub-Published by Fintage Publishing B.V.

Twilight

Words and Music by Jeff Lynne
© 1981 EMI APRIL MUSIC INC.
All Rights Reserved International Copyright Secured Used by Permission
Reprinted with Permission of Hal Leonard Corporation

Other Permissions

INTRODUCTION

Death Is Not "The End": One Agnostic's Journey on the Bumpy Road to Belief is a journal of real supernatural events. Three hours before the Christmas Eve of 2003, the soul of Max Blau departed from a hospice in Tempe, Arizona. Yet, in Oxford, England Christmas Eve had already arrived. There in Max's former home sat his loved ones, grief-stricken upon hearing he had died on their most loved and celebrated holiday. Then just hours after Max's purported departure, incredible things began to happen in Oxford, and in Arizona as well.

Despite the terrible sadness caused by the untimely death of Max, my husband and dearest friend in all the world, I soon realized that things were not as they seemed. During Christmas week alone, I began to receive telephone calls from loved ones and friends dear to us. Oddly, some of the callers sounded happy, if not downright joyful just after Max had left us! In fact, his sisters and a few of his close friends called to tell me their uncanny stories. From the outset, these tales had a strange effect on me. You see, I was agnostic back then. I had no beliefs one way or another. Nevertheless, after hearing these strange details, I decided to do what I did best – sit at my coffee table and take notes.

After obtaining an advanced degree, I worked for twenty-five years as a statistician in education, health care and government, remaining, as ever, a curious person. So when these incredible events began to take place, I knew I would have to get the details down on paper if I ever wanted to do a little investigating of my own. Then later, to validate these written accounts, I sent reports to those who had kindly taken the time to tell me their stories. If there were any truth to these rare claims, my notes would have to be corroborated, and the required corrections made.

Then on New Year's Day, two days after Max's burial, I began to have odd experiences of my own. In fact, I soon became a party to some mind-boggling happenings in places like my home, restaurants, cafés, gardens, and even during my first trip to England! As these unbelievable events hit me, I attempted to sit still long enough to type up the stories. Then before long, I had created a computer document for every event that I had logged and saved in a calendar. Despite the bizarre goings-on, I managed to keep track of most events, including the dates and times of day. My background in psychology and years of recording research data had certainly come in handy. Nevertheless, as you will see, my journal is not written in clinical form. It is mainly written in story form.

In **Death Is Not "The End"** the supernatural phenomena – both explained and unexplained – are called *events*. My story begins with the mysterious events of December 23, 2003. It ends with the eye-opening revelation I experienced on December 23, 2004, the first anniversary of Max's death.

Through research conducted following the fifty-odd incidents and encounters (and odd they were), I classified the events into a number of unique categories:

> the shifting and displacement of physical objects in and around rooms; apparitions and other spirit encounters; synchronicities and extreme coincidences; automatic writing; numinous dreams; the movement of an undated coin; intelligent haunts; residual haunts;

uncanny telephone activities; electrical demonstrations, malfunctions and breakdowns; object alteration; third eye phenomena; spirit communications received through clairvoyance, clairaudience and clairsentience; soul travel; spirit guide communications; telepathy; validation of rare events based on the frequency of repetition of the events; validation of rare events based on statistical hypothesis-testing; and the discovery of a corroborating written record found after the occurrence of a rare event.

In the Post Script sections following a number of the stories, I examined the events in detail and review subject matter related to the event. The post scripts, as discussed below, are reserved primarily for post-event research and commentary. Though a number of happenings have been left unexplained, clarification is offered and interpretations are made whenever feasible.

The timeframe of *Death Is Not "The End"* is December 23, 2003 through December 23, 2004. Regardless, these supernatural, mystical and synchronistic happenings went far beyond the boundaries of one journal year, changing my life completely. Then because of the rare and challenging life changes I continued to experience over a subsequent eight-year period, I continued journaling. After all, the supernatural happenings did not end simply because one journal year had ended. Not by any means! Consequently, I continued to chronicle both the fathomable and the unfathomable for years to come. Nevertheless, my focus shifted because of a notable increase in synchronistic events, intuitive perceptions, signs, and exceptional communications.

As my intuitive side came to the fore, I sought to develop and further understand my newfound abilities under the guidance of Sunny Dawn Johnston of Sunlight Alliance. In 2006, while watching a news program on television, I learned of Ms. Johnston's amazing intuitive abilities and angel work at The Sunlight Alliance Healing Center in Glendale, Arizona. I called her office immediately and began to take her classes on: Mediumship, the Angels and Archangels, and the Law of Attraction, to name just a few.

Then in the summer of 2007, I began to suffer from an infirmity that affected my constitution – my whole being. This long-term illness also involved my sight – that is, my physical vision, rather than my intuitive vision. Suddenly, I could not see the long columns of numbers I worked with daily. However, this was my job! Often the pages were blurred or weaving back and forth. Many weeks later, after trying so hard, I was forced to leave my work of twenty-two years as a consulting statistician. This was the only kind of work I had been formally trained to do. It was a scary time for me as I joined the ranks of the unemployed. How would I – how could I – continue to make a living?

Still, I could write and type with eyes unfocused or even closed, so I continued journaling, whenever I was physically able to do so. This task did not require reading or reviewing columns of numbers. Regardless, my lengthy journal still had to be rewritten and edited before it could be published!

Three and a half years and fifty-five doctors later, I finally found a doctor who properly diagnosed my illness. This wonderful naturopath treated me (and is still treating me) for endocrine disease: thyroid disease and hypoadrenalism, the stress disease. As a result of my doctor's amazing endocrine program and all the awe-inspiring happenings I have experienced since 2003, I see now that I have truly been blessed – with perseverance, renewed energy, and a brand new perspective on life. Then too, because I have kept a detailed log for many years, my notes are ready to be formalized beyond my first journal. I look forward to the prospects with joy and anticipation!

Since my beloved Max went to the light, our bizarre, poignant and often comical communications have been rare. Nevertheless, he still visits our earthly plane of existence from time to time, most notably on special occasions. You see, Max loves parties, get-togethers and helping people of all kinds. What an incredible communicator he was and always will be!

In addition, I have heard from other visitors as well: my dearly deceased father, my paternal grandparents, my step-father who later passed at the age of ninety-five, angels, spirit guides, and family members of friends and classmates. Many of these beautiful encounters have happened subsequent to the writing of this journal, to be revealed in a future book. Nevertheless, some of these exchanges took place in 2004 when I was first introduced to my spirit guide. I am pleased to present such stories in *Death Is Not "The End"*.

Journal Entries. My journal contains seventy-one entries, beginning with the events of December 23, 2003 and ending with the incomparable happening of December 23, 2004. In this work, I delineate *over 50* awesome events, spanning a year and one day. The last day is too mind-blowing and too meaningful to be excluded from this tome. Indeed, it is the *sine qua non* of my journal!

Over fifty refers primarily to recurring events. You see, other events occurred in 2004 that were left undocumented. That is, I did not take the time to document each *type* of event more than once. If the same event happened several times, I told the story just once. The most repetitive events I experienced were these: an uncanny incident in "The Toaster Trick"; Max curling up on the couch with me; an electrical episode noted in "The Hair Dryer Affair"; and Max's spirit visitation in a church garden. Though I described the toaster trick soon after it happened, this incident occurred approximately two or three times a week for many weeks in 2004, and on into 2005. Therefore, I witnessed the phenomenal toaster trick at least twenty times – a conservative estimate.

More than fifty of the seventy-one journal entries are based on unusual, unnatural and meaningful events, such as spirit messages from Max, coincidental electrical events, and several other untimely deaths that occurred soon after Max passed away. In this sense, my journal is episodic in nature, unlike a diary of daily activities, thoughts, and concerns. The general narrative and the accounts of our loved ones were written in the **past tense**. In contrast, I wrote what I call the "cameos," i.e., my stories and observations concerning the extraordinary happenings, in the **present tense** in an effort to glue the reader to the scene.

Event Recording. Due to a meticulous bent brought on by working with numbers, I have included dates and times of day at the top of each entry. In this manner, associations and interpretations can be drawn for a better understanding of an event. Because the moon has an effect on nature, phases of the moon are included as well. At the start, I had not yet made the decision to record every observation or to keep track of dates. Later, as I began to keep more exacting records, I expressed my concerns over the neglect of a few particulars. In these cases, an estimated date/time is provided, such as Wednesday Afternoon or 1/xx/04.

The phenomenological data were initially logged as events, then told in story form. However, some information was subsequently removed. For example, if I witnessed an event that I was later unable to recall in any detail, I then excluded the event from my journal. Likewise, I excluded two separate accounts received in early 2004 from two of Max's dear friends, a man and a woman. Both are friends of mine as well. Since then, I had been unable to reach either of the two for corroboration. So I decided it would be best to remove the stories which they had initially described to me over the phone. However, I can say with confidence that the first event happened to the man while he was walking in the woods, approximately a week after Max died. The second event concerned a phenomenon that the woman said she witnessed in my home while I was vacationing (writing) in Sedona. She had been pet-sitting and watching my house for me. The nature of the details surrounding each of these events is somewhat fuzzy. However, I do know this: both the man and the woman told me their stories with great enthusiasm. They both appeared to have been stunned by what they had seen and heard. The dear man has since moved away with no way to contact. And despite my voice messages and invitations, my friend and confidante (the woman) has not entered my home since the day she witnessed the uncanny event. Now I am unable to reach her at all. Though my friends tell me I ought not wait around, I miss her and have hopes that she will call me one day.

Despite the years gone by, I still bring a pen and a long sticky note pad with me wherever I go. As I wrote the first draft *of **Death Is Not "The End"***, I never thought, as a few friends suggested, that the recording of all that data would be too tedious a job to undertake. Quite the contrary, I felt comfortable with this idea because the happenings were either so beautiful or so wacky that I felt compelled to get my observations down on paper. Keeping track like this, meant everything would be of record, ready to read and review. This way I could tell my mother and closest friends the amazing stories without dithering. Later, I found myself fleshing out accounts on my laptop – before work, after work, on the Wednesdays of my four-day work week, and on weekends too. Because of this, I was confident I would not be relying on old memory. Before long a journal was born. Lives were forever changed, perhaps mine most of all.

Song Lyrics. These awesome events often arrived with a song – on the radio, via musak, while I was sitting in a café, or in the office where I write. *A number of the songs actually described the events as they transpired, lending a synchronistic quality to the whole experience. These songs had become part of the experience itself.* Even today, as I remember seeing Max's spirit on January 3, 2004, I still hear the song "Unchained Melody." This soulful song was an integral part of my mystical experience that day. You see, approximately five minutes <u>after</u> Max appeared on the arm of my sofa, I changed the television channel out of habit. On hearing the song, "Unchained Melody," I looked up, and there before me was the movie *Ghost*, while Max's spirit hovered above the arm of my sofa. I was stunned!

People are incredulous when they hear this story, thinking it could not possibly have happened. It sounds surreal – too good to be true, they say. Objectively I agree with them. But I am here to tell you that, to my downright amazement, it happened. And in all humility, it happened to me. My ghost story happened just as I told it. Why would I delete this account from my journal, simply because it is too far-fetched for people to believe? I am here to convey to the best of my ability my story – *the whole story* – about the amazing phenomena experienced by our friends, loved ones, and me. And I am so happy to be telling it!

Sound became an integral part of my journal, and my journey. Because of the song lyrics and sounds that were linked to key incidents, as in the amazing ghost encounter, these lyrics give the reader a more complete picture of the event. S/he can then visualize and perhaps even feel or hear the experience from the perspective of the one who witnessed it. Such meaningful lyrics and melodies, have a way of adding dimension to my written stories. Where legally permitted, one to four lines of song lyrics have been included in my journal entries. Otherwise, the song titles alone have been included, along with the appropriate footnotes. All required permission standards have been followed, with respect to the use of song lyrics and the proper referencing of all songs in the book.

Post Scripts. The post script sections of my journal fill an important need. Post scripts provide a way of separating the events from issues concerning the events. In this manner, no true story is ever changed or manipulated beyond the necessary revisions for clarity, grammar, punctuation, style and the like.

While refining the book, I expanded on the stories by adding post scripts where there was a need for definitions, further research, and/or commentary concerning an event. Therefore, post scripts are reserved primarily for:

- My questions or comments concerning an event
- Definitions or descriptions of phenomena related to an event
- Key information from theories of consciousness
- Related information from quantum theory: for example, where an event may connect with, or have roots in, a scientific model (such as string theory, m-theory, or parallel universes)
- New material related to the story or linked concepts, as in the "Law of Attraction"
- Logical analysis of an event
- Statistical analysis of an event, where possible
- Interpretation of an event

In addition to the post scripts, Journal Entry 34 contains information on quantum physics and The Theory of Everything as related to uncommon phenomena. Journal Entry 59 sheds light on the third eye.

I do not pretend to have all the answers. In that sense, I have not attempted to analyze or interpret every event documented in this book. Some stories are brief and self-explanatory in terms of the typical conjectures put forth to make sense of the phenomena. Although I have attempted to describe the happenings in detail, some events simply defy description and rational explanation. Though I have provided post scripts after certain journal entries and interpretations, I encourage you to take a stab at it. Get together with friends and read the stories. Analyze and interpret the amazing happenings to your satisfaction. This is half the fun and joy of the book. The other half is the stories themselves.

Please note: Due to the sensitive nature of the subject and as a protective measure, most of the names have been changed in my journal. Nevertheless, the real names of some people have been kept with their expressed permission. I have retained my pen name and the nom de plume of my deceased spouse, Max Blau, as well. Every person, place and event documented herein is real. Yet despite my best efforts to capture in writing the quintessence of a supernatural happening, certain events have left me baffled, no less in the year of this publication.

I continue to keep records of rare and unusual events. Yet there is more than enough to tell, based solely on the breathtaking year that followed the death of my beloved Max. I humbly present my story to you, dear reader: ***Death Is Not "The End": One Agnostic's Journey on the Bumpy Road to Belief!***

~Mandy Berlin
Chandler, Arizona

PREFACE

People claim to have unique experiences all the time, yet they share common elements of experience with others. Consequently, they form clubs and associations, sharing knowledge, information, fun and friendship. Some experiences are exclusive to the individual, especially at given points in time. For example, there is just one President of the United States. No other person in the world today is having his presidential experience. Now take a look at our great universe. Witness the awesome phenomena that cosmologists, quantum physicists and other scientists are just now discovering. Sir Isaac Newton would roll over in his grave!

Because certain people have never witnessed a phenomenon does not mean the phenomenon does not exist. Look at all the wonderfully weird species of fish that oceanographers have discovered in the past decade. No one had ever seen these species before, yet they existed. Indeed, they have been thriving in all their glory at the bottom of the ocean.

Now apply these concepts to certain rare phenomena, generally unseen, which many refuse to believe exist. These phenomena are dubbed "rare" simply because a large number of people have never seen them. This does not mean that the phenomena, like the weird fish, do not exist or that a rare event never occurred. Many mind-boggling wonders, miracles and manifestations happen all the time. In fact, rare phenomena are being documented all over the world. Take a look around. Keep an open mind. Go beyond your comfort zone. The possibilities are endless!

~Mandy Berlin

FOREWORD

Beyond the puzzle-filled world of the mainstream sciences, a new concept of the universe is emerging. The established concept is transcended; in its place comes the in-formed universe, rooted in the rediscovery of ancient tradition's Akashic Field (also called the A-field) as the vacuum-based holofield....

Thanks to information conserved and conveyed by the A-field, the universe is of mind-boggling coherence. All that happens in one place happens also in other places; all that happened at one time happens also at all times after that. Nothing is local, limited to where and when it is happening. All things are global, indeed cosmic, for all things are connected, and the memory of all things extends to all places and to all times.

~ Dr. Ervin Laszlo

Part I

THE HOPE

Tuesday, 12/23/2003
Tempe, Arizona
(Wednesday, 12/24/2003
Oxford, England)

The Night Max Left

"Knockin' on Heaven's Door" [1]

Max left our world three hours before the Christmas Eve of 2003, at nine p.m. sharp. In life, my Max had never been late for any important occasion. Death was no different. Some say at fifty years of age, he died too young. Others say he lived a full life. As I see it, young or old, Max moved on too soon.

I wasn't just devastated - I had lost the love of my life. For over sixteen years, Max and I had shared everything – and I mean everything – the good, the bad and the ugly. Thankfully, we had shared many beautiful and wondrous moments together before learning that a slow-growing cancer had infested his body. Max's doctors said the tumors had been growing for at least a year, perhaps two. Then they shook their heads and said, "There is nothing we can do."

The last seven months of Max's life were *the ugly*. Nevertheless, Max and I always said, where there is life there is hope, and we wrote poetry to help us live with adversity. When all possible measures had been exhausted, they moved my Max to hospice. Alas, I was finally forced to help him let go.

---

[1] Dylan, Bob. "Knockin' on Heaven's Door." *Pat Garrett and Billy the Kid Soundtrack.* Columbia. 1973. LP.

When Max died, I knew (like I was always afraid I'd know) that it was not just the company of a man I'd miss. It was Max.

Max, the funny one, who'd get down on his knees and tease me, and hurry me along while I put on my makeup… I seldom kept a straight face when he was around. Max, the serious one who worked weekends, even into the wee hours of the morning… I brought him food and stayed with him, sometimes all night. Max, the brilliant man who read all manner of books, even my own (dry) statistics manuals. He said he wanted to know more about my work. Max, the grumbling one (I grumbled as well) as we cleaned up the yard in one hundred degree heat. Max, the strong-willed one who, as a child, pedaled his tricycle fiercely across the Sahara Desert so he could spend the day with his father at the airport where he worked. Max, the caring man, who listened to strangers' stories and talked to them all night, instilling in them a sense of hope. Max, the careless one, who almost lost an eye because he was trying to get an important job done. Max, who loved to gaze at the moon and show me all the constellations… the mind-blowing nights we watched the bejeweled comet in the sky!

How could I not love him forever?

۩ ۩ ۩

After my darling died, I compiled a book of our poems, pictures, and stories. It is a tribute to Max and to all cancer victims and their loved ones – a scrapbook entitled *For the Time Being* (AuthorHouse, 2007).

Nevertheless, the story I am about to tell you is not so much about my sadness as it is about Max and my joy. Perhaps you might think, if she lost her spouse, how could she possibly talk about her joy, especially if she really loved this person? Well, I must say that along with the shock and grief that came with the loss of my beloved husband and friend, something extraordinary arrived at my door; it was something I never expected and will certainly never forget, not even in a lifetime! When these incredible things began to happen, I was agnostic. For over thirty years, I had no beliefs – in God, or angels, or in life after death.

❧ ❧ ❧

When I was a child I had some beliefs – the beliefs of my parents. You see, I attended Catholic school in a lovely little Midwestern town called Cuyahoga Falls. I wore my beanie and school uniform and went to church every day, as dictated by the nuns. In fact, I had become quite good at parroting prayers and verses from my missalette.

My grandmother thought I was a saint, but what did she know?

Maybe I was sedate in high school; I was certainly too shy to talk to boys. They must have thought I was rather bookish. Yet, no more than a week after attending classes at Kent State University, my life began to change. See, when I dropped off my books and took off my glasses, attractive young men began showing up at my door – a singular experience for any young woman, especially me.

Even so, I didn't comprehend much of anything about myself or life, until my first semester at the university. Soon I was steeped in studies and loving every minute of it. We had been focusing on the scientific method. I really liked that method: designing studies, observing and recording data (the hard evidence), and performing statistical analyses. We even learned how to transform data into something called information. It was great!

Before long, I began to question everything in existence, including my mother's concept of a distant place called heaven. I certainly had no hard data for that. In fact, I was becoming a real skeptic. And so my childhood fantasies of heaven and a divine maker seemed to evaporate before you could say "Christmas break."

Then I left Ohio for sunnier parts unknown. After working and going to school part-time for years, I received my bachelor of science degree in 1981 from Arizona State University. However, being the avid student, I promptly signed up for six years of doctoral studies in educational psychology, and I became a research scientist, a statistical consultant by trade. After all, what better way to conduct studies and analyze all that hard data my professors were always talking about?

On weekends, I went out with friends. Soon I would meet my British sweetheart at a bar in Tempe, Arizona. In that hot, smoke-filled room, I learned something rare: chivalry is not really dead. You see, Max actually offered me his chair – a defining moment in time. And after a six-year courtship full of fun and travel, we married in May of 1992. Max studied feverishly and became a life safety systems designer, while I continued to do the consulting work I loved. We both worked hard, sometimes six or seven days a week. In spite of it all, whenever we had a three-day weekend, Max would say, "Hey, pup, let's get outta Dodge!"

So we packed our bags and backpacks and tooled our way up some scenic route to Prescott, or Sedona, or the Mogollon Rim. Over the next ten years, we traveled throughout the western region of our great country. At night, we camped out under the stars. In the morning, we drank coffee from tin cups by clear running streams. How could I forget that old cotton safari hat he wore with "Jambo!" printed on the front, in big bold letters. So many happy times, I cherish them all, yet I see now that the most wondrous thing we had was love.

In those months of grief, anger, and guilt (because Max was dead and I was not), things began to happen that set me to wondering about life and death. These uncanny happenstances simply did not fit into my agnostic world. Nevertheless, I knew that if I ever hoped to make sense out of the unimaginable incidents we were beginning to experience, I would have to stick with the scientific method – to observe and record all the data.

❧ ❧ ❧

Just after Max died, two of his sisters began to have unusual experiences. Though I was feeling broken to have lost my husband and dearest friend, their phone calls happened to catch my attention. In fact, their stories sounded just plain strange. So I gathered up all the strength I could muster and began to take notes over the phone. *If nothing else,* I thought, *perhaps this exercise will take my mind off the daunting lack of Max. I must at least try!*

So I sighed and picked up my pen, though I certainly did not comprehend one wit of the goings-on. Little did I know, my notes would form the beginnings of a meticulous log of supernatural events.

Paulette was the first to call from her home in Sonoita, Arizona. She said Max had appeared to her in a dream at about eleven p.m., approximately two hours after he had passed away. Despite her sadness on hearing the terrible news of her brother's death, she sounded almost comfortable and strangely accepting of it. *How odd,* I thought. But I didn't want to jump to any conclusions, so I just listened.

In Paulette's lifelike dream, Max had been joking around with her. "Hey, I feel fantastic, Paulette, more alive now than ever!" She said they'd been "tipping a few," watching the late shows together. I was shocked. How could they have been tipping a few? Max was dead. Along with my surprise, I felt put off. *If Paulette's dream contains any ounce of reality,* I thought, *am I so happy to hear that Max – in all his aliveness – is having a grand time without me?*

I shook my head. *Oh, it's just a dream.* Regardless, I continued to jot things down.

Now, after all the mind-bending events I have witnessed since Christmas week of 2003, I look back in joy and amazement over

Paulette's vivid dream. As she ended the story, she cried, "Mandy, my dream seemed so real! Imagine my confusion and disappointment when I woke up to find Max gone. How could that be?" For Paulette, this was an encounter of some sort, which resulted in a sense of disorientation and disillusionment once she truly understood that Max had died.

But was he forever gone?

You see, Paulette's dream was just the beginning.

A few days later, Max's middle sister, Char, called from Oxford, England. She proceeded to tell me about an incredible march, of sorts. She had been sitting in her bathroom when, out of the blue, footprints appeared on the rug. The tracks were not of her own making, Char said, "Because, Mandy, they appeared to me one by one, while they were being made!" It was as if an unseen crusader were trampling on the rug. Char was appalled, yet amazed, watching in disbelief as the mind-boggling footprints materialized right in front of her!

Soon after Char's encounter with the uncanny, the family phoned to inform her of the sad day. They said her beloved brother had passed at nine p.m. Mountain Time in the hospice in Tempe, Arizona. Then Char realized something amazing: accounting for the time differential between England and Arizona, the mysterious footprints had materialized on her rug *not long after Max had died*. In fact, this bizarre phenomenon had taken place on the morning of December twenty-fourth, Christmas Eve in Oxford.

I can just hear Max now. "Happy Holidays, guys!" he seemed to say. *You just call out my name and you know wherever I am, I'll come running to see you again...*[2]

We played that song for him all night – the night he died.

---

[2]   King, Carole. "You've Got a Friend." *Tapestry.* A&M, 1971. LP

Wednesday, 12/24/2003
Christmas Eve
Chandler, Arizona

Christmas Eve Thunderstorm

I'm not paralyzed but I seem to be struck by you...
You'll probably move right through me...[3]

At around two o'clock in the morning, I awoke to a deafening boom as torrents of rain whacked the windows, not unlike the bombing of London. Lightning bolts lit up our living room like Grandma's colossal Christmas tree – all happening *in Arizona*, in the heat of the night, in the dead of winter – a mere five hours after Max had left our world.

Too fearful to make a run for the bedroom without him, I rolled myself into our pathetic old afghan, my makeshift security blanket. Thunder bellowed like Thor himself as another bolt blew, and another... and *yeow*, a shocking third! Cowering in a corner of the living room, I screamed like a banshee. *Maybe I'm leaving my body... no... more like my mind.* Then, without warning, a blast hit our roof, or so it seemed.

Thankfully, the house hasn't toppled. Yet, I thought. *It's just those daylight detonations besieging an overwrought mind.* Reaching this cosmic conclusion, I surfaced like a cave dweller ready to view the world. "What a strange phenomenon," I said aloud, as if this meager stab at a scientific approach might bring me some relief. It didn't. For another bolt blew and all I could do was cringe and crawl back to my corner. Fingers trembling, I managed to reclaim my ragged afghan.

---

[3]   Finger Eleven. "Paralyzer." *Them vs. You vs. Me.* Warner Bros, 2007. CD.

Glancing up at the ceiling, I cried in silence, *Oh, how I miss my Max, a man I never thought I had taken for granted.*

But somehow, I did. I must have.

No matter my sorry words, the storm showed no mercy as bongo sticks pelted the patio table. Perhaps in an act of defiance, I finally got up enough pluck to fling open the living room blinds and confront my tempest. Staring out into the mist and an all but visible backyard, at last, my sentiments softened as I remembered how much Max loved the rain. Whenever storm clouds threatened, he'd lift the garage door and call me out to catch the sights. Together, in our little haven, we'd watch nature fling its fearsome fireworks, and smell the sodden earth and the sweet, wet grass. There I felt happy, at ease in Max's company, protected in his arms. Sometimes it seemed he called me out to see the storms just so we could connect and share those beautiful moments of closeness and camaraderie. Yet, even as he and I both became a part of my cherished past – a past so new and troubling in its very finality – the thought of our thunderstorm moments somehow had the effect of allaying all my fears.

Soon the winds blew the clouds high as if heading out to chase some distant folly. At long last, I managed to amble my way back to bed – well, the sofa. Punch-drunk, I nearly sat on my tabby cat. "Oops, Tiggi, digging at that old afghan! Here, come sit next to me," I said, pressing on a pillow, soon to become her paw partner. Rolling and tumbling around a bit more, we finally found our comfy spots and settled in for the night.

I don't recall waking up again, until dawn.

JOURNAL ENTRY 3

Saturday, 12/27/2003
Chandler, Arizona

Fritz and Baby Steps

*Out on the ocean of life my love
There's so many storms we must rise above...*[4]

Relentless rays streamed through the blinds as if bent on constricting my pupils the whole day. I had planned to sleep in, but then thought, *Well, maybe I'm not so lethargic after all.* I glanced up at the carefree Van Gogh sprigs on the wall. Oddly, they reminded me of roasted beans and a superb aroma.

Before long, I was vertical and downing a rather stiff cup of coffee in the kitchen. *Mmmm... now that I'm nearly in the mood, I think I'll tote my mug out to the patio and take a look at the wreckage left from Wednesday's Wail... or was it Whale?* Despite some lingering lassitude, I find myself doing more than surveying. Cup in one hand and broom in the other, I sweep a little, sip a little.

Soon, I'm gathering palm fronds and detritus. "For posterity," I say, as I throw the debris up against the shed. All the same, I know full well I'll have to go back and bag the stuff later.

Then, out of the blue, I hear a strange scuffing noise.

Hey, what? I turn and, from the corner of a bleary eye, catch sight of a bespectacled something peering over at me, and my property.

I move in to investigate.

"Oh, Fritz, you startled me!"

---

[4]   The Moody Blues. "The Voice." *Long Distance Voyager.* Threshold, 1981. LP.

"Sorry, neighbor," he shouts. "Hey, how about that doozy of a storm?"

Walking up to the fence, I stop short and greet his hat. "Man, I've never seen anything so electrical! In Arizona, in the winter? Wow," I say, shaking my head.

Creases form around Fritz's eyes as he scrunches up his nose. "You know that was Max, don't you? No one loved the rain and storms as much as he did."

"Fritz," I say, dropping the broom, "I've been wondering what's going on."

"Lady, don't you know? He's here!" Fritz, a man in his sixties, sports a boyish grin holding nothing if not kindness and generosity. "Max did that for us. So we'd know he's okay."

Like a timely maharishi, Fritz's tranquil nature has a way of sweeping over me, like honey being poured on my head and shoulders. "Everything is okay," he said.

"Hey, thanks Fritz."

"Don't thank me, Mandy. Thank him!" he says, gazing at the trees like he sees him.

After our chat, I start to feel pretty perky. *Is it Fritz or just the coffee?*

Maybe I'm starting to recuperate. By the day, by the hour? Regardless, I know that progress seldom moves in a linear fashion as one would expect, or hope. Sometimes it takes baby steps: two steps forward, one step back.

Salvaging the rickety broom, I return to the walkway by the side of the house. *Baby steps.*

Where did that idea come from?

Oh, from the movie, What About Bob?[5] In this movie, baby steps is the title of a book written by the renowned author and psychiatrist, Dr. Marvin (played by Richard Dreyfuss). The good doctor decides to share his book and teachings with wild and wacky, Bob Wiley (actor, Bill Murray). Later, the egotistical doctor attempts to take a vacation without Bob, his devoted patient… where the fun begins. Chuckling, I recall the goofy yet philosophical way Bob taught his own psychiatrist how to behave, and in due course, how to live.

Baby steps, I sigh and shake my head. Then, in a while, I take up where I left off – clearing my path, picking up the pieces of my life.

---

[5] *What About Bob?* Dir. Frank Oz. Perf. Bill Murray and Richard Dreyfuss. Touchstone, 1991. Film.

Visitation On New Year's Day

My sorrow today reminds me of the touching song, "Afterglow"... [6]

All morning I had been lying on the sofa feeling sorry for my dear, sweet husband taken so young by the ravages of cancer. Yet, I was feeling sorry for myself as well. I knew it would be hard after Max died, but not this hard.

In spite of all that, I realized I had to stop the wallowing.

❧ ❧ ❧

If I can just get up and go to the dining room. I must at least try to do something. I don't know, maybe I'd like to go see his flag, folded so neatly by the beautiful flowers – a sea of lavender and gold amidst sprays of baby's breath.

Even the red, white and blue bunches seem to rise and salute me, front and center. I brush a pretty petal with a fingertip, but my hand begins to tremble as I draw close to his banner. I just can't contain it any longer. Bending down, I begin to sob before Max's flag as one would weep at the Wailing Wall... thoughts of his sadness, and my inability to alleviate his pain. Then at once, the sight of our friends and loved ones paying their respects before his casket. His requiem, the beautiful

---

[6] INXS. "Afterglow." *Switch*. Epic, 2005. CD.

military ceremony – all sounds and images flooding my mind in a moment remaining no less than a decade in my heart.

I know that I must let him go.

Exhaustion sets in… I'm wilting before the posies. But as I stoop and breathe, I feel my hair brushing up against his flag – and in a flash comes a single-minded sound – rising up from the back of my medulla oblongata.

I let out a shriek as a strange, yet familiar disturbance whirls about my head! "What's happening?"

Shaking, I turn toward the noise. "What?"

"What are you saying?"

Now the sound starts to fade.

Still, I know *something or someone is here.* I stop to listen, for what?

That buzzing sound again, but I just can't make it out. Gaining confidence, I shout, "Louder, I can hardly hear you!"

At once, like a blast from infinity, the words "SOCKS UP" echo off the back of my neck. "Oh God! What's this?" I'm sure that a sentence is being formed, though I am unable to decipher all the words. What I hear is, "*Blip… blip… SOCKS UP… blip….*" Though the masculine tenor is deep and close to my head, his pitch is strangely high. This is as precisely as I am able to describe it to anyone who has never experienced anything so odd.

SOCKS UP, I think, *how sibilant the sound! I know it first-hand.* The blare of it falls at the back of my head between my neck and right ear. Yet, its resonance is higher than any normal sound.

Regardless, I would know that sound anywhere. "It's Blau!"

"Max?"

❧ ❧ ❧

Even as I acknowledge the essence of my deceased husband, I ponder the thought of white noise coming from (dare I say it?) another dimension.

As a statistician of over twenty years, I know that the incredible racket I'm hearing is not white noise because that signal is random. White noise has no pattern – zero, nada. On the other hand, the commotion I'm hearing appears to be coming from an intelligent being, an entity creating a detectable pattern which emerges in the form of a sentence. And because of the unique sibilant sound of his consonants and the overall familiarity of the tone, I am certain it is Max… or his soul, *or his something or other.*

Bear with me. It is difficult to formulate the words for what has happened. You see, a revelation of this magnitude requires a whole new vocabulary on my part.

Years ago, I had read a few articles on rare and uncanny phenomena and had seen a couple of Hollywood movies about it. One time in the early nineties, Max and I went to a psychic fair just for fun. We even saw an astrologer that day. But as an agnostic scientist, I hadn't given the supernatural much thought. As one who attempts to remain objective – without becoming closed off to the incredible possibilities life engenders – I neither believed nor disbelieved in the existence of such phenomena. And despite my mother's assertions, year after year, I held no personal beliefs in life after death. Perhaps I thought we would all be sucked up into the cosmos and become one with the subatomic particles, like the song, "Dust in the Wind."[7] No consciousness, no thought, no real existence. Then Descartes' expression, "I think, therefore I am" would become, "I do not think, therefore I am not." Of course, after death, no one would be saying these words because no

---

[7] Kansas. "Dust in the Wind." *Point of Know Return.* Kirshner, 1977. LP.

one would be around to have any thoughts… just a collective cluster of particles floating around the cosmos.

Well, at least that's how I looked at life early on the morning of January 1, 2004.

.ೱ. .ೱ. .ೱ.

Now, as SOCKS UP reverberates in my brain, I have become still and focused, ready to receive. Straight up, I stand, surveying my dining room from a brand new perspective. I turn in the direction of Max's voice and put forth a question:

"SOCKS UP? I mean, what on earth are you trying to tell me?"

No uproar now, not even a peep. *Maybe I'm too soft.*

"Hey, I don't get it," I yell. "Tell me more, I want to know!"

Nothing. Now what?

So I take a deep breath, lower my head, and listen.

Well, who'd ever think?

The strain on the other intelligence is far more apparent: "PUUUUULLL YOUR SOCKS UP, MAAAAATE!" He hollers as if talking to his own toddler!

Faster now, like a seasoned instructor, "PULL YOUR SOCKS UP, MATE!"

Oh man, I'm feeling weird. I'm starting to slip into something… strange… what's happening?

.ೱ. .ೱ. .ೱ.

One day when I was a child, I was involved in a weird situation on the railroad tracks in Point Pleasant, New Jersey. Hiking along, I caught my sneaker under one of the tracks. Feeling off-balanced, literally and figuratively, I was unable to dislodge the shoe, or even my foot, from the steel girder. Glancing back through failed spectacles, I caught sight of a shimmering light in the distance. Squinting hard, at last I was able to make out a train, no more than a block away from me. "Oh geez!"

I struggled to break free. Then amazingly, I managed to dislodge my foot from the merciless grip of the track. How I did this, I will never know. Suddenly, I stumbled off the cinders and plummeted down a hill, rolling onto someone's lawn. The blaring steam engine whizzed by my head. My ears began to ring as I realized the magnitude of my fortune.

Then my brain went numb.

I must have come to because a woman who looked like a lovely angel appeared from nowhere with a hot, wet towel. She said something I could not make out. Then she washed my face and hands, and helped me up. My legs were shaking a bit, but soon I began to collect at least some of my senses. Then I thanked her profusely and carried on my wobbly way to drum practice at the VFW Drum and Bugle Corps.

I was late for practice, but who cared? I was just happy to be alive!

♪ ♪ ♪

Thoughts of this incident rush to the forefront of my brain, causing me to see that I am about to go into a state of shock if I do not do something, fast. I plop down on the dining room chair and try to collect myself, taking deep breaths to shift away from any ensuing state of helplessness – because whatever is happening in my dining room, I do not want to miss it. Now breathing deeper, I rub my neck and head. Soon I begin to feel more grounded. So I get up and make a turn to my right. All at once, I hear Max pontificating in my ear, "Like, hey luv, do you get it? Hmmm?"

"My God!" I see, or perhaps intuit, a haze of white light coming through to my right. Awestruck, I turn to find a shimmering light, certainly more welcome than any locomotive on the planet. Long and thin, it is as if his core (his soul?) is being pulled through an infinitesimally small hole. Lengthwise, it finally expands in my own dining room – seemingly shape-shifting to adapt to this three-dimensional world.

"Oh God!" If I hadn't been confident it was he whom I knew, I might have feared such an awesome sight – the essence of Max in profile!

I have tried to relay this information with as much detail and accuracy as possible. Regardless, to this day, I do not know if my eyes were opened or closed when I first caught a glimpse of Max's phenomenal spirit. I believe my eyes were open, but it was like observing a hologram flared out in mid-space. Was I viewing his presence, or was his image somehow being transmitted directly into my brain/mind from another location, another space?

I did not know then and I do not know now.

🎗 🎗 🎗

Trying to maintain, I hear him roar, *"PULL YOUR SOCKS UP, MATE!"* Seems he has lost all patience with his flabbergasted pupil. Stumbling on a chair, I cry, "My God!" as a previously unknown reality begins to sink into the cerebral cortex of my brain. Water streams down my cheeks, yet I do not feel any fear nor sadness, just a deep sense of wonderment and joy.

I can't… I don't… Max, you're here! I say without uttering a word.

Suddenly, I stop and remember what seems like light years away – there is a woman sitting in the guest room at the other end of the house. *Wait, my mother is still here.*

How could I have forgotten?

I so want her to see and hear Max, to bear witness to this bizarre and beautiful experience, to share in my discovery. To share in my delight.

But even as I attempt to holler, "Mom, come here now!" I find myself unable to speak, much less shout. I am mesmerized by the sights and sounds in my dining room. I want to look at this thing closely, to turn it around like a dodecahedron in my brain; I want to try and make sense out of what I once thought was impossible – to retain, if only for a moment, the inspiration sweeping across my errant soul.

Waves reverberate through my mind and body as I stand before the table with my thumb pressed on a star. *Max, if there's a seventh heaven, I am knowing it now.* Reverently, as one might hold the cloth of the Holy Grail, I hold his flag and put it up to my cheek.

"Thank you for giving me this… this unbelievable *thing!*"

"I love you so!"

Yet I can hold on no longer. Soon I slump down and fall into a blissful state of nothingness.

Post Script 1

Resurfacing who-knows-when, I find myself sitting on the chair which I had luckily, collapsed onto. Feeling good, I got up and smoothed out the flag and rearranged all the lovely things on the table. Then I grabbed a sorely-needed cup of coffee and ate a handful of nuts. Eventually I started to feel great, or so I thought, so I decided to go in the living room to write. Yet, no sooner did I sit on the couch, than I relaxed completely and fell into a deep sleep.

Waking up about an hour later, I felt energized.

☙ ☙ ☙

Now I'm sitting at the coffee table on this lovely Arizona afternoon, attempting to collect my thoughts. I am shaking my head, pondering the unthinkable, the previously unimaginable. Nevertheless, I do not have to imagine a thing. All I have to do is think and remember.

Regardless of what I must do today, I must first get my thoughts down on paper. The writing will be the easy part. I can certainly retain my notes in confidential files, but how can I tell her? How can I tell anyone? I am sitting here just about to pinch myself. If my mother comes in and finds me this way, she will think I have lost it totally. How will she or anyone receive this far-fetched, if not mind-bending news? How can I possibly explain to anyone what happened in my home today? It was awesome and beautiful! Aside from an immediate sense of confusion and incredulity, I felt no fear.

However, won't they think it disturbing? Won't they think I'm just another grieving widow who has gone off the deep end? I can barely believe it myself. Yet, it happened, this I know.

Post Script 2 - Cognitive Dissonance

Much later, I realized I had been experiencing *cognitive dissonance*, the psychological term for the feeling of uneasiness which tends to occur after experiencing anything contrary to one's paradigm of reality or belief system. The Einstein of Parapsychology, Dr. Dean Radin, has been utilizing time-honored methods in **psi research**[8] to investigate further into the unexplained and other rare phenomena. In his book,[9] Dr. Radin sheds light on the concept of cognitive dissonance:

---

[8] **Psi research** is research into parapsychological phenomena, including paranormal cognition, paranormal action, extrasensory perception, psychic phenomena, recurrent phenomena (such as hauntings), remote viewing, and other similar processes/causes which are difficult to explain or, at times, simply unfathomable.

[9] Radin, Dean. *The Conscious Universe*. New York: Harper One, 1997. Print.

This is the uncomfortable feeling that develops when people are confronted by "things that shouldn't ought to be, but are [per Leon Festinger and colleagues]...." There are three common strategies for reducing cognitive dissonance. One way is to *adopt what others believe....* A second way... is to *apply pressure* to people who hold different ideas. This explains why mavericks are often shunned by more conventional scientists and why there is almost no public funding of psi research.... To function without the annoying pain of cognitive dissonance, groups will use almost any means to achieve consensus. The third way of reducing cognitive dissonance is to *make the person who holds a different opinion significantly different from oneself....* The distressing history of how heretics were treated in the Middle Ages and the more recent "ethnic cleansings" of the last half-century remind us that witch-hunts are always just below the veneer of civility. The human psyche fears change and is always struggling to maintain the status quo.[10]

Because of my agnostic point of view, the event of January 1st, though wonderful and beautiful, resulted in feelings of cognitive dissonance. Such strong feelings emerged, in part, because the events of this day contradicted my thirty year belief that death is the end. In addition, I simply could not fathom how to share my experience with others – even my own mother – without coming across like a crackpot or a fool. That very afternoon, I began to feel anxious. *Yes, I would like to talk about what happened, but what if my story is rejected? Worse yet, what if I am rejected for telling it?* Regardless, I know what happened like I know

---

[10] *Ibid*

the back of my hand. How can I narrow the gap between what I saw and heard and what others might think if I even choose to tell them?

Consider Dr. Radin's first strategy to reduce cognitive dissonance: *adopt what others believe.* Because of my father's training (to be discussed in Post Script 3) and because of the phenomena that simply did not go away, I began to dig in my heels a bit. Before long, I was not only unwilling but unable to capitulate to the status quo, i.e., to the notion that this event and the subsequent events I experienced did not happen. I do not need to receive the acknowledgments of a room full of people to tell me what I saw or heard or to tell me whether it was or was not real. I have always been a rigorous statistician and researcher, whose faculties of observation are very good. I would not feel the need to see or hear a second instance of the January 1st event, or any of the other events hereby recorded, to reassure myself that they happened. They happened.

Dr. Radin's second strategy to alleviate cognitive dissonance is to *apply pressure* to those who hold different ideas. Though I have not applied any pressure to anyone, I have chosen to reveal my accounts – to provide data and information concerning these phenomena – to give people everywhere the opportunity to read my journal and decide for themselves. My greatest wish is to give hope to those who are destitute of the very word. After having experienced over fifty rare events in one year alone, including the related events witnessed by our loved ones, I could not, in good conscience, keep these accounts to myself. As a statistician, I recognize the relevance of the need to know. In this way, readers can compare the phenomena, as detailed herein, with the documented accounts of others who have observed or have otherwise experienced similar occurrences.

Dr. Radin's third strategy for easing dissonance is to *make the person who holds a different opinion, significantly different from oneself.* I personally have never attempted to make anyone similar to or different from myself. People are who they are – *viva la difference!* Yet, based on email messaging and off-the-cuff conversations, I have noticed that some people tend to form sharp distinctions right away, and that is their choice. Nevertheless, as my own cognitive dissonance began to subside over a period of weeks (months?), I slowly began to reveal some of my supernatural experiences to a select few, i.e., loved ones and friends. Little did I know, I would be feeling my way through bumpy terrain a lot longer than I had ever expected.

Post Script 3 - The Aftermath

Regardless of what anyone might think or believe about the supernatural, one thought remains in my mind: Max's awesome words. The phrase he used was certainly haunting me in more ways than one. I wondered if I had ever heard, "Pull your socks up" before – perhaps years ago in a movie? I could only guess at the meaning, but that wouldn't get at the crux of the issue, and I needed to know.

So, I searched online for the idiomatic expression, "Pull your socks up" and I discovered it has more than one conversational meaning. Here is a rather lighthearted treatment written by Betty Kirkpatrick:[11]

> "Pull one's socks up" is an idiom cliché used to mean to make an effort to do better. It is often children who are at the receiving end of this cliché, as "If you don't pull your socks up you will find yourself repeating the year," although its use is not confined to them. In origin it refers to smartening oneself up by pulling socks up that

---

[11] Kirkpatrick, Betty. *Clichés: Over 1500 Phrases Explored and Explained.* New York: St. Martin's Griffin, 1996. Print.

have slipped round one's ankles, a common problem for
schoolboys wearing short trousers.

If the above interpretation doesn't characterize Max's life as a lad in
Africa and England, I don't know what does. Max was a schoolboy in
the British school system. In light of the January 1st event, I believe
Max used this expression to give his errant pupil (me) the "what for."
Perhaps he came in worriment over my condition or maybe just to say,
"Hey luv, I'm still kickin' around!" In any case, I found Max's visitation
and his words and sentiments to suggest a rather supportive way of
chiding me. It appears he was also cluing me in to the phenomenal
potential of all that exists – showing me there is more to life and death
than what we see with our corporeal eyes!

I don't pretend to completely understand what happened on January
1st, but one thing I do know is, it happened. From the time I was two,
my dad, George, taught me to trust myself – my thoughts, feelings, and
yes, even gut instinct. *And I do, Dad, that I do.*

After all, he was my first hero! Gut instinct is how he survived
World War II when his ship, the aircraft carrier USS WASP, sunk
following direct hits by four torpedoes. Those terrible hours, swimming
in the boundless waters of the Pacific Ocean, paddling in circles without
a life jacket. As a pharmacist's mate, he had doled out all the floatation
devices to his crew. Then somehow, amidst the crisis and confusion,
he neglected to save a life vest for himself. Still, he kept his courage
and plunged from the burning ship into the murky waters far below.
Eighteen hours later, a ship rescued him and the men he swam tirelessly
to reach, the lucky ones like my dad, who managed to keep afloat in the
endless waters of the Pacific. Of the WASP's 2,247 crew members, 173
men lost their lives and over 400 sustained injuries. Forty-five planes
went down with the ship on that terrible September day in 1942.

My father was fortunate enough to live another twenty-eight years to tell the story. Now he's up there, too – with Max – wherever that is! Most of our loved ones are up there now.

Post Script 4 - Consciousness

Because of Max's mind-blowing appearance on New Year's Day and the subsequent events I witnessed, for which there are no adequate nouns, adjectives, or verbs, my desire for more knowledge grew until it became a passion. Later, after having experienced a number of rare and unusual events, I started reading books and articles on topics as diverse as the universe and the cosmos, the supernatural, the metaphysical, consciousness, the spiritual, the intuitive, the paranormal, research into psi phenomena, and so forth. Then about three years after completing the first draft of my journal, I stumbled across a wonderful book by Ervin Laszlo, cosmologist, twice nominated for the Nobel Peace Prize. In the passages below, Laszlo talks about cosmic and human consciousness:

> In the great chain of evolution, there is nowhere we can draw the line, nowhere we could say: below this there is no consciousness, and above there is (91).
>   ….Nobel laureate biologist George Wald said, rather than emerging as a late out-growth in the evolution of life, [mind] has existed always. Essentially the same notion was put forward by Apollo astronaut Edgar Mitchell. All things in the world, he said have a capacity to "know…." The higher forms of knowing… have their roots in the cosmos…. (91).

Laszlo tells us that the stuff of the cosmos – the world, the galaxies, matter and mind – are not separate or distinct. Rather, they are all aspects of the reality of the cosmos.

....In the in-formed universe our brain/mind can access a broad band of information, well beyond the information conveyed by our five sensory organs. We... can be, literally "in touch" with almost any part of the world... or beyond.... (91)

When we do not repress the corresponding intuitions, we can be in-formed by things as small as a particle or as large as a galaxy. This, we have seen, is the finding of psychiatrists and psychotherapists who place their patients in an altered state of consciousness .... It was also Mitchell's outer-space experience. In a higher state of consciousness, he remarked, we can enter into deep communication with the universe.... (91)

We can reconstruct how... non-sensory, information reaches our mind.... according to the new physics, the particles... and galaxies... emerge from the... quantum vacuum.... They are dynamic entities that read their traces into the vacuum's A-field (Akashic field), and ... enter into interaction with each other. A-field traces – the holograms they create.... persist and in-form all things.... (91-92)

The author intimates that this is true of our bodies and brains as well. Everything we experience in a lifetime corresponds to cerebral functions:

.... all things in the universe are... oscillating at different frequencies. These oscillations generate wavefields.... When the wavefield emanating from one object encounters another object, a part of it is reflected from that object, and a part is absorbed....The interference of the initial and the response wavefields creates (a)... pattern... effectively a hologram. It carries information....

> We can tune our consciousness to resonate with the holograms in the A-field. The transmission of information in a field of holograms... occurs when the wavefields that make up two (or more) holograms are "conjugate" .... (like) resonance. Tuning forks and strings on musical instruments resonate with other(s)... tuned to the same frequency .... (92)
>
> The "phase conjugation" that transmits information in holograms... occurs when two... wavefields contain synchronized oscillations at the same frequency..... Even when the wavefields contain oscillations at different frequencies, if they are in harmonic resonance... they produce a coherent channel of communication. In that case a pathway of nonlocal information-transmission is created..., from the quantic to the cosmic.... (93)

Laszlo says that when we remember something or have an intuition that we've experienced a particular phenomenon (like déjà vu or déjà vecu), we recall the information from a hologram, a record of our experiences.

> Our brain... can also resonate... with the holograms of other people, especially with those with whom we have (or had) a physical or emotional bond.... The most widespread... are sudden revelatory intuitions of mother and lovers when their loved ones ... undergo a traumatic experience (94).
>
> ....By entering altered states of consciousness in which our everyday rationality does not filter out what we can apprehend, we can open the roof to the sky. We access a broad range of information that links us to other people, to nature, and to the universe (94).[12]

---

[12] Laszlo, Ervin. *Science and the Akashic Field.* Rochester, VT: Inner Traditions, 2004. Print. Reprinted with permission.

Journal Entry 5

Friday, 01/02/2004
Waxing gibbous moon
Around noon

Dead Butterfly in Max's Truck

Like the poignant song "Butterfly" did I keep him too long? [13]

Before going shopping Mom and I decided to get a decent start, so we stopped for brunch at the local pancake house. With all that had happened since the summer, I literally woke up and realized we hadn't been to the mall in about a year. For that matter, we hadn't done much of anything frivolous since the Christmas of 2002.

I wanted to remedy that, so I asked Mom if she'd like to go to brunch and the mall, and she agreed wholeheartedly. "Okay, but let's make a day of it, honey!"

"Great idea, dear!"

So after a delightful meal and some "chewing of the fat," we moved on to the corner gas station. As I filled the tank of Max's truck, it occurred to me that the water and tires ought to be checked. In fact, I hadn't even driven the vehicle since one worrisome night in November – the night I had to rush Max to the hospital. It was hard to believe so much had happened in only two months time. It just dawned on me this morning that Max's so-called jalopy has been long overdue for a good run. He'd always kept it in great condition, and I would like to do the same. You see, I have no plans to sell his truck – it has so much

---

[13] Carey, Mariah. "Butterfly." *Butterfly.* Columbia, 1997. CD.

life left in it. I want to use it for hauling boxes and things that would never fit in my car.

While the tank was being filled, I hopped back in the truck and searched for the tire gauge that Max kept in the door compartment on the driver's side. Oddly, the pocket was empty except for... except for...

🦋 🦋 🦋

"What's this?"

Something small and yellow wedged in the corner.

"Hmmm, it's so tiny." I'm craning my neck, trying to peer into the narrow compartment.

"Oh, God."

"What, dear?" Mom asks.

"Look," I say, as I gently pick up the hapless creature by a wing.

Softly, I set it the palm of my hand.

"Mom, it's a dead butterfly."

"Oh my!"

All morning I'd been doing well, but somehow this curious find has the unexpected effect of setting me off. I want to get out of the truck, but I can't. Mom puts her hand on my shoulder, and as my arms hit the steering wheel, tears burst forth.

But it doesn't make any sense. *I just saw Max yesterday. I know he's alive.*

Somewhere.

So, why am I crying?

Despite my bewilderment, I'm reliving the incredible sounds I'd heard less than a day ago: *"Pull your socks up, mate!"* His resonance and those amazing words are ricocheting through the nooks and crannies of my brain. Soon, amidst the veil of tears, I find myself grinning at Mom. She smiles at me with a puzzled look on her face. Now I'm laughing and crying like a fool, wiping my cheeks with the long, accordion-like stream of Kleenex that Mom is frantically trying to pull out of a square box. Soon, she bursts out laughing, bunching the barrage into a big ball.

Chuckling, I say, "I must be about as ridiculous as that big blob of paper, but I just don't care." Finally, my hands are dry. "Okay, all right, let's hit it before the crowd beats us to it."

"That's my Mandy, love you."

"Love you too, honey."

Then, reaching for the keys, I realize I've lost track of the butterfly.

Looking down, I catch it on my lap. "Whew, can't lose this baby," I say as I pick up the little creature by a wing. "Will you hold her for me, Mom?"

"Sure, darling. Here, I'll wrap it in Kleenex and put it in my zipper pouch."

"Thanks dear," I say and turn the key. Glancing right, "What a pretty specimen, don't you think?"

"I do, honey."

"Think I'll keep her."

🦋 🦋 🦋

On our way to the mall, we passed a recreational area that somehow jogged my memory of a lovely Saturday Max and I had last spring. We'd spent almost the entire day romping through a butterfly exhibit at the Desert Botanical Gardens in Phoenix. I thought, *Maybe one of those millions of butterflies flew away and landed in Max's truck.*

But we didn't take the truck, we took my car. I'm sure because Max took a picture of me standing under a Palo Verde tree and my red sedan was in the photo. Though I sometimes have trouble remembering names and even appointment dates, I often remember visual minutiae

31

like this. Maybe it's because we had such a great time with those glorious butterflies and being there together on that wonderful spring day, that I can still see those pictures in my mind. I mulled over them night after night, after we learned Max had cancer. They are engraved in my mind and heart forever.

So I realized we hadn't taken Max's truck, but this left me puzzled. Where had the little butterfly come from? We seldom saw them in the yard and Max kept his truck parked in the garage anyway. Then, since last June, he hadn't been driving much at all. We'd begun traveling together – mostly in my car – mostly to go see doctors and spend time browsing through shops and stores. We knew that one car was the only way to go. Somehow, in all its sadness, cancer had brought us closer together.

I suppose my butterfly question will always have more than one answer because there are just too many unknowns to pin anything down, so to speak. Suffice to say the little lady (fellow?) came fluttering into our lives from nowhere, wriggling its way into the cab of Max's truck. Yet, two things I do know:

(1) Classically, a dead butterfly is considered to be an omen of death. Perhaps my knowledge of this ancient portent had set me off, realizing I'd found the little creature in Max's truck not long after he died.

(2) Paradoxically, a butterfly is also considered to be a symbol of Everlasting Life.

With respect to the first point: Max owned the vehicle but I don't know if he actually saw the dead butterfly in the truck. If one wants to entertain the idea that this omen has any viability whatsoever, did the fact that the butterfly succumbed in Max's truck make him a marked man? Still, for the omen to have any effect, wouldn't the person have to notice the butterfly? Just being near the creature might not be sufficient for the omen to have an effect.

Vagrant thoughts on a rainy day.

I decided to ignore the first point and focus on the second. After all, wasn't it the idea of everlasting life that moved me to keep the little yellow and brown beauty?

As we drove on to the seemingly unattainable mall, at last I announced, "Mom, I'm going to preserve the butterfly in glass... in honor of Max."

"Why, I think that's a great idea, dear."

Glancing right, I checked her profile and did a double take. *Never noticed how much she looks like June... Cleaver, that is.*[14] As I started to smile, an unsettling thought came to the fore. Whether or not Max saw the dead butterfly, I was the one who picked it up. Does this make me a marked woman?

Chewing on it awhile, I decided there's no point in even thinking about it. *After all, thoughts become things.*

Where have I heard that phrase... and what if it's true? I thought, as I put my hand on Mom's arm. By and by, we made it to the mall and I whipped the truck into the parking lot, second row. *Not bad for a Friday.*

"Well, here we are!"

"At last!" she whooped.

Post Script 1

My butterfly was encased in glass, but much later. I'd kept it in a green glass jar for several years. This worked better than I'd expected

---

[14] *Leave it to Beaver.* Prod. Joe Connelly and Bob Mosher. CBS. 1957. Television.

because the butterfly simply did not deteriorate! Then, one day as I was editing this entry, it occurred to me that I had ignored my beautiful butterfly way too long. So, that very day, I started leafing through the yellow pages and searching online for a lepidopterist. Well, my search ended up taking some real twists and turns. In fact, it took weeks to find anyone who could do a proper job. Then, through several chance coincidences, I finally found an out-of-town lepidopterist more suited to the situation. Well, the dear man was not only an incredible butterfly collector but a retired MD as well. So, after our phone conversation and a couple of emails, I was invited to his home.

The doctor and his wife were most gracious and welcomed me in with a smile. Soon I was showing them my butterfly and telling them the story. Then they showed me some of their phenomenal specimens and some lovely photographs of Sulphur butterflies, like mine. The doctor said the Sulphurs are of the family Pieridae. He said he'd pin mine up and make a nice frame and encasement for it. In fact, he and his wife designed an encasement displaying my butterfly in the center, with another Sulphur above it, and one below it. They also gave me a second encasement containing three more butterflies of the Pieridae family, all for my home. I wasn't elated, I was bowled over!

Yet, this is not the end of the story. On the day the doctor and his wife walked me through their home and showed me their magnificent butterfly collection – hundreds of rare and awesome specimens – I learned that their son had passed away approximately three weeks before. I was so sorry to hear this happened to such a nice couple. Sadly, I expressed my condolences, but I felt it just wasn't enough.

🦋 🦋 🦋

A few years after Max died, I started counseling people who came to me in grief. You see, before my life as a statistician, I'd studied psychology in graduate school for six years and counseled teens and adults for three. Then, while writing the first draft of this book, the grief work just naturally began to take shape. It all started on the streets as I met people in restaurants, stores and shops, primarily because so many were experiencing losses due to death and other extraordinary circumstances: foreclosures on homes and businesses; job losses; bizarre accidents; hurricanes; floods; earthquakes and sometimes even tornadoes; and even people who had moved to Arizona from other states. Often I would find myself consoling someone in distress because a loved one had recently died of cancer, just as my Max did. I could certainly identify with this person's plight, to say the least. I offered hope and encouragement based on my experiences of 2004 and the loss of other loved ones.

More recently, I have been running into people in distress because a sister or a brother committed suicide years ago. Such cases are often difficult, especially if the survivor is unable to gain a sense of peace and closure. All of these cases are sad, but I must keep in mind my sincere hopes for them: that perhaps through my stories and those of others like me, they may come to know that the end of this life is just the beginning – there is so much more to come!

One of my challenges is to know when and how to broach the subject. After all, these dear people are not simply grieving in the moment. Some have been mourning in silence for years. It is a delicate subject. I must first consider whether or not to tell them my story. If they appear to be amenable, then I must also consider whether to tell them now or later, and decide when they are better able to comprehend it. Sometimes even I have difficulty comprehending what happened to me. Why would I expect anyone else to make instant sense out of it, much less one in distress?

Hindsight is often a wonderful teacher. Over the months it occurred to me, because of the extraordinary series of **synchronous events**[15] (which happened during the three-week period before I was actually able to reach the good doctor), that our meeting was meant to happen at a later date. Otherwise, I would have been phoning him when his son had passed away. Somehow I felt the angels were guiding me, running interference until the time was just right.

When I returned to receive the two lovely butterfly encasements that the doctor and his wife had taken the time to make, I brought them a copy of our family scrapbook, *For the Time Being.* I sincerely hoped that the book would give this quietly grieving family a sense of comfort and hope. I had told them about my agnostic past and my recent about-face, caused by the extraordinary events that happened after Max's alleged departure. And before going home, I gave them one of my journal stories, chosen just for them.

. . .

In retrospect, it is mind-boggling how the universe seems to be moving me toward people, places and events involving grief and loss. I feel inspired to help those who are dealing with loss to receive the joy of the ultimate promise: that there is more to life than what we see, beyond the grey veil! My desire is to give people something of value to take with them on their journey of discovery and renewal.

---

[15] **Synchronous events** or synchronicities are sometimes referred to as coincidences. However, a true synchronicity involves an interconnection that goes beyond coincidence. **Synchronicity** is defined as the experience of two or more events, that are apparently causally unrelated or unlikely to occur together by chance, that are observed to occur together in a meaningful manner. The concept of synchronicity was first described by Swiss psychologist Carl Gustav Jung in the 1920s. Beitman, Bernard, Elif Celebi, and Stephanie L. Coleman. "Synchronicity and Healing." N.p.,16 Mar. 2001. Web. 25 Aug. 2011.

Post Script 2

Book revisions are eye openers. As I completed my third revision of this journal, I was dumbstruck.

Did my own delay in letting go of Max happen because I was able to see and hear his spirit – to know that he was still a part of my life, as all spirits will always be part of our lives? No matter what we are able to see or hear – or not – all who live must let go of the departed, paradoxically even as we receive the hope and promise of eternal life. We must continue to live our lives completely until it is time for that Grand Metamorphosis – of death and life again! Sometimes we let go of those who have died fairly quickly; sometimes only a little at a time. I realize that my process of letting go took, not months, but years to achieve at a deep and abiding level. I finally understood that to really love Max, I had to release him like a "Butterfly" rising high in the sky…[16]

I have Sunny Dawn Johnston to thank for this beautiful release. [17] It happened in October of 2009, during a private session in which Sunny, through her years of intuitive experience, helped us resolve a terribly unsettling situation that occurred at the hospice the night before Max passed away. Through this awe-inspiring session with Sunny, our unfinished business was at last settled, freeing Max's soul to progress to a higher plane of existence. Though I knew he had already transitioned to the Other Side, he had still been coming back to visit us from time to time. Only this time, I felt his beautiful, courageous spirit depart from our home. This left me not in sadness, but in joy with a boundless feeling of unconditional love. And it hasn't gone away. I share it now with the living.

---

[16] Carey, *op. cit*

[17] Sunny Dawn Johnston, Psychic Medium of Sunlight Alliance in Glendale, Arizona

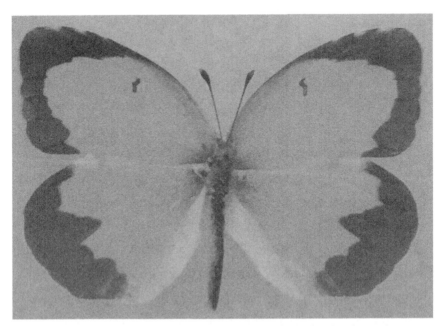

The butterfly found in Max's truck three days after his funeral.

Saturday, 01/03/2004
Waxing gibbous moon
Around 7:30 p.m.

Apparition and the Movie *Ghost*

"One Sweet Day" [18]

Our dear friend Tessie went home today. For over two months now, she'd been coming and going, spending all of her spare time with Max and me whenever we called. Now she needed some time for herself – to rest and recuperate in her home with her dear family. Yet, we were all trying to get some rest, including our friends and loved ones who had returned to their homes earlier. Seemed we had more success some days than others. Grief is lopsided, time immaterial.

Well, today was a quiet one. Last I knew the cats were lounging in my room and Mom was reading in her hideaway, the guest room. I'm happy for that.

Alone now, I curl up on the sofa (where else?), thinking it's time to do a little meditating. Since Max died, I've done it a couple of times. For me, this is a calming, mind-clearing process, a great way to work through difficult times.

Now, as I go into my meditation, I tune out the blare coming from the television set. (So, why didn't I turn it off? No idea, it just didn't register.) Sometimes when I work at home, I leave the TV on all day. I like the company.

---

[18]   Carey, Mariah. "One Sweet Day." *Daydream*. Columbia. 1995. CD.

So despite the buzz, I sit up, close my eyes and go into my deep-breathing exercises. First, I focus on my feet, then legs, abdomen, and so on. This exercise has the effect of grounding me as brain waves shift to the tranquil state of *alpha*. Then comes *theta*, a more hypnotic state of being. Under normal circumstances, *delta* or true sleep follows *theta*, but I forestall it by remaining mindful.

Out of the blue, I feel a soft tail brush up against my leg. Oh, it's my black-and-white cat, Allie. Still, I continue to breathe even more deeply now, feeling so relaxed and free. In my mind, everything is light and airy, but slowed down as the colors change in my field of view. Soon I am aware of an image forming to my right, just above the arm of the sofa. Allie's mewing, fairly quaking at my feet. I want to pick her up. But instead I try to keep her as tuned out as the TV while focusing on the awesome sight building like a hologram before my eyes! First, a head comes into view – a serene, smiling profile not unlike that of Max – with flecks of gold highlighting brown hair. He's wearing a white gauze shirt with a soft, checkered design. A golden aura surrounds his being as he relaxes on the arm of the sofa. In physical terms that wouldn't make much sense. Nevertheless, his spirit may take respite anywhere.

Slowly, I shift my head and body to focus on what appears to be my Max. I am dumbstruck by his brilliance! Now I can hardly hear Allie's sounds, though I know she's still twittering. *Can she see him too?* On any ordinary night, I'd boost her up on my shoulder, yet I find myself rapt in the moment, unable to move.

Is this truly happening?

It seems so real.

Regardless, my reluctant mind begins to wend its way back to the living room, the real world – or so it seems. Yet, Max's spirit lingers on like that of an enchanting suitor. Perhaps because he's still around, I'd like to recapture one of those cozy times we had, watching old movies.

40

So, in this exhilarated state, I'm running my fingers over the chair and between the seats. *Where's the remote?*

What a brash creature of habit!

Fumble… fumble…

Okay, got it. I dial around, not expecting to find anything or anyone as fascinating as the spirit next to me.

But just as weird and wonderful thoughts come to fruition, a familiar face cuts across the television screen. There, before me is Patrick Swayze slow dancing with Demi Moore in the well-known scene from the movie, *Ghost*.[19] Swayze's Sam is a who was murdered by his so-called buddy. Now I can only watch incredulously as Sam's spirit glides around the room with his sweetheart who is very much alive – all achieved with the help of the wacky medium, Whoopi Goldberg's character. The poignant song, "Unchained Melody", resounds in the background:

> *Lonely rivers sigh 'wait for me, wait for me'*
> *I'll be coming home wait for me…*[20]

"My God," I say to Max, or Allie, or any other creature who might be listening. "Is this just another bizarre coincidence?"

"On second thought, Max, I don't have to ask you that question."

Meanwhile, I realize that the television and my words might tend to stir things up. Right or wrong, it happens – Max's image begins to fade. But it doesn't matter because the pure magnitude of his presence stays with me. Water streams down my cheeks as serenity, like a soothing afghan, wraps 'round my shoulders. I am one with the Universe.

---

[19] 19. *Ghost*. Dir. Jerry Zucker. Perf. Patrick Swayze, Demi Moore, and Whoopi Goldberg. Paramount, 1990. Film.

[20] The Righteous Brothers. "Unchained Melody." *Unchained Melody – The Best of the Righteous Brothers*. Curb, 1974. LP.

Post Script 1

It is difficult. No, it's almost impossible to describe the awe-inspiring thing that I just witnessed and expect to succeed in getting the information across in any rational, human way. The English language has no words.

Not long after living and breathing the quintessence of Max, while watching the synchronous scene from *Ghost,* I attempted to tell my mother. I felt so energized, so immortal, so jazzed! Regardless, I knew I would have to tone things down a bit to make it easier for her to understand.

Well, that was the plan.

As I walked down the hall, I rehearsed what I'd say and how I'd say it. Then I tapped on my mother's door but it was already ajar. Quietly, I peeked in to find her folding sweaters. What a run-of-the-mill sight to see: Mom folding clothes just after I experienced a mind-blowing vision of Max! The word *incongruous* comes to mind. Though we both fold our laundry and do mundane chores as a matter of daily living, I began to feel sorry for her. Soon I came to the vast realization that I would have to adjust my story further downward to make it more believable and understandable for Mom.

It didn't work.

Her response: a genuine smile and an "Oh, that's nice, dear," not unlike that June Cleaver again. Then she went about her business, putting clothes away as if I hadn't even said a word. As if I weren't there! Maybe that's what bothered me most. I left the room shaking my head, and as I marched down the hall, I realized my hands were shaking too.

What's the use? I sighed and plopped down on the couch.

Oh well, what the heck. On some level, I knew I had to pipe down and think about it – try to take my mother's stance after hearing this far-fetched story. Perhaps it was frightening to her or maybe she thought it was just a tall tale. But that was certainly not the case.

No matter, I knew I had to give my mother the benefit of the doubt. It was obvious. She never intended to make me feel bad. I mean, she's just human. How many people on this planet have ever heard a story like that? Probably not many.

Even so, I just wanted to give her a glimpse… perhaps help her see that there is more to life than the clothes we fold… more than the material world we see, hear, touch, and smell each morning when we wake up. *Can she not see how joyous life is? Does she not know how beautiful death is? Where does one end? Where does the other begin?*

Are not life and death simply different aspects of the same extraordinary reality? I never saw it this way before, but now I understand that the continuum continues. I'm not being facetious. Isn't this what a continuum is supposed to do? Death is just another part of the continuum of life.

Post Script 2

The problem concerning my mom was my fault. Being as enthusiastic as I was, I actually blew my description of Max. Was it hubris on my part to think I could possibly tell my mother what happened and expect her to understand? Maybe so.

Or maybe I should have waited a bit longer. A more composed manner would have added weight to my no-doubt mind-boggling portrayal of Max and the coincidental movie to boot, not to mention my conjectures on the subject. Still, I have to give Mom credit for keeping a cool demeanor. Perhaps she thought I'd been dreaming or maybe she was hiding unease. She has always been good at that.

In any case, I did not find Max's ghost to be frightening at all. He was uplifting and magnificent! I will never forget this beautiful experience. Right now I feel so close to Max, a spirit being, and so far away from any living creature I can think of.

From now on, I know what I must do.

I must keep things to myself.

JOURNAL ENTRY 7

Sunday, 01/04/2004
Waxing gibbous moon
Evening

My Dream and *The Evolution Angel*

Until the dolphin flies and parrots live at sea – Always
Until we dream of life and life becomes a dream…[21]

I had been napping on the sofa where I seemed to be spending much of my time, of late. Despite my weariness or perhaps because of it, something beyond awe-inspiring happened to me tonight. I am so at a loss to describe it, or do it justice of any kind. I can barely understand what transpired, yet alone explain it in any comprehensible way. However, I will try. I must at least, try.

I find myself waking up from a profound sleep. My thoughts and feelings are beyond description as I cry out, "Max… Max!" I feel as if the top of my head has busted loose, but it is a joyous feeling, not a sad or bad one. For in my dream, I am being held by an incredible being. His enormous, empathic eyes are those of my darling, yet he appears in singular form. The only image that might even come close to depicting this magnificent spirit is, oddly, that of an amoeba – like those viewed through a microscope in biology class. The difference lies in his infinite intelligence and in the vastness of his form, taking up the entire field of view with my eyes closed. (How shocking when years later, I read a book describing a spirit as an amoeba, discussed in the post script below.)

---

[21] Wonder, Stevie. "As." *Songs in the Key of Life*. Motown, 1976. LP.

This *magnetic force*, this intense and overwhelming energy is moving toward me in a surging form as he embraces the wholeness of my being with love and the beauty of all things noble and bright. The core of his spirit shines a violet blue and his aura emits sparks of light all around us. This force, this pureness and wholeness of love, is in an eternal state of flux – waves of compassion envelope me and I find myself screaming, "Max, Max!" Then, as I fall further into something I can only describe as rapture, I thrash about, yelling, "Dear One, I love you so!"

Alas, from the very movement of this tumultuous encounter, I soon awaken. Stunned beyond belief, I rub my eyes and run my fingers over my face… dripping with perspiration.

Wait a minute!

I sit up and touch my gown… *drenched.*

☙ ☙ ☙

Tonight before I go to sleep, there is just one thing I must do. I must get down on my knees and thank God for this, this inconceivable wonder of life and death.

Post Script

I had written the above entry in January of the year 2004 and the remaining entries over the span of that same year. Then, due to a long-term illness involving visual difficulties, I had not gone back to rewrite my manuscript for grammar, syntax, the inclusion of numerous post scripts, and so on, until four-and-a-half years later. While doing so, I ran across an amazing book written by Todd Michael, an emergency room physician.[22] As he was attending to both the living and the dying

---

[22] Michael, Todd. *The Evolution Angel: An Emergency Physician's Lessons with Death and the Divine.* New York: Penguin, 2008. Print.

in the ER, Dr. Michael said he began receiving communications from the spirit world. Some of his most extraordinary encounters occurred with messenger spirits whom he said had come to help the deceased cross over. The good doctor also said that exchanges began to occur with the newly deceased – souls who had departed in the hospital. In this extraordinary book, the author refers to Spirit as the Evolution Angel which is also the title of the book. Nevertheless, the entities informed Dr. Michael that they have no need to take on names, because all spirit creatures of God are as one Spirit.

With respect to my journal, what struck me most was a phenomenal exchange that took place between Dr. Michael and Spirit. I believe this communication connects with my dream in a mind-blowing way.

> **Doctor:** When you are not manifesting (i.e., creating) here as you have described, do you have a form of some kind? What are you made of exactly?

> **Spirit:** *To understand our true nature, think for a minute about an amoeba. An amoeba is a bit of living protoplasm enclosed by a single continuous cell wall. This protoplasm can form projections called pseudopods. They remain attached to the larger organism at all times and derive their energy from it.*
> *We are projections of the Great Spirit, the Great Light. Although we appear in some ways to be independent, self-contained creatures, we are not. For that matter, neither are you.*

> **Doctor:** So you are made of light?

> **Spirit:** *Yes and no. We are even finer and more etheric than light itself. We are very nearly pure consciousness.*

But for all practical purposes you may think of us as beings of light.

Doctor: I still don't understand. Do you have a distinct "body" that is made of light?

Spirit: *Not exactly. As I said, we are best described as fluid beings.... This is one of the main differences between us and human beings who are caught in a relatively stable form....*

The difference... is a matter of degree.... Whereas you may take months or years to change your form, we can shift and change from instant to instant.... We have escaped the illusion of solidity... we flow perfectly and with no effort. (Michael 30-31).

JOURNAL ENTRY 8

Tuesday, 01/06/2004
Feast of the Epiphany
Day before full moon
Early morning

Another Amoeba Formation

Today I heard the song "Mr. Dieingly Sad."
The title and the waves in the song
remind me of Max and the amoeba in my dreams...[23]

Upon awakening, with eyes still closed, I'm seeing a dazzling amoeba-like formation of a golden hue. The form gushes forth, then ebbs like the tide. On close inspection, it appears to be made of tiny particles like pixels on a television screen.

Exquisite!

The image remains with me for another fifteen seconds or so. Then it collapses into minuscule flecks like dust flickering in a beam of light. Still, an adequate description of its beauty eludes me.

It shimmers so.

Then, in a puff, it's gone!

---

[23] The Critters. "Mr. Dieingly Sad." *Younger Girl.* Kapp, 1966. LP.

Journal Entry 9

Thursday, 01/15/2004
Third quarter moon

Commotion in the Kitchen

Just like a ghost, you have been a-hauntin' my dreams...[24]

Sunday my mother left town to return to her husband and their home in Nevada. I miss her already but John needs her, too. He is getting up in years and can no longer fly or drive beyond the city limits. Otherwise he would have made the trip with Mom to attend the funeral and be with us. All three of us, John, Mom and I, felt badly that he was unable to make the trip. On the other hand, his children and granddaughter called him daily while Mom was gone and often spent the night with him. We were thankful for that.

So, my mother took the bus, her favorite mode of transportation when I am unable to fly with her to take her home. She loves to look at the scenery despite the desert terrain, and catch the view as it changes from town to town – that is, wherever there are towns to be seen! Contrary to popular opinion, many of the towns in Arizona and Nevada have green grass and trees. How lush? Well, that's another question depending on the aridity and the time of year. In January after a measurable rainfall, the trees and grass are often green and sometimes very picturesque. Mom and I especially love the colorful array of desert wildflowers set against a mountain scene.

Almost every year after Mom's Christmas stay, Max and I drove her home. This gave her the added advantage of stopping to visit the places

---

[24] Classics IV. "Spooky." *Spooky.* Imperial, 1968. LP.

she missed while riding the bus. The last time we all enjoyed having tea and delicious cakes at a charming restaurant in Wickenburg, a quaint desert town northwest of Phoenix. Then we proceeded northwest on Route 93 to a town called Wikieup. With a general store, a café, and a gift shop, Wikieup is not much more than a ghost town. Mom enjoyed browsing through the clothing racks and jewelry cases to hunt for "just the right" Indian gifts for John and the family. Max and I savored our coffee as we chuckled at Mom trying to decide which of ten items she would choose. "Oh, what the heck, I'll take 'em all!"

Yes, I miss my mother very much and I miss John too. Still, I have been somewhat preoccupied since Mom left town. Along with the hectic job I just returned to and working long days, I come home to find the dishes moving around on the kitchen counter! Tonight and several times in the past week, some of the them actually flipped off the rack and crashed to the counter. Other dishes shook, making a weird clamor in the rack. It is as if they are behaving like living organisms with an energy all their own.

What mechanism might be causing these strange activities? We haven't had any earthquakes and I wasn't anywhere near the dish rack when the dishes started flipping around and flying off the rack, or otherwise changing position. Amazingly, none of them broke. Still, I should have been paying more attention when these activities first began, but I've been very focused on several projects for work. However, if this should happen again, I'll try to be more diligent and take notes. It's funny because I always keep pens and sticky notes on my kitchen counter. They have certainly come in handy since all the commotion began.

Journal Entry 10

Thursday, 01/22/2004
Around 6:00 a.m.

The Toaster Trick

*I came back to let you know
Got a thing for you and I can't let go....*[25]

Wow, the toaster trick happened again.

Since Max left, our toaster has been acting up – "behaving" quite strangely I must say. How else can I put it? On some mornings when I fix my breakfast – coffee, cereal and a slice of toast – the toast pops up and stays in the toaster. (I imagine this is the normal situation for most people.) Yet, about two or three times a week now, I've noticed that *amazingly, the toast pops up, flies into the air and lands right on top of the toaster.*

One time, the toast missed the top of the appliance and alighted like a bird on the counter. Mostly though, as if by an invisible sleight of hand, the toast lands on top of the toaster and stays there. What a sight to see – makes me "flip" every time! It's like someone is saying, "Madam, your toast is served" or "See, I can make you laugh after all!"

I am here to tell you that the toaster trick never happened before Max died. No, not once. Our toaster worked normally then. In fact, it still works fine but with value added: *the toast pops up, flips in mid-air, becomes parallel to the counter, and lands on top of the toaster.*

It's as if the toast is presenting itself to me so that I might further delight in eating it with butter and jam.

---

[25] Caldwell, Bobby. "What You Won't Do for Love." *What You Won't Do for Love.* Sin-Drome, 1978. LP.

Post Script

Max used to make my toast in the mornings, though not every day. He only did it if I was running late or had work to do before driving to the office. Seems like he's still here helping me get to work on time. "Hey, did I tell you I love you today?" he used to say. Now I tell others that way, like I'm Max.

JOURNAL ENTRY 11

Saturday, 01/31/2004
Waxing gibbous moon
Afternoon

More Deaths in the Family

"Don't Let the Sun Catch You Crying" [26]

Uncle Lou left us. We didn't hear of his death right away because his family lives in Ohio. Sad to say, we've been out of touch for years. It's a good thing Aunt Leila in Florida sent an important email informing us of his passing.

Yesterday I managed to get a long letter written to Lou's wife, Patti, and my cousins whom I haven't seen since I was nineteen. Their father was so good to me when I was a little girl. I will never forget his bellowing laughter as we watched the football games together, or how he smiled and sang me a song as he bounced me on his shoulders all around Grandma's backyard. "Watch out for my hydrangeas, Lou!" she'd yell.

I sent Patti a floral centerpiece to place on their dining room table. Still, it never seems enough. I'm so sorry I missed his funeral.

❧ ❧ ❧

Wish I could say that was the end of it, but things are coming in bunches now. I received word from Max's cousin, Melissa, who lives in England – her father, Uncle Vince, died *three days* before Max. I'm

---

[26] Gerry and the Pacemakers. "Don't Let the Sun Catch You Crying." *Don't Let the Sun Catch You Crying.* Laurie, 1964. LP.

stunned and feel awful for her. She lost not only her father but her cousin. You see, Melissa and Max had been very close since childhood.

Post Script

It has been a year of sadness for Max's family and mine. Yet, somehow I take comfort in my newfound belief that our dearly departed are still alive and together once more. Because of the things I have seen, heard and sensed since Max died, I believe this to be true. I have been trying to get this idea across to some of my loved ones and friends who are now grieving other losses, but even while lunching privately, I'm finding it difficult to discuss these rare and unusual events that have happened of late – to let them in on a little secret *(wink wink)* – without catching a shade of doubt or discomfort in their eyes.

No matter, I still hope to send out a positive message. How much I choose to reveal depends on the individual. I find that some people are receptive and like talking about the supernatural. When this happens, I enjoy the discussion and tend to be more open about my experiences. Other folks are not so amenable. I sometimes have to choose my words very carefully, for fear they'll think I'm just out there somewhere.

The basic message I would like to get across? Keep an open mind; there is more to life and death than what we see.

Above all, I've learned that when it comes to someone who has just lost a friend or a loved one, the less said, the better. It is easy for the grieving person to become overwhelmed so it's best to just be there for her, to listen and provide what comfort is possible. As time goes on, she may start to feel more open to talking about life and death. Then, when the time is right, I might tell her a story or two and share some of my deeper thoughts on *life after life.*

Regardless, it is obvious that there are some people who just aren't open to discussion. In this case, it's usually counterproductive to try to bring someone around concerning the issue he has been dead against all his life. I have to leave things alone unless he should at some point happen to bring up the subject. Yet, with a hard-core skeptic, that may never happen.

Before these incredible experiences, I was a real skeptic myself. I mean, what were the odds I would ever have a revelation like this in my lifetime? As a statistician I'm sure I could come up with an appropriate estimate, but that would be superfluous. I feel lucky beyond belief! Thanking the cosmos every day for the amazing things I have experienced in my life, but mostly, for all the wonderful people I have known and loved.

JOURNAL ENTRY 12

01/xx/2004
Time unknown

Max Curls Up with Me

This journal entry is like déjà vu
and the song "Coming Back to You" by Macy Gray [27]

I labeled this journal entry 01/xx because, when so many wild and curious events began to take place, I hadn't been keeping a record of everything. I do remember, though, that when this event happened, I'd been meditating a lot – praying for peace, fortitude, knowledge and understanding.

And so, right around this time, I'm lying on the sofa when out of the blue, I get the sense that my husband, a disembodied spirit, is curling up around me. I am barely awake. Even so, I'm able to discern powerful thought-forms and emotions surging toward me in waves. I doubt this will make much sense to anyone, but this is the only way I can describe it: I can just about hear Max's voice as if it is light years away, yet I distinctly hear him cry out, "M-a-n-d-y, I love you."

"Mandy, I love you!"

Then, without forethought and certainly without any effort, I find myself screaming, "Max, Max, I love you too!" Then I pause, waiting for a response, but I can't hear a thing. So I say, "Where are you? I mean, I can feel you, but where are you?"

Then, I hear him say, "Mandy..." but I am unable to hear the rest of his words. Like the blips from a bad radio signal, his sound simply

---

[27] Gray, Macy. "Coming Back to You." *Déjà Vu (Original Soundtrack)*. Hollywood, 2006. CD.

fades into a hum… then nothing. And as his voice drifts away, so does his being.

Still, I do not feel alone or empty, and I glide into a bottomless sleep.

.ℐ. .ℐ. .ℐ.

These incredibly heartfelt, if not impassioned moments happened about four or five times over a three-week period. Nevertheless, I am at a loss because I cannot fully comprehend what took place. But in light of all that has happened since December of 2003, I decided to try to capture and make note of these beautifully compelling thoughts and feelings coming through to me. Sometimes the forms arrived as symbols and visual patterns, sometimes as emotions, and other times as words of the English language – all having Max's unique, resonant quality.

Regardless, my words do not and never will do justice to these overpowering experiences.

Post Script

As the receiver and object of the above thoughts and feelings (in essence, a part and parcel of the informal study at hand), I am unable to verify what I have seen or heard. Nevertheless, I do not believe these visions, sounds and sentiments are coming from me, i.e., solely from my mind. In general, this puts me into the dubious category of object of the event in question.

Is Max, then, the subject? It would seem so. However, some would say that I am the subject and object as well, i.e., the only creature playing a part in the entire scenario. Apart from any commentary at large, I find that as these sounds, sights and sentiments arrive in my field of consciousness, they appear to be extraneous to my being. They are

57

flying toward me in what I can only describe as *shock waves*, soft yet loud – another contradiction – at least on the surface. These waves are filled with an intense energy, or what appears to be a consciousness of their own.

Forgive me. It is difficult to talk about these notions in any humanly intelligible way, but I do hope you will bear with me. It is my best effort at explaining such awe-inspiring yet incomprehensible encounters.

JOURNAL ENTRY 13

Sunday, 02/01/2004
Waxing gibbous moon
Evening

Max's Last Day and Ring Movement

Oh, little darling of mine, I can't for the life of me
Remember a sadder day...[28]

I have always kept my journal notes tucked inside a large calendar. Now, as I search for my scrawl of February 1st, I am struck by the picture of a snow-capped mountain on the calendar page. And there is a quote from my childhood hero, Madam Marie Curie: "Nothing in life is to be feared. It is only to be understood."[29]

Madam Curie's words befit the story I am about to tell. To preface this inexplicable event, it is meaningful to backtrack a bit to December 23rd, Max's last day. At approximately four-thirty in the morning, I received a telephone call from the hospice nurse. "You must come right away," she said, "Max is failing fast!"

Why did her call not surprise me?

Because at three-thirty in the morning, I'd had an awful dream. By the time the woman phoned, I was already up, holding my head in my hands. Try as I might, I could not get my wits about me. Yet despite my fatigue and angst over the daunting dream, the nurse's call worked like a cattle prod: in twelve minutes flat, I got dressed, kissed Mom good-bye, and drove to the hospice – a true record for the turtle that I am!

§ § §

---

[28] Simon, Paul. "Mother and Child Reunion." *Paul Simon.* Warner Bros., 1972. LP.
[29] Bueler Mortuary. *Inspirations: 2004 Calendar.* 2004. Print.

By the time I arrive, Max is in a terrible state, unable to utter a word. *How unlike Max,* I say to myself, wanting to ignore the troublesome signs. He seems aware of my presence because as soon as I come to his side, his head begins to move.

Frenetically rocking, he opens his mouth several times as if trying to tell me something of vital importance. But to my great sadness, he is unable to utter a sound.

Dumbfounded, I just stand there. I cannot even say, "Hi, luv." And in the emptiness and clarity of dawn's first light, I grasp the reality. *His time is near.* In a state of total terror, I realize that I will have to be the one to give Max the encouragement he will need to move on. Oh, how I do not want to do that.

How can I do that? I don't want him to leave!

Like an automaton, I stand there trying to comprehend what is happening to Max.

He is not going to be able to speak.

Not now.

Maybe not ever.

Oh Lord, help me! Help me do something for him! You see, I am speechless too. Now, without any true awareness, my agnostic self is praying. Stumbling on my own feet, I feel the weight of the words about to slip from my mouth. With incredible sadness and all the anticipation of the moment, I touch my dear husband's arm and kiss him on the curve of his handsome brow.

At once, words spewed forth. I do not remember what I said; I just knew I had to say something, *anything* to give him strength – and faith – to give him something to take with him. Still, I prayed he would stay longer if he could. So I told him of my hopes and wishes for his future... *whether here, Lord, or elsewhere,* I thought. And, in that eternal moment, the Agnostic One found herself pleading for the certainty of an *elsewhere*. I also prayed that Max might hear me. For, despite all his movements, I did not know if he was physically capable of understanding my words.

❦ ❦ ❦

All of a sudden, my ears begin to ring as spiky sensations bombard my head. *I'm losing it!* And there I am drifting alongside my husband, somewhere in outer space. We are floating along in the nether regions without a care to behold. How else can I describe it? Perhaps we are having a lighthearted moment together.

Nevertheless, I realize I must pull back and wield a strong grip. *You have to find a way to carry on for his sake.* So I take some deep breaths and will myself back to his bedside. In seconds, I'm looking through the hospice window at the beautiful luminarias on the lawn. This gentle scene has a quieting effect on my mind, perhaps even on my body. At last, something called composure rights me and I slip back into my skin, returning to the current state of affairs or what we commonly call reality.

Okay... all right... I can do this.

At last, I am able to convince myself that it's true.

Words pour forth as if coming from the mouth of a bystander. Surprisingly, I seem to have saved my most meaningful thoughts and sentiments for last. "Max, I hope you can hear me because this is important." His eyes are barely open, as if he might lapse into a stupor at any moment. He isn't moving around much now.

Still, I have to trust he can hear me. I mean, what other choice do I have? Well, I suppose I could just keep quiet. But that might add to the feeling of hopelessness.

No, I won't go there. I have to talk to him, for the two of us.

I take his arm and hold him near. "Sweetie, I put your wedding ring on a silver chain. It's hanging by the mirror in your bathroom."

61

How I'd hoped he'd be coming home to wear it again, but I won't tell him that. In his sorry state, I don't want him to feel beholden in any way. Lord knows, he'd been pressured enough by the doctors into doing that toxic chemo.

Now, things being as they are, I can think of only one more thing to do. In a lurch, at last I right myself and clear my throat. *Okay, here goes....*

"Darling, I hope you don't think this sounds weird," I say, trying on the trace of a smile.

"You see, I've been doing a lot of thinking lately, and I wonder if you would let me know... if uh, when *(how should I say this)* ... when... when you arrive? I mean, when your journey takes you to that special place... the one you always talked about... that wonderful place where we would all meet again?" I try so hard, but the water won't stop.

In silence, I turn just before I start to weep. How ironic, I'm praying he won't hear me now.

🐾 🐾 🐾

Life is strange. For over thirty years, I'd had my doubts – so many doubts that I soon found myself living the life of one who has no beliefs. And before Max came along, I lived it to the hilt. During our sixteen years together, Max had been the one so firm, so resolute about the existence of life after death – not just as a thought – as a foregone conclusion. For this reason, I wanted to underscore his beautiful confidence and remind him of his unwavering faith. But now I see something more that I may not have grasped on a conscious level that day. You see, throughout his long period of illness, Max had had such a dastardly time of it – first with Meniere's Disease, then with the rare cancer so difficult for the doctors to diagnose, and finally with the toxic cancer treatment and the wicked survival rate of less than fifteen percent. With all of the changes we endured, the feelings of displacement and defeat tended to bubble just below the surface of the fiery caldron. It seemed almost fair and perhaps even venerable that these feelings should take hold, especially toward the end. But were they Max's feelings or were they mine? Or were they shared between us? I don't know. Sometimes I wasn't even sure where Max ended and I began. I just knew that because of the horribly untenable situation he was facing, I had to buoy him up, to give him another reason to believe!

Maybe I wanted to give myself a reason too.

But if ever there was a reason for me, it was Max.

🌢 🌢 🌢

A year or two ago, Max and I had been watching one of the universe shows and we got into a rowdy discussion about parallel dimensions and multiple universes. Scientists sometimes call them **multiverses**.[30] Well, not long after our night of chitchat and fond revelry, Max came home with a novel called *Parallelities*[31] that he raved about for weeks.

Then later, right before Max had been moved to hospice, I found the dog-eared book on his bathroom counter. Beyond curious, I put down my cleaning cloth, sat down on the toilet seat and opened *Parallelities*,

---

[30] The **multiverse** (or meta-universe, metaverse) is the hypothetical set of multiple possible universes (including the historical universe we consistently experience) that together comprise everything that <u>exists</u>: the entirety of space, time, matter, and energy as well as the physical laws and constants that describe them. The term was coined in 1895 by the American philosopher and psychologist William James. The various universes within the multiverse are sometimes called parallel universes. Rees, Martin. *Before the Beginning.* Reading, MA: Helix Books, 1997. Web. 25 Aug. 2011.

[31] Foster, Alan Dean. *Parallelities.* New York: Del Rey, 1995. Print.

right then and there. After reading just a couple of pages, I could see that the author had captured the concept of parallel dimensions in an everyday novel sort of way – very well indeed. I stashed the book in my purse and took it with me to read after work when I went to see Max at the hospital. Sometimes I'd read a page or two as he napped or whenever I went to get his tea and jello. He seemed so happy to know that I'd picked up a book of his, a book he valued.

But how could I have known this off-the-wall novel would become the inspiration for my last words to my love?

Well, I couldn't have known, except perhaps at some premonitory level.

The Urban Dictionary defines a **premonition** as an early warning about a future event.[32] Seems I'd already had a preconscious feeling about it. On the other hand, maybe I just took the information I had at my disposal (from the book and the Universe programs) and used it to help Max face the kind of uncertainty that was becoming more certain with each passing day.

In Dr. Larry Dossey's book, *The Power of Premonitions*,[33] he tells us:

> Premonitions represent anti-mystery. They convert the unknown into the known, sometimes saving our skin by alerting us to impending disasters or health problems.
>
> So we encounter a paradox: surprise, mystery, and not-knowing are important for our health, but the eradication of surprise via premonitions can also work to our benefit. We need to make a place in our life for both the known and the unknown, for certainty and uncertainty.

---

[32] Max. "Premonition." *Urban Dictionary*. N.p., 17 Sept. 2004. Web. 26 Aug. 2011.

[33] Dossey, Larry. *The Power of Premonitions: How Knowing the Future Can Shape Our Lives*. New York: Dutton, 2009. Print.

"Either-or" doesn't fit us well as humans. We are complex creatures, able to participate in multiple meanings and disparate interpretations simultaneously. It's when we relax into ambiguity that we are most human.

Future knowing is a valuable quality, but we should hope that it never eradicates *all* the mysteries of life…

In the years before Max died and during my earliest flurry of note-taking, I hadn't invested much credence in concepts like **premonitions** or **postmonitions**.[34] In fact, I had never even heard of postmonitions until much later. I'm aware this may sound contradictory, given the postmonitory dream I'd had about Max at three-thirty on the morning of his last day. But, back then I didn't understand what was happening to me, or to him. I had no labels or definitions for monitions of any kind.

I have kept the details of my dream in confidence as this is not the intent of my journal. Nevertheless, I learned that what I'd seen and heard in my dream had taken place in Max's room – miles away – a few hours before I'd had the dream while sleeping on my sofa. Then, when I arrived at the hospice, Max's nurse told me what had happened to him during the night. Yet, despite already knowing what had taken place because of the content of my dream, I did not receive validation from the nurse until hours later. At the time, I wasn't seeking validation of any kind or even thinking along those lines. The facts concerning Max's terrible night were revealed by the nurse who detailed this information

---

[34] A **postmonition** is dreaming that something happened after it happened, without knowing it happened. Say you had a dream about an earthquake (randomly), about an hour after there was an actual earthquake, but you didn't know there was one until the next day when you wake up. This would be a postmonition. NyteTerror. "Postmonition." *Urban Dictionary.* Urban Dictionary, LLC., 4 June 2009. Web. 26 Aug. 2011.

upon my arrival at the hospice, leaving me in a state of shock and disbelief – because I already knew what she was going to say before the words left her mouth.

I decided not to tell the nurse about my dream or let on that I already knew what had happened to Max before I got there. You see, I couldn't even discuss it with her because I needed to talk to those near and dear to me about this incredible experience. Since then, I have shared judicious bits of information about my postmonitory dream with my mother and a few close friends. The rest will remain as it was, locked away in my heart.

♪ ♪ ♪

Returning from a needed rest and three bites of a tasteless sandwich, I walk down the halls toward my sweetheart's room, looking forward to the sight of his thin, handsome face. Out of the blue, the back of my brain gets a jolt about as powerful as an electric shock… and I know what I must do.

"*Parallelities*, Max!" I holler and rush to his side.

"Remember that cool, crazy book, and the Universe shows?"

Max is moving again – head darting back and forth.

"Darling, do you think you can try to, uh…."

How to say this?

"Max, when it's time, do you think you could tell me… when you arrive?"

"When you get to that wonderful place… your parallel dimension?"

"I know it will be a beautiful place, so safe and free! That's where I see you, darling."

Please let it be.

"Maybe we can even meet…."

There, someday perhaps?

Then, out of the blue, I find myself gathering, if not courage, then something else… momentum… as another thought flies to the fore.

Okay….

"Honey, your ring in the bathroom? When it's time, and you get to where you're bound, would you uh… come back and move the ring and the chain?"

"Move them off the handle? Well, I don't know if it's possible. But if you can, then I will know that you are doing just fine."

I had never believed in stuff like this, ever. But Max and I had heard some stories about objects moving in people's homes after their relatives passed away. We'd talked about it a few times, back in the early nineties. But we were joking about it, thinking it was weird or bizarre.

"I hope my idea doesn't sound strange to you, Max."

He does not respond. He is not moving now, so I doubt he hears me. Still, I do not give up hope. "Sweetheart, if you think this is a ridiculous idea or if you find it's just not possible, know this: either way, I understand."

"I love you."

Now Max is moving his head wildly, to the left and right, and back again. He opens his mouth several times like he's about to speak. How I'd hoped to hear him say something, anything. And though he may have heard me, I just don't know. Yet, one thing is very clear – his head started to move as soon as I said, "I love you."

I content myself with that beautiful thought. Smoothing back the hair that never left the head of my brilliant lover, I kiss him on the cheek and put on a paltry smile. "Get some rest now, darling," I whisper.

"We'll talk again in a little while."

How did I know with an already grieving heart that that would never happen?[35]

.⁣.⁣.

Dithering about the room like a headless turkey, I spotted a chair and slumped into it. *Nothing more to give. Nothing to receive.* I had reached the point of no return. Alas, I resigned myself to the certainty of uncertainty, the lopsided face of the trickster. Until that sad day, I had never experienced the depths of such a one.

Then my darling lapsed into another coma. Upon receiving word, our friends and loved ones hurried to the hospice to be there with Max in his last hours. At nine p.m. sharp, Mom, Tessie and I counted ourselves among the lucky to be with Max as he flew from his body for the last time.

Nothing in life is to be feared. It is only to be understood.

In the weeks and months that passed, I checked Max's bathroom to be sure his wedding ring remained untouched. To that end, I closed the door softly behind me and kept it closed at all times. There were no incidents nor accidents – our delightful, ornery cats never had the opportunity to do their toilet paper deeds in Max's bath again. There were no earthquakes nor planetary events that might tend to cause a silver chain or ring to move.

Then today, the first day of February, I walk into Max's bathroom to find that the chain and his wedding ring have moved halfway off the handle. So I check my calendar. It is one month to the day since Max came to me in spirit, and cried out, *"Pull your socks up, mate!"*

---

[35] Nevertheless, on that tumultuous day I knew nothing of what I know now – that Max and I would be blessed with the inconceivable opportunity to continue our conversation – beyond the grave.

Post Script 1

Did Max's being move the chain and ring? Does this halfway position mean he is halfway there – that much closer to his destiny? Or did some nameless thing cause the ring and chain to move? In the last analysis, I have no way of knowing for certain.

Once more, the trickster reveals his lopsided jowls.

Nevertheless, I'm not that troubled by the ambiguity of the situation. We seek to comprehend and often, with an appropriate analysis, we are able to draw reasonable conclusions. But just as often, we simply do not understand. In some cases, we never will. That is, until we die.

At first, it came as a shock and then a comfort to find the chain and ring so disposed. I am nothing if not grateful for the inherent possibilities of life, and death! Do we not realize that death is a big part of life? Though we may not be aware of it now, the continuum goes on, beyond our world and into a vastness that we do not yet understand. But just because we do not yet understand it does not mean that it does not exist. How many things do we not yet comprehend *that really do exist?* An infinite number, no doubt.

Post Script 2

For so many years, my statistician-scientist side dismissed concepts like premonitions and other soft psi notions. My life's work had been based on solid evidence, and hard numbers. "The facts, ma'am, just the facts!" Max would tease. Even so, he was about as analytical as me! Regardless, I had no time to quibble over what might have been, or what might be, or what could possibly happen (barring my own beloved mathematical forecasts). My eyes were focused on "what is" or "what is most likely to occur," based on time-honored quantitative methods and rigorous calculations. In essence, my life revolved around the collection, analysis, and interpretation of the seen – the hard data.

It never occurred to me that the unseen (what we might never be able to measure objectively) is also a part of what is.

It never occurred to me, that is, until now.

As anyone can see, my life has changed by leaps and bounds since Max died. In fact, my life had already begun to change not long before he left this plane of existence. Unwittingly, I was fast approaching something called an epiphany. But if the truth be told, this sometimes bewildering process had been bubbling and stewing for some time. Am I having more than one kind of epiphany? Or does one epiphany encompass different landscapes? Since I'm steeped in the process, I wouldn't know. How do I observe myself as subject/object? How does anyone observe her thoughts or actions objectively?

Nevertheless, I know that meaningful change doesn't happen overnight. This includes what we as a species tend to fear – that necessary, tumultuous, and often incomprehensible thing called an adjustment period. Periods in the plural is more like it. I have begun to grasp the reality of it in hindsight, especially while journaling. Those transformative "Aha!" moments often pop out as I record an event or remember something meaningful that happened many years ago.

One of the most exciting things about keeping a journal is this: since you are maintaining a dated log of detailed events (like psi activities) you are apt to go back and unearth connections or links between events that you hadn't noticed before. What an eye-opening venture, and adventure! Try it a while, I think you'll like it. But don't give up after just one week. Carry that notebook, cell phone, or even a big pad of sticky notes with you, and jot down your observations. Then type up your notes formally if you are so inclined. Connections may take a couple of months or even longer to detect. The amazing thing is that you won't have to dig too deep to find the links and patterns, thanks to your log of events and the labels you created to assist you in your search.

Journal Entry 14

On or around, 02/02/2004
Waxing gibbous moon
Time unknown

Max Appears to Tessie

Go ask Alice
I think she'll know...[36]

Tessie, our dear friend, phoned me and told me something incredible. She had been daydreaming in her room when Max appeared to her in a vision. She said she was awake when it happened, rather than simply seeing him in a dream.

Tessie said Max appeared to be young, perhaps about eighteen years of age. His hair was longer than usual and rather wavy. She told me he appeared to be euphoric, marching back and forth with what looked like a long pole that he would sometimes twirl and tap on the (seeming) ground as they talked. He wore a white shirt and a pair of blue shorts that looked like a uniform – clothing that Max might wear for school sports, such as field hockey or soccer.

Before Tessie's remarkable vision faded, she said that Max told her adamantly, and I quote:

Remember what the dormouse said,
"Feed your head...."[36]

Incredulous, I quizzed Tessie further and she said that this is what she heard Max's spirit say. In looking back, he had apparently taken

---

[36] Jefferson Airplane. "White Rabbit." *Surrealistic Pillow.* RCA, 1967. LP.

these words directly from the song, "White Rabbit" (Slick, 1967). Please note that the name of the band was subsequently changed to Jefferson Starship.

Readers might wish to try and translate the meaning Max had intended. I decided to take a stab at it next.

Post Script 1

To my mind, when Max quoted the awesome words, feed your head, he meant that while we are here, we ought to be reading, learning and expanding our minds. Of course, there is the drug culture innuendo and all the implications that can be derived from the "White Rabbit" lyrics. One could probably write a treatise on this song alone, not to mention Lewis Carroll's wonderful work.[37]

Post Script 2

Not long after hearing Tessie's account, just for fun I called Max's brother, Mark. Did he happen to remember his school colors? "Why, they were dark blue and light blue," he said. Of course Max's colors were the same. I then realized the blue shorts Tessie saw in her vision do not contradict Mark's statement, and that the clothing appears to be part of a school uniform.

Another interesting note: out of the blue, I remembered that Max and Mark had each held the Wellington School record for Javelin Throw, Mark's in earlier years. In fact, Max seldom hesitated to remind me he had topped his brother's record around 1969 or 1970. Both brothers had learned how to throw spears from the proper source – the

---

[37] Carroll, Lewis. *Alice's Adventures in Wonderland*. London: MacMillan and Co., 1865. Print.

boys of Rhodesia, now Zimbabwe. They played games with the young Rhodesian lads when they were just tykes themselves. What better way to learn?

Could the long pole in Tessie's vision that Max sported so proudly have been a javelin? I mean, an intended javelin, as in Max's communication to Tessie?

Tessie knew about none of the above facts until I phoned her later. She sounded surprised and delighted to hear about Max's javelin throwing record and his school colors. These details also tend to provide validation for her vision. Regardless, I believed Tessie's account from the start. As a good friend, I knew she would have no reason to tell me a yarn, knowing how serious I am about the writing of my journal and the accurate recording of narratives.

Above all, isn't it fantastic that Tessie received corroborating evidence for something as ethereal as a vision?

Journal Entry 15

Tuesday, 02/03/2004
Waxing gibbous moon
Time unknown

Max's Friend Passes On

"Where to Now St. Peter?" [38]

Max's dear friend, Jack, died of cancer on this date. He leaves his wife, Debbie, and their two grown children.

Not more than a year ago, Jack and Debbie had moved their belongings and their lives to their brand new home in Tucson. Max and I were lucky enough to be introduced to them through his group, the Thai Laos Cambodia Brotherhood (TLCB). I especially remember the nights we cracked jokes and told stories at the relaxing TLCB dinners and get-togethers. It came as no surprise that not long after the first year of festivities, Max and Jack became buddies who kept in touch frequently.

Now I am so sad for Debbie, not only because she lost her friend and husband, but also because she is new to the Tucson area. Her children live in other states and she only knows a few people in Tucson. This makes it very hard for her during an already difficult time. I'm going to ask for some time off to drive down and stay a few days with this lovely, courageous woman.

Jack's death came unexpectedly. In December, he and Debbie had taken the drive up to see Max after his transfer to the ICU. No one knew Jack had cancer too, not even Jack. I am stunned to have lost our

---

[38] John, Elton. "Where to Now St. Peter?" *Tumbleweed Connection*. Uni. 1970. LP.

fun-loving, down-to-earth friend. He and Debbie were so supportive when Max died. I will never forget their heartfelt cards, their calls and their many kindnesses.

Post Script

As I complete my final edits, I am happy to report that I did spend some time with Debbie that spring. We had a heartbreaking, but awesome time talking about our men, our families and our lives with them. But I am so sad to say now that Debbie, too, died of cancer and heart failure in May of 2008. However, I feel comforted knowing she is with Jack.

I was grateful to have an opportunity to give Debbie and her children copies of our book, *For the Time Being*, a family scrapbook and memoir. Debbie cried for joy when she saw Jack's name at the top of the "In Memoriam" page. This book contains many of Max's poems and illustrations as well. We wrote it for our families and for the surviving loved ones of those who died of infirmities like cancer, but never did I expect that Jack and Debbie would be leaving so soon. Now their dear children are the survivors.

JOURNAL ENTRY 16

Friday, 02/13/2004
Third quarter moon
Around 3 p.m.

Candy for the Oncology Staff

Despite the stress and heaviness of cancer,
I never felt that Max was a burden.
Through it all, this song came to mind,
"He Ain't Heavy, He's My Brother" [39]

Today I bought some Valentine candy and made up some cards and took them to the oncology ward at the Desert Hospital where Max had lived for many weeks before being transferred to hospice. When I checked in at the front desk, I was surprised to learn that several of the nurses and most of the staff I knew had left. Some were gone for the day, while others no longer worked in the Oncology Ward. I began to wonder what the turnover rate was like.

Fortunately for me, I recognized a couple of Max's nurses as they were doing their rounds. So I went over and thanked them personally for their hard work and kindness toward Max, the patients, our family, and our friends. When Max was around, some of us used to camp out with him or sleep in the lounge down the hall. Regardless, the people in oncology always made us feel welcome no matter how much work they had to do. As busy as they were today, I considered myself lucky to have a chance to talk with two of the nurses I knew. Then I left the cards and

---

[39] The Hollies. "He Ain't Heavy, He's My Brother." *He Ain't Heavy, He's My Brother.* Epic, 1969. LP.

candy for them to share with the rest when things settled down, if indeed they ever did!

Though it was a bit difficult to return to the oncology ward, I felt privileged to have the opportunity to thank at least some of the staff and to share my thoughts and sentiments with them. Their job is a challenging one. I can only hope it is as rewarding as it is demanding for these wonderful, dedicated people.

Journal Entry 17
Saturday, 02/14/2004
Around 10:00 a.m.

Valentines for Max - Lunch with Mel

Because days come and go
But my feelings for you are forever...[40]

For Valentine's Day, I decorated Max's flag, parked on the counter
between the dining room and the kitchen. My countertop is blue and
the banner, set in a cherry wood triangle, matches the surroundings.
His banner rests back-to-back against my dad's, displayed in triangle
form as well. (They look handsome together!) The counter is long, so
there's plenty of room for the flowers and mementos I like to arrange
around the flags.

Around noon, I decided to make the hour's trek to the Veteran's
National Cemetery in Cave Creek. Then, with the help of a
little plant wire, I managed to weave my valentine card into a red
and white bouquet, placing it at Max's headstone. The cemetery
personnel request that each grave be decorated with artificial flowers
instead of fresh cuts. Though not my style, I must say today's silk
arrangement looked real. Maybe someday I'll get used to the rules
and regulations.

I fiddled around with Max's bouquet to get it just so. Then I said
a few prayers that Max used to say and asked him how he was doing.
"Max, I pray your new life is as beautiful as I see it."

"No, more beautiful."

---

[40] Papa Roach. "Forever." *The Paramour Sessions.* Geffen, 2006. CD.

What was that murmur I heard trailing behind me as I tiptoed back to the car? Must have been the wind....

❧ ❧ ❧

Considering freeway traffic and the time spent in contemplation, the trip to and from the cemetery normally takes about three hours. Driving, this time toward Phoenix, alas, I was getting too pooped to pop. This would never do because I had plans to meet my girlfriend, Melinda, for lunch – er maybe a mid-afternoon meal. Racing like mad toward our meeting place, I barked, "Girl, you've got to get with it!" So I turned up the oldies and popped out the handy wipes. Speeding and sponging off my face, I sang along with the Beach Boys, Fleetwood Mac, and yes, even the Troggs. Though I wouldn't recommend multi-tasking on any freeway, this happy change of pace seemed to do it for me.

By the time I pulled into the parking lot and saw Mel's easygoing smile, I had pretty much recharged my batteries. As I zipped into a tree-lined desert spot (a contradiction in terms), I thought of something that took me off guard.

Geez, I haven't seen Melinda in years.

Eight, ten? I don't even know.

I do know that for the past few years, Melinda had been living in California with her husband. Unfortunately, right around the time I lost Max, Mel went through a rough divorce. She then made the complex decision to buy a home in Prescott Valley so she could return to her old stomping grounds. Though this made it easier for the two of us to get together, we saw that it would probably be best to meet somewhere about halfway. Even so, the shorter drive was mine.

Kind of Mel to make the longer trip.

Needless to say, with all we'd both been through, we were in a difficult way. We had some serious catching up to do. Perhaps this is why Melinda and I spent the rest of the day at the restaurant, going from lunch to happy hour... and on into dinnertime cocktails. We laughed and cried and talked for hours that seemed more like moments in time.

JOURNAL ENTRY 18

Friday, 02/20/2004
Evening

Prayer to Hear Max Again

My prayer is to linger with you
At the end of the day
In a dream that's divine...[41]

Despite all of the incredible happenings that have given me hope, I see that I'm starting to miss Max again. For one thing, I miss his voice – the one I heard on New Year's Day *nine days after he died*. So, tonight I prayed that I might hear him again.

---

[41] The Platters. "My Prayer." *Encore of Golden Hits-The Platters.* Mercury, 1960. LP.

Journal Entry 19

Saturday, 02/21/2004
Early afternoon

My Prayer is Answered

I heard Max's voice in an amazing way.
Was he beside me, as in "Hey There Delilah"? [42]

In light of the prayer I said last night, what happened today was truly extraordinary. Still, it shouldn't seem so surprising if we believe that our prayers are answered.

♪ ♪ ♪

"The remote's broken," I said while attempting to change the channel. "Nothing's happening."

Hmmm... becoming a familiar scenario, isn't it?

All right... okay... let's check the batteries. Finally, I got off my duff and went to the garage. *Let's see, where did Max put the battery pack?* Rummage... grope... fumble fumble.... *not here I take it.*

Before long, I ambled my way to the kitchen to look in the hutch by the phone. Well, after tossing out some junk at the top of the pile, I spotted something. "Yay, a whole pack of double As!" I hollered like an anthropology student on her first dig.

Regardless, I didn't stop there. You see, whenever I find a pile of stuff, I have to poke around till I hit bottom. *Hmmm, what's this?* And there, underneath the batteries like a lost pup, was the handheld recorder Max used to keep in his pocket. I chuckled remembering

---

[42] Plain White T's. "Hey There Delilah." *All That We Needed.* Fearless, 2005. CD.

how he liked to tape his project notes and other vagrant thoughts while sitting in traffic; a great way to make the most of otherwise wasted time.

But I wondered if the old machine still worked. Soon to find out.... I jerked the contraption out from under the rubble. It's a wonder I didn't break the darned thing.

Fumbling around, I finally notice something. "Geez, there's a tape in it," I holler, as if my mother were still around. So, I set it on the counter, press "Play" and turn it up full-blast.

No sound... nada.

Okay, maybe it's reading the end. So I rewind the thing and press play again.

In order to maintain some semblance of patience, I sit back on the barstool and tap... tap... tap. It's like a day goes by.

At last, a buzz... a treasure unearthed from a time gone by as I perceive a familiar timbre. Sitting up, I say, "Man, it's Max." Like a small child who has just opened her first Christmas gift, I'm in total awe. *The recording may have been made back when, but this is happening now, for me.* I brush back a tear because the tiny ribbon has captured the character and tone of Max's voice so beautifully. *It's like he's here right now, talking to me.* Bowled over by his words and thoughts, I'm powerless to keep the water from my eyes, so I just let it flow.

From the start, I'd been amazed at the nature and depth of Max's ideas. His tendency to think outside the box had a way of defying time-tested notions: catching people off guard, testing me all the time, and sometimes even inciting me to riot. We had so many heated (yet fun and thought-provoking) debates. I think one of Max's primary purposes here on earth was to challenge people, and that he did, but in a rewarding way. After sitting down to dinner with Max, you went home with more than you came, whether a thought, a feeling, insight into something new, or perhaps even a totally different reality to ponder. I can truly say no one ever left our table indifferent.

The recording ends. I eject the tape and try to drum up a title. "Hmmm, I've got it," and with a felt tip pen, print the words:

On Art and Life: The Philosophy of Max Blau

As if he can hear me, I say, "I'll keep this tape forever, Max."

"Promise!"

But I must remember to make copies for our friends, so I scribble a note and pin it up on the board in the kitchen. "Hey guy, I hope you don't mind, I titled your tape."

You see, Max never titled any of his work unless his employer requested it. He even disliked borders or frames around works of art. Guess that's another way he thought outside the box. In fact, Max reviled titles, labels and limitations of almost any kind, just as he despised the way people are often labeled.

In short, Max was my hero. But how could you possibly tell?

♫ ♫ ♫

As the last rays of a blazing sun reflected off the patio chimes and onto the living room rug, I sat cross-legged on the floor and replayed the tape. It relaxed me to hear Max's calm voice and his amazing views on life. And as the glittering lights danced on the blue rug, I listened to the tape again and again. Before long, day turned to dusk and with a wrinkled sleeve, I wiped the salty crust from my face. "High time for a nap," I said, gaping and lifting my arm just enough to pull down a pillow. Then, before you could say *short circuit*, I slipped into a stupor.

Hours later, I awoke to patio chimes proclaiming another blustery night. And, as I got up and watched the cut glass flicker in the light, this way and that, it dawned on me that Max's tape had seriously – if not joyfully – diverted me from my noontime plans. So I pulled up the remote and installed the new batteries, at last. Then, reverting to the channel surfing of yesteryear, I did a little test.

"Okay, everything's working fine. Just needed batteries, that's all."

♪ ♪ ♪

Humor has a way of relaxing me. So I dial around in search of a sit-com before bedtime. After all, it's Saturday night. Yet, despite my desire for a little lighthearted entertainment, thoughts of the day capture my mind like an old time movie. Soon I realize that I don't need a TV set at all – the show that's burning my brain has me rapt.

One by one, the events of the day materialize like pictures moving in string formation. And what they reveal is astounding:

1. The remote control is broken
2. But is it broken or are the batteries dead?
3. I search for batteries in the garage and hutch
4. Finally, I find an unopened pack of batteries in the hutch
5. Now I find Max's tape recorder, <u>buried just underneath the batteries</u>
6. Then, to my amazement, a tape of Max's voice is still in the machine

Ironically, in the formlessness of the dark, the undeniable sequence of events unfold, shedding light on an unseen reality. Like an airborne portrait, the big picture virtually hits me in the back of the head. "Oh my God," I cry, looking up at the ceiling like I can view The Man. "How did I not see?" I ask, arms outstretched.

Last night I prayed to hear Max's voice. And, in less than twenty-four hours, You answered my prayer!

Post Script

Much later (okay, I'm a tad slow), I finally recognized the tacit confirmation that was sent my way. The upshot was this: first, I asked to hear Max's voice, *"the one I heard nine days after he died."* Then through what I can only describe as a brilliant celestial maneuver, in less than a day, all the powers that be caused me to search for the batteries, which brought me to the tape of Max's voice. The batteries were right above the tape recorder, of course. This clever maneuver confirmed what I already knew in my heart: *that the voice I heard nine days <u>after</u> Max died was the same as the voice on tape, the one he'd made not long <u>before</u> he died.*

Of course it was Max, all along.

Friday, 02/27/2004
First quarter moon
Around 7:00 a.m.

The Eye and the Untangled Necklace

Half asleep, I found a pixel-like eye winking at me. Strange, I've never seen anything like it – an eye winking while my eyes are closed. What's this about?

Even so, my mind starts to drift, wondering if one eye winks or if it actually blinks.[43]

Suddenly, I open my eyes and look around. *Oh, it's too early in the morning for this.*

"It's Friday, and I have to go to work. So let's get on with it!"

After some toast and a shot of café au lait, I return to the knots in the necklace I'd planned to wear today. Due to another riotous week at the office, my eyelids had begun to clamp shut way early the night before. And as I continued to work on the knotty (naughty) necklace, my head began to bob like a buoy lost at sea. Well, it wasn't long before Magoo tossed the wicked chain on the coffee table. "Ach, no luck there."

Oh well, let's try again tomorrow.

꙳ ꙳ ꙳

---

[43] Reminds me of the "sound of one hand clapping." Does one eye wink or does it blink? I leave this madcap question for the reader to sort out.

So I put my mug down on the coffee table and pick up the necklace, only to find something shocking, if not downright impossible: the chain is smooth.

Then I feel a lump… the one in my throat, as I say, "What?"

"The knots are gone!"

This is just plain weird. Before I went to bed last night, I was sure the chain had several tangles in it. Despite oncoming delirium, I struggled for almost an hour to remove them. To no avail. Sure I was frustrated, I couldn't even get one knot out!

Baffled, I turn the necklace over in my hands and wonder: *Could those little knots have come undone when I tossed the chain on the table?*

Nah, no way. Hunkering down on the sofa, I sigh, remembering how I used to leave my jewelry for Max – right there on the coffee table. He had a knack for getting the kinks out of almost anything. In fact, he seemed to enjoy the challenge of fixing things and would have most any kinky piece ready to wear in the nick of time.

Well, we must have been a match of sorts because, week after week, month after month, I'd find new stuff for him to fix. Yet, he never seemed to mind.

Hey guy… I hope my smiles said something about how I felt whenever you fixed things for me. But just in case, I want to say thanks again, hon… not only for being adept at repairs, but because you never seemed to lose your enthusiasm in doing things – day after day, year after year.

JOURNAL ENTRY 21

Monday, 03/01/2004
Waxing gibbous moon
Late afternoon

An Unexpected Gift

Like the singin' bird and the croakin' toad... [44]

I received an unexpected package from a prominent bookstore in England – Kenneth Grahame's classic, *The Wind in the Willows*,[45] Max's favorite book when he was a lad. His brother, Mark, used to call him Toad after one of the author's incorrigible characters.

But who sent me this wonderful book? I see no name or return address on the package.

Post Script

Months later, I receive a call from Char, Max's sister. She said, knowing how much it would mean to me, she'd thought about mailing me the book all along. Of course, it had to be Char who sent it, though she wouldn't actually admit to it.

What a delightful book! I love the colorful characters and all their misadventures – great lessons for children, young and old.

Thanks for your thoughtfulness, Char. I will always treasure this timeless work of art.

---

[44] Croce, Jim. "I Got a Name." *24 Karat Gold in a Bottle.* DCC Compact Classics, 1994. CD.

[45] Grahame, Kenneth. *The Wind in the Willows.* Abr. ed. London: Walker, 2000. Print.

PART II
A LIFE FOREVER CHANGED

Wednesday, 03/24/2004
Noontime

Max's Notes and an Extraordinary Find

I memorize every line
And I kiss the name that you sign...[46]

My mind is blown. In the process of ransacking drawers, I discovered a stack of Max's legal pads that I had stashed away before the funeral. Back then, I was too distraught to even glance at them. It's amazing what a couple of months can do. I'm beginning to feel a bit stronger. So I decided to start the day by pitching stuff from drawers and boxes. Well, I ended the day by safeguarding an unexpected treasure – one you might say is *beyond this world.*

To shed light on today's phenomenal experience, I must backtrack a bit. You see, Max had always been a good communicator who spoke his mind more often than not. And in many ways, he was a man of letters. He usually kept a pad in his pocket to jot down notes of import as the mood struck him. Sometimes I'd even find used up legal pads in strange places like bathrooms or in the garage. For as much as Max enjoyed the free exchange of ideas, he also liked to retain important facts and figures, albeit not so tidily. As a design engineer, he preferred to keep the stats in his own notebooks rather than relying on outside sources. In fact, Max's record-keeping tendencies saved his employer more than once – like the time the mainframe crashed and they needed data for a critical customer meeting – Max at the ready again.

---

[46] John, Elton and Bonnie Raitt. "Love Letters." *Duets.* MCA, 1993. CD.

Sometimes I'd find a notebook containing one of his hand-written poems or a cartoon sandwiched between reams of engineering codes and company acronyms. What a joy to discover his spur-of-the-moment creations!

So today, while cleaning out drawers, I stumbled across the stack of legal pads that I'd been too distressed to even look at in December. Then an irresistible thought came to mind. *Maybe I'll find one of his poems, just like I found "The Seashell" not long before he died.* (This inspiring poem is provided in Post Script 2.)

Soon, I found myself carrying the whole pile of pads to the dining room. I set them lightly on the lace tablecloth as if they were the king's mail.

Then, as I pull up a chair by the window, I begin to feel uneasy. For, despite six years of graduate study and the necessity to read several books a week, I hesitate to disturb this scruffy pile. *Grad school was no big deal, but this stack is about two feet high.*

I have never felt so intimidated.

Where to begin? I sigh.

Before long, I see that there's a pad sticking out about halfway down the stack. The pages are dog-eared, the cardboard tattered.

"Hmmm, what do you say little miss," I ask The Tig who's mauling my shoe. "Shall I start here?" I ask as I finger the tattered notepad.

Tiggi flicks her ear and curls her tail into a cordial question mark.

"You want to know too, don't you?"

She looks up at me with her big, green eyes and lets out a mindful mew. (After all, she is a lady.)

"Aw, me too," I say, rumpling her scruff. And, in a not-so-ladylike way, I jerk the tattered pad from the pile. How the other pads remain in place, I'll never know.

Furtively, as if someone besides my little side-kick might be watching, I glance down at the first page to find Max's fuzzy scrawl – the sorry handwriting he had developed so painstakingly after his first stroke. The lump in my throat now feels like a boulder. I want to stop, but I can't. Something's spurring me on.

Moving forward, I see that the top page is full of Max's hospital notes. Even while under the care of several nurses, he'd managed to keep a log of meds, dosages, dates and times. Despite burning images of days and months gone by, I force myself to go on. Any poem or sketch created by Max would be worth so much more than the few trying moments required to uncover them.

But amazingly, what I run across is not something I would ever have imagined – no, not in a lifetime! For, about halfway down the crumpled page, I am finally able to decipher an entry dated November 22nd, the anniversary of President Kennedy's assassination. At first, it appears to be a dreadful log. Max had been talking about the terrible fate of our thirty-fifth president. No doubt, he was also sad because of his own plight. He'd been preparing for his first round of chemo after the stroke that happened on the day they installed his porta-cath. I remember how hard he'd worked to reclaim some semblance of his neat-looking script.

I must stop and wipe the water away.

Pressing on, I find that Max had scribbled something beyond belief – given his daunting circumstances and the event that happened to me nine days after his death. For there, in an apparent effort to buoy himself up, he had written:

"I must pull my socks up."

"Wait a minute!" My hands are trembling, I can hardly hold the pad. My mind starts to drift and I flop down, glancing back at the ephemeral notepad as it slides across ceramic tile. Stunned, I just sit there watching Tiggi lick my arm.

❧ ❧ ❧

In time, my senses clear and I feel the blood rush to my head. Still a bit unsteady, I shudder my way across the room and thankfully spot the notepad at the far end.

Soon feeling more with it, I pick up the pad and dust it off. "If nothing else, Tiggi, I must understand what is happening here." So I boost us up – Tiggi, the pad and me. Then, leafing back quickly through the pages, at last I find the page dated November 22nd, and my eyes lock on four incredible words. I examine them again and again, as if they had been written in Sanskrit:

"...*pull my socks up*"

My God. Max had written these words after his first stroke. He apparently wrote them to buoy himself up. *Yet, these are the very words I heard him say on January 1st after he died.* This time he said them to me, in an effort to buoy me up:

"*Pull your socks up, mate!*" *he said.*

I look up at the ceiling and cry, "Max, this is what I heard you say when you came to me, nine days after you died! You said, '*Pull your socks up, mate!*' as if to admonish me for not – *for not believing* that nothing in life is ever lost. You gave me the old 'chin up' just as you gave yourself that day in the hospital."

Unfettered by it all, Tiggi sighs, passing out on the table. Her paw is still clinging to the page like a bookmark as I sit there, rapt in thought. Now I too have marked off the page – I'm holding it like validation in my hands!

Post Script 1

What is the validation? It is the code, "Pull … socks up…," the words Max had scribbled down on his tattered legal pad no more than a month before he passed away. <u>This is the code that matches the words Max's soul revealed to me on January 1st, two days after his own funeral.</u> His words form the structure and meaning of the cipher that no one can refute – not even me.

On the first day of the New Year, Max returned from the grave to tell me what he had already told himself thirty-one days before he died: "Pull your socks up!

This mind-bending corroboration ventures beyond the realm of belief and into the realm of the knowing. I will cherish it forever!

Post Script 2

As noted previously, I am including one of Max's poems. The last two stanzas are especially beautiful to me. True to form, Max left his poem untitled, but I call it *The Seashell*. He composed it on Saint Patrick's Day, four months before he learned that he had cancer.

Or did he already know?

> *I am a Seashell,*
> *I am the Message,*
> *I am the Sender*
> *and the Sent.*
>
> *I am an example*
> *of the Creator,*
> *As are you,*
> *and none other.*

I am the Recipient
and the Dreamer,
The bringer of Memories
and Hope,
The center in the Maelstrom;
the keeper
of the Flame.

And you, the Sender and the Sent,
the Message and the Mood,
the keeper of Aspiration.

Know then, that we are one,
as all are one in dreams this day.
We live upon the shores of destiny,
And reinvent them daily in ecstasy.

Life is the bliss of action,
Death, the bliss of reflection,
The time to wish,
Of return and renewal.

By
Max Blau

JOURNAL ENTRY 23

Wednesday, 03/31/2004
Waxing gibbous moon
Morning

The Death of Another Loved One

Praying for the healing rain
To restore my soul again....[47]

I am very sad to record the passing of Uncle Clyde on this date. I just learned of his death because his son, Nate, telephoned me from England. I am feeling especially troubled because Nate and his family are suffering the loss of their dearest father and grandfather, and also because I had planned to visit Max's Uncle Clyde this summer. For the past few weeks, I've been working on my vacation plans which include a trip to Oxford, England to visit Max's guardians and family. Well, dear Clyde was in the forefront of my thoughts and intentions – after leaving Oxford, I'd planned to go see him for the very first time.

Though Uncle Clyde and I had never met, somehow I felt I knew him. You see, for the past decade, Clyde, Max and I had been sending letters back and forth across the sea, especially after the death of Cynthia, Clyde's beloved wife.

I was so hoping to meet him. I regret that I didn't go sooner.

Yet, no matter how sad I feel, I try to console myself with this conviction: Clyde is *there* with Cynthia, Max, and Uncle Vince, and all those who have already made the journey to the Other Side. Of this, I have no doubt.

---

[47] Clapton, Eric. "My Father's Eyes." *Pilgrim*. Reprise, 1998. CD.

Post Script

Now I'm revising my plans to include a weekend stay with Nate, Chloe and the girls who live in Surrey. Sure looking forward to it!

So why are the days moving along at a turtle's pace?

JOURNAL ENTRY 24

Saturday, 04/03/2004
Waxing gibbous moon
Noontime

Max's Fifty-first Birthday

My visit to the cemetery reminds me of the beautiful song
"Landslide" by Stevie Nicks [48]

I am writing this journal entry almost a week after the fact. April 3rd would have been Max's fifty-first birthday. I know I paid him a visit that day because it was the day before Palm Sunday, but I can't remember driving to the cemetery or doing much of anything else for that matter.

Did I leave him a garland or a bouquet? I can't recall. The scene is murky to me now like coffee dumped on a watercolor painting. Yet my mind's been more like jello all week.

Maybe longer.

Still, it's not like me to forget. I'm a visual person and Max's birthday was an important occasion for us. At the very least, we'd go out to dinner. Sometimes I'd bring him a fresh bouquet or a box of candy and a big card – one with a joke in it, of course.

Max had his ornery days and, like anyone, a blue day here or there. But more often than not, he was a real cut-up, wearing that old, khaki safari hat from his time in Africa. I remember him fondly that way. Sometimes when he walked away from me, he'd hunker down, bending his knees, becoming shorter and shorter with every step. Soon, I could hardly see him at all – crouching, waving, meandering his way into the sunset.

---

[48] Fleetwood Mac. "Landslide." *Fleetwood Mac.* Reprise, 1975. LP.

Wednesday, 04/28/2004
First quarter moon
Early morning

No More Tangles

Getting ready for work, I stomped back to the bedroom to look for something to wear with my new grey suit. For some reason, I had left the suit in the guest closet. On the way, I whipped out a rather alluring rose-colored scarf and stopped short at the bed.

"How did this happen?" I exclaimed. For there was my silver necklace, draped across the king-sized comforter like jewelry fit for a queen. What's more, there were no tangles in it!

"How is this possible?" I said in sheer amazement. "What's going on?"

Last night I had fallen asleep on the sofa. Too dozy to read, I watched a little TV and fooled around with my silver necklace. I mean, the darned thing had about five knots in it! So I worked on it till the show ended, but even with such dogged determination, I hadn't loosened a loop. The protuberances appeared to shrink, looking more like the subatomic particles the scientists were talking about on NOVA. I rubbed my eyes and before you could say "miniscule", my head began to bob just above the coffee table. When I came to, I found the tangled chain draped across my hands like rosary beads.

Now no longer caring about the tangles that remained, I knew it was beyond me. *Yawn.* Time to give it up for the night.

Yuck, still have to brush my teeth. Grunting my way to the bathroom, I tossed the knotty necklace on the bed. "I'll do it tomorrow – with tweezers." So I brushed my teeth and slipped into my polka dot PJs just in time for a comedy show. And somewhere between chuckles and cushy couch pillows, I slipped into that blissful state of freedom commonly called unconsciousness.

♪ ♪ ♪

Yet, even as the rays of the morning sun flicker across my bedroom wall, I walk in the room to find my silver necklace arranged on the bed, just so. No twists! No tangles!

I gasp and shake my head. "How is this possible?"

To be sure, I remove my bifocals and bring the necklace up to my nose. Smiling, I say as I start my inspection, "How sweet, it shimmers in the light."

But something isn't adding up. "Hmm, no knots." I turn it over and over. "Not even a kink. How can this be?" I shake my head and plop down on the bed. *I couldn't have loosened the tangles while I was sleeping....*

No, I can't even do that when I'm awake.

Soon I'm up, draping the silver chain 'round my neck. Then looking up toward the ceiling, I shout, "Hey darling, wherever you are... thanks for helping me out in a pinch!" Brushing back a tear, I mull over the scarf. *Maybe I won't wear this after all.* Then fastening the little clasp and straightening the chain, I say to Max. "Maybe I'll just wear your necklace... by itself. In memory of all the good things we had."

"Most of all, each other."

Post Script

I'm getting that déjà vu sensation again. Didn't this happen before?

Yes, of course it did. In checking my calendar, I see that a similar event occurred on February 27th as documented in Journal Entry 20. Just another coincidence? Much less likely, methinks.

No, I'm not sleep walking, nor am I sleep-fixing necklaces – absurd the thought, though someone will surely ask. When we first started dating, Max used to fix my jewelry. Somehow he managed to keep up the tradition throughout our marriage. He seemed to enjoy the challenge of repairing broken clasps, lifting little loops… disentangling tiny ties.

In contrast, witness my vexation in manipulating small objects of any kind. I enjoy abstract thought, but the thought of tiny items in disrepair? Well, that just about sets me into a tailspin. Of course, this is Magoo speaking. If my vision were better, perhaps I'd find fixing things amusing, like Max.

Well, maybe he was just being nice.

Anyway Max, you know I've always appreciated your help and thoughtful kindness… I mean, don't you know? I sure hope so. No matter the task at hand, you had a way of making it fun… love you, guy.

Saturday, 05/01/2004
Waxing gibbous moon
Around 4 p.m.

A Spirit Guide Speaks

Then take me disappearin' through the smoke rings of my mind…
Far from the twisted reach of crazy sorrow…[49]

I can't seem to recall the date this wonderful event occurred, but I believe it was on or around May 1st. I know it happened at about four o'clock because I usually meditate around that time of day, at least when I'm home. I've been meditating a lot the past month and plan to continue with this practice. The deep breathing clears my mind, tends to alleviate grief, and consequently helps me sleep. Because of a health issue, I did some research and learned that meditation is a great way to retain the health we have or to return an ailing body, mind and spirit to healing mode.

Mandy's motto: *an ounce of prevention is worth a shot.* So I ordered more meditation CDs. So happy to find they arrived on time for the weekend.

Well, after doing the Saturday chores, I glanced down at the mystifying stack of disks and books I'd arranged on the end table. *Let's try this one,* I thought, as I slid the *Spirit Guide Meditation* CD from a

---

[49] Dylan, Bob. "Mr. Tambourine Man." *Bringing It All Back Home.* Legacy, 1965. LP.

book by Sylvia Browne.[50] "I've never attempted to contact a spirit guide," I said to Tiggi, my tiger-striped confidante.

"So, what have I got to lose? Who knows, maybe I'll learn something." Tiggi's tail shot up, then curled in approval.

"I see you agree!"

❧ ❧ ❧

Sitting up straight on the sofa, I wiggle around and get comfortable while trying to keep my feet flat on the floor. Soon, with Ms. Browne's recorded guidance, I slip into the deep-breathing process and begin to feel calmer, more relaxed. Then the author calls to mind several pathways that I'm now visualizing in my mind's eye: a lovely field, a gazebo, and so on.

Slipping away, before long I hear her say that it is time to make my request.

I clear my throat. "Okay, here goes...."

I say it aloud, with confidence. "What is the name of my spirit guide?" For some reason, I think I'll have to wait awhile to hear anything. Not so....

Truly, no more than a few seconds elapse when I am thunderstruck to find the colors shifting in my field of view. Waves of violet, green and gold surge before my closed eyes. Then, at once, I hear a gentle voice as clear as the crystal chimes ringing on my patio! There is no mistaking his name.

"Charlemagne!" he says.[51]

---

[50] Browne, Sylvia. *Contacting Your Spirit Guide.* Carlsbad, CA: Hay House, 2002. Print.

[51] During today's meditation, I learned that Charlemagne is my spirit guide. Charlemagne also conveyed the idea that he is a spirit being not to be confused with Charles the Great, the Frankish king of old.

JOURNAL ENTRY 27

Sunday, 05/02/2004
Waxing gibbous moon
Around 11:00 a.m.

Max's Churning Computer

Darlin' come on listen to me,
I won't do you no harm...[52]

Today I glanced through the files Max kept on disc. I knew that hundreds of his files were contained in several directories. So having set aside a block of time, I decided to review all of them, delete those of little value, and retain those that seemed important. *I'll just copy the "good" ones to CD.*

Then I can dispose of Max's computer, I thought.

One time not long after he died, I logged on to his machine to search for some documents. The computer ran well that day – no problems whatsoever. Luckily, I found the needed files in no time at all.

❧ ❧ ❧

So with every confidence, I sit down at Max's computer and boot up. But about three seconds into the logon, I hear a nefarious noise, a thud followed by an ear-splitting bellow. "Whoa!" I jump up from my seat and back away. You see, the computer's bawling like a car that won't start in the dead of winter. Stunned, I move about halfway down the hall. *Wouldn't want to get any closer to the thing. I mean, what if it*

---

[52] Lennon, John. "Whatever Gets You Thru the Night." *Walls and Bridges.* Capitol, 1974. LP.

explodes? Now that may sound silly, but believe me, I am not willing nor even able to get any closer to the roaring roadster – or in Max's case, the "Croakin' Toadster".

Suddenly, as if the computer is changing tune, it starts to make a chugging sound. "Oh God, it's dying!" I want to turn it off now, but I can't. *That might screw up the hard drive. I can't lose any of these files. They must be backed up.*

"Stop, stop!" I scream like a fool.

Then, *as if on cue*, the chugging actually *stops!*

"WHAT the HECK?" I shriek, as if a few fricatives might placate the pounding in my chest.

Nevertheless, on hearing the happy hum of the CPU, I begin to pull myself together... somewhat... and plop down on the chair. Still I'm not getting anywhere, staring at the clock like this.

Okay, after that bizarre scene, coffee's not desired. It's required. Lunchtime.... Besides, I must give the old guy a break.

"Oh, sorry dude, you're not that old," I say. You see, we must try to appease the Toadster.

♪ ♪ ♪

After a welcome lunch, I'm armed to the teeth with a humungous slice of peach pie and my trusty mug. Then, on the way back to the office, I holler at the ceiling, "Hey, Max!" in case he's around. "Honey, I won't delete anything from your hard drive except garbage. I promise."

"Darlin' come on listen to me, I won't do you no harm..." I'm singing that Lennon tune, boogying with pie and coffee. *Behaving myself unlike some toadsters we know....* So I set my reinforcements on his desk and sit down with purpose, something like the operator of a guided missile system.

I clear my throat.

"Okay, alright, here goes…."

"DEFCON Three…"

Hesitation.

"DEFCON Two…"

My hand reaches out to the computer.

"DEFCON One!"

And I press the button.

Lifetimes in that one moment.

Eventually some beeps and clicks. *What, no racket?*

I exhale and check the hard drive. *Nothing weird at all.* So I take another breath, and wait, and wait…

Click… click… click….

I breathe out and say, "Right," as the machine boots up.

"Yes!" I cry, arms to the sky.

Breathing more freely now, I say to my ineffable one, "Guy, the computer's finally behaving itself." (As if he doesn't know.)

Soon I'm reviewing the files without further incident, working long into the night.

Post Script

Since that strange Sunday, I have logged on to Max's machine several times. And I am relieved to report that nothing creepy has happened since then. Just the same, I've decided not to dispose of Max's computer – no, not for a long, long time!

Journal Entry 28

Saturday, 05/08/2004
Waning gibbous moon
Around 4:00 p.m.

Book Flies Off the Shelf

This chapter calls to mind that great song by Carlos Santana,
"No One to Depend On" [53]

I had so much success with my last meditation, I decided to do it again. *Better not wait too long,* I thought, *or I might lose some je ne c'est qua, whatever I'd already learned.* So I returned to Sylvia Browne's CD, as discussed in Journal Entry 26. Then based on her guidance, I decided to use my meditation time to find out what I could, or perhaps should, be doing with my life.

But first, to underscore the upshot of today's incredible event so it makes sense to the least and most circumspect alike, I must backtrack a little and tell you about my lifelong situation.

As a youngster, my IQ tests revealed above average ability in the mechanical domain. Regardless, I have little experience with things of a mechanical nature. In fact, it is probably closer to the truth to say that I have *no desire* to do anything mechanical, like changing an oil filter or even installing handles on kitchen drawers. That is, I could do it, but would I? Probably not – zero patience you see.

On the other hand, maybe I like to pummel nails into walls, because I enjoy hanging pictures. So out of necessity, I learned how to wield

---

[53] Santana. "No One to Depend On." *Santana III.* Columbia, 1971. LP.

a hammer at a young age. I won't tell you what Max had to say about my veteran hammering skills.

Was it because of my lack of mechanical *savoir-faire* that I married the most complementary man for me – the one and only Max Blau – a guy who liked puttering around the house, repairing cars, troubleshooting computer systems, fixing electronic equipment? He was an engineer by day and mister fix-it by night. Well, not every night!

To beat all, Max whistled while he worked. Maybe I liked that most of all. And when you consider his intellect, along with all the other wonderful traits he possessed, it didn't take long for this girl to fall in love. Perhaps you can see that there were other losses that came with the greatest loss of all, the loss of my dearest Max.

To add insult to inconceivable injury, this woman, who admits to being all thumbs, owns a home she is ill-prepared to maintain. A common widow's lament, I do believe, though it was probably a more frequent cry in my mother's day. Women of today are much more proficient at repairing almost any kind of contraption, be it a car, a computer, or perhaps even a crane (though I confess, that would scare me to death).

Now I find myself just getting by when it comes to the mechanics of things. Sure, I change light bulbs. Last month I broke down and installed a new air filter. Then I did some patch painting *(hey, really something there)*. But when the toilet broke, well that's when I said, "Time to find that handyman coupon." I used it, of course, with no compunction at all.

Then to make matters worse, more (and even bigger) things have been breaking: the garbage disposal, Max's truck, and even my car! I suppose I should have expected it, because I just haven't monitored things like Max. Now that he is gone ("on holiday," I say), I have truly been in deep doo-doo – driving an hour each way to my responsible job (many of my partner's reports and mine cross the governor's desk), muddling through piles of paperwork at home, and trying to keep the house and yard clean – all while attempting to cope with my blues over Max's demise. Yet these things I have done faithfully, albeit not perfectly, as ways to keep my mind occupied.

However, the stress of the mechanical situation is beginning to take its toll. The thought of trying to repair broken machinery has set me into a tailspin! So I hired a couple of repair men who fixed most things, but soon, they both beat feet. "No more, can't do it!" was the general refrain. I have been wondering why, because I paid them well for their toil. Then it occurred to me: might they have had strange experiences too?

(Months later, I would learn of an uncanny incident that had happened to one of the men. In retrospect, this could have explained why he left, nevermore to return. He is a neighbor of mine, but he simply shook his head and said he could not go inside my home anymore.)

Despite all the odd goings-on, or perhaps because of them, I simply had to get away from it all.

.♪. .♪. .♪.

Late in the afternoon of this amazing day, I sit down on the sofa and begin to meditate, seeking nothing more than to let go of all worries and concerns. Sitting up straight, I breathe in and out, following Sylvia Browne's guidance on CD. However, I am able to offer no natural nor scientific explanation for what is about to happen.

I'm starting to drift into a kind of meditative stupor – that incredibly harmonious state of relaxation and bliss. Soon, with Ms. Browne's promptings, I pose my meditative question to the universe:

*I'd like to know what I ought to be doing with my life right now –
what should I focus on?*

Thoughts and images swirl around in my head... *perhaps I'll go to a
day spa, or even get a new job, or write another book, or travel to England
or Egypt.* Eyes closed, feeling relaxed and free, I continue to breathe
deeply, happily. Yet never in my life did I expect to receive a response
to my question so quickly, *so outrageously!*

No more than seconds later, I begin to hear just audible noises rising
up in the background. At first, I think the sounds are coming from the
compact disc. Feeling composed and in control, I continue to breathe
deeply as images of the pyramids float around in my head.

Soon, out of the blue, comes a long, low series of rumbles, building
into a crescendo like a fine drum roll. Then I hear a TRIP, THUD,
POP and a thunderous BOOM!! Chills whisk at the back of my neck
like frozen fingers. I jump up. "It's in the dining room!" I shout,
running like a fool – no place to go, nowhere to hide. "Oh, what am I
doing? Haven't a clue," I exclaimed. My nose is nearly pressed up to the
front door but I am too scared to turn and face the unknown.

Soon my curiosity gains momentum like a colossal cat crouching
on a fencepost on a moonlit night... overshadowing all my fears. I
whip around and yell, "Ooohhhh man!" (as if this could possibly scare
off the harbinger of heinous deeds), and bolt into the dining room like
a sun-crazed runner. Skidding on slick tile, I stop short. "'Whut' the
heck?" There, in the middle of my dining room floor, sits a tome long
since abandoned. Yet the book is not setting on the floor, it is sitting
there as if it owns the property, as if it's saying:

*Now that I have your undivided attention,
Madam, take a good look at me!*

I stand speechless, rapt in disbelief as an awesome reality becomes all too apparent. For, in less time than you can say *whiz-bang*, I know that this book did not just fall off the shelf.

Humor me – allow me to explain how I know this – and to reveal what it implies.

I had never read the book that is staring up at me from its Machiavellian place on the floor. But I do remember that Max had read it sometime around the mid-nineties. He said he found it instructive and practical for his work and hobbies too. Me, I had no desire to even open the book, so when Max had finished reading it, I set it on the bottom shelf. "For future reference," I said, tongue in cheek.

Then I forgot all about it.

Now I see that the books on the bottom shelf are tilting into the slot where I'd set the forgotten volume long ago. This would be expected. But, as I move and breathe, I realize that this book was ejected by force – by some awe-inspiring energy, generating all the pops and booms I heard as the book flew off the shelf. You see, I found this tome in the middle of the dining room floor, more than three and a half ceramic tiles away from the bookcase.

I surmised that if the book had simply fallen off the bottom shelf, about three inches from the floor, it would have landed closer to its now-empty slot. But the book did not land anywhere near the shelf. In fact, this tome seems to have flown across the room, after having been expelled from the bookcase by some inexorable force – a force so powerful it caused all the weird and wacky noises I heard, from the time of the rumble until the time the book hit the floor!

One thing I can say for sure: no earthquake, tremor, thunderstorm, tidal wave, monsoon, or car crash occurred anywhere near my home today, and my cats had been sunning themselves in the back bedroom at the time. That is, no creature nor human (not even me) had been anywhere near my dining room when the book flew off the shelf. I should qualify that by saying, "no being that I could detect in any visible way."

So, what is the name of this dilapidated old volume?

How to Fix Damn Near Everything[54]

I just stood there, stunned, afraid to pick it up. Soon, I heard a voice, the one in my head: *makes sense, of course, my God!* And, as the title of the book registered in my brain, I did the only thing any rational human being could do. I got down on the floor and doubled up, tears of laughter streaming down my cheeks. Never did I believe what Max used to say when something mystifyingly funny would happen. "Mandy, God is a joker," he'd cry, with a little tear of joy in his eye. Though I'd often laugh with him because of his joy and delight over the weird and wonderful, I held no conceivable archetype of my own. I just didn't believe – until now.

Post Script

Rational analysis. I received a swift response, specific to my meditation question. The title and sheer presence of the book, *How to Fix Damn Near Everything,* connected directly to my lifelong situation: a lack of mechanical know-how because of my unwillingness to learn how to fix things. This resulted in the avoidance of mechanical work, except perhaps for light duty or to request the assistance of a repair person. The title of this tome played to the obvious – the thing I've been trying to ignore which, I freely admit, has become a real impediment in my life.

---

[54] Peterson, Franklynn. *How to Fix Damn Near Everything.* New York: Wings, 1977. Print.

In fact, on the date of the event, several appliances and devices in my home did not function properly or were broken altogether.

Yes, this off-the-wall phenomenon addressed my mechanical problem in a direct way, and I can only shake my head in amazement.

At this point, some readers may prefer to skip the experiments and statistical tests, provided below. If so, you may wish to continue with the paragraph labeled "Test findings". This includes Dr. Dean Radin's incredible commentary on the test results and the occurrence in my home!

Force experiments. *How far would the book have landed if it had simply dropped off the shelf?* Out of curiosity, I did some book tapping tests to determine the estimated distance the book would land (on ceramic tile) after tapping it until it dropped off the shelf.

I encourage readers to try this experiment at home using a hardcover book with the approximate dimensions of 9-1/2 x 7-1/4 x 1-3/8, i.e., the size of the publication, *How to Fix Damn Near Everything.* Try to find a book of about the same weight, i.e., two pounds, 1.3 ounces. For all trials, conduct your experiment using the same bookcase, preferably in a room with a tile floor. The bottom shelf of the bookcase should be approximately three inches off the floor. Perhaps this is a standard measure for many bookcases. (Please note: since I have accumulated a number of books, they tend to remain upright on the shelves with little or no slack between them). In like manner, place the books on the bottom shelf so that there is little slack between those books and the book you have chosen for your experiment.

Then, review the preliminary and main experiments, as discussed below, and begin your trials. Simply tap the back of the book while exerting the least amount of force as described in the main experiment. Use a tape measure, of course, to gauge the distance between the fallen book and the bookcase. You may find some variation in distance based on whether the book lands on tile, wood, carpet or concrete. All other things being equal, ceramic tile should produce results similar to mine.[55] After each of the thirty runs, record the result in inches including a fraction, i.e., like 5-1/2 or 6-1/8. Annotate any unusual observations concerning how the book landed. Then do some simple arithmetic. Calculate the mean (average) distance in inches over the thirty trials.

Although the following experiments were not conducted in a laboratory setting, I have attempted to conduct them using established methods and procedures, i.e., in as scientific a manner as possible. To that end, I enlisted the assistance of Lorraine, an outside observer who was not aware of the book-flying incident nor my writing with regard to this event. First, I trained her on the standardized measuring procedures, then on recording the numerical data, and finally, on how to annotate any unusual observations with respect to the way the book landed. She then obtained the measurements (30 in each of the two experiments) and recorded her observations.

Preliminary "normal force" experiment. This preliminary experiment was designed to simulate what is likely to happen under normal conditions. For this set of thirty trials, Lorraine was first instructed to use a moderate or normal amount of force while tapping the book in back (alternately from the left edge, then center, and then the right edge of the book). As the book left the shelf, she then observed how it fell and landed. That is, did the book roll, pitch, fly or otherwise drop in an uncommon manner? How was the book positioned after landing? Lorraine then took all thirty measurements and recorded the data.

Results of the preliminary experiment establish that, over all trials, the book landed in a normal manner, i.e., either face up or face down, settling a mean (average) distance of 6.8 inches from the shelf. No

---

[55] To standardize the measurement process: after the book fell, the end of the book closest to the bookcase was measured from the center point to the bottom of the shelf (at the center point of the vacated slot).

unusual movements or out-of-the-ordinary sounds occurred, i.e., no rumbling, rolling, flipping, flying, popping or banging took place during any of the thirty trials. Perhaps a book of a different weight or size would have fallen and landed anomalously when tumbling from a higher place on the shelf. In this experiment, the statistical results comparing the mean of 6.8 inches with the event value of 48 inches were highly significant ($p < .0005$). This finding reveals that *less than five times in ten thousand* will this event occur by chance.

On the day of the May 8th event, the book landed in the middle of the dining room floor, over three and a half ceramic tiles from its location on the bottom shelf. The same process had been used to measure the distance from the shelf to the book, each tile measuring 13.5 inches square. *At the outset, it was determined that the book landed over 48 inches from its place on the shelf* – a distance 6-1/2 times greater than expected based on the normal force results, i.e., a rare event, indeed.

Main "least force" experiment. Because the preliminary results were highly significant, the main experiment was conducted to simulate what is likely to occur under least force conditions. That is, for each of the thirty trials, Lorraine was first instructed to tap the book using the least amount of force or movement possible to cause the book to drop off the bottom shelf. She was also instructed to tap the book at back center only, i.e., no tapping to be done on the left or right sides of the book. All other conditions remained as discussed in the preliminary experiment. Lorraine then took all thirty measurements and recorded the data.

For ease of calculation, fractions were then converted to decimal place values. The main experiment distances per trial and the mean distance are provided in the table, below:

Trial	Distance (in inches)
1	4.25
2	4.75
3	4.75
4	4.25
5	4.75
6	3.75
7	4.50
8	4.50
9	4.50
10	4.75
11	4.50
12	4.75
13	4.50
14	4.50
15	4.50
16	4.75
17	5.38
18	4.75
19	5.00
20	4.75
21	4.88
22	4.38
23	4.50
24	3.13
25	4.75
26	4.75
27	5.00
28	4.50
29	4.50
30	4.25
Mean	**4.56**

Main experiment descriptive results. Results reveal that the book landed a minimum distance of 3.13 inches and a maximum distance of 5.38 inches. The distribution of values is skewed slightly to the left. However, the numbers cluster to a large extent around the mean distance of 4.56 inches. Therefore, when applying the least amount of force possible, the book tends to land, on average, about four and a half inches from the shelf. In all but one case, the book landed face up or face down. During Trial 13 the book landed open with the binding flush against the floor, a distance of 4.5 inches from the shelf. Over all sixty trials, this was the only inconsistent occurrence. In fact, no book rumbling, rolling, flipping, flying, or shooting across the room took place during any of the trials, including Trial 13.

Main experiment results versus the event. These findings shed light on the fact that the difference between the least force results and the book flying event is great. *On May 8ᵗʰ, the book landed over 48 inches from its location on the bookcase – a distance 10 times greater than what we would expect based on the results of the "least force" experiment.*

One-sample t-test analysis. How can we determine what this difference means? One time-honored way is to perform a statistical analysis on the above numbers. First, I state my premise as a *working hypothesis,* writing my belief or expectation in statistical terms: *the sample mean of 4.56 inches is significantly less than the specified value of 48 inches.*

To test my hypothesis, I select a probability formula applicable to this scenario, a one-sample t-test. (This process is based on the laws of probability and statistical indicators like the sample size, mean, standard deviation, and so forth.) Plugging my numbers into the formula, I am testing my expectation against the null (no difference) hypothesis. Chance says that there is no difference between the sample mean and the specified value. Then, in contrast to the null, my working hypothesis says "there is a difference" – the sample mean is significantly less than the specified value.

Test findings. Results show that the sample mean of 4.56 inches is significantly smaller than the specified value of 48 inches (p < .0005). This outcome is highly significant, i.e., the smaller the value of p, the greater the significant difference between the sample mean and specified value. The results were off the charts, limited only by the tables in my statistics manual which exclude extremely small criterion values, i.e., infinitesimally small numbers are not necessary to report.

The findings reveal that the May 8th event would have occurred solely by chance less than five times in ten thousand, i.e., an exceedingly rare event. I relied on the tables in my statistics manual because I did not have the statistical software to obtain further computer output. Yet, because this finding is so rare, no further calculations are necessary. Regardless, I had a very interesting email "conversation" with the eminent Dr. Dean Radin concerning the "book flying" incident. With his permission, I am providing Dr. Radin's thoughtful elaboration on the t-test results and the event that happened in my dining room:

> …a t score of over 800 has a p value that is so close to zero that it isn't calculable. E.g., a z score (standard normal deviate) of 30 is associated with p = 10e-198, so the results of your test are much, much smaller than 5 in 10,000. More likely greater than 1 in a trillion trillion trillion trillion … etc. I.e., this wasn't chance. Something threw that book.[56]

Conclusion. Despite the fact that this experiment was not conducted in a laboratory setting, blind experimental procedures were followed

---

[56] Radin, Dean. "Re: Attachment for you…" (Mandy Berlin). 8 Aug. 2011. Reprinted with permission.

with the assistance of an outside observer who took the measurements, made the observations and recorded the data. Classical statistical tests were then performed to compare the sample data against the event after both the preliminary and the main experiments. I performed these tests in as rigorous and scientific a manner as possible. Auxiliary calculations are available upon request.

In both experiments, the highly significant differences in distance suggest a momentous difference in the degree of force delivered. These findings, along with Dr. Radin's remarkable statement, provide more than enough robust mathematical evidence necessary to draw the conclusion that the "Damn" book did not simply drop off the shelf. Rather, it appears that a force (beyond the natural?) "caused" the book to exit the shelf and soar across the room.

As previously discussed, I have ruled out the possibility of extraneous factors, like people, pets, the weather, an accident, or any other environmental factor that might on the odd occasion cause a similar situation to occur. If any of these aspects had been in operation, they might have had the effect of moving the book or even knocking it off the shelf. However, these potential causes have been eliminated because they never entered into the picture at the time of the event. Though I was sitting in the living room when the book left the shelf and did not see the "high jinks" firsthand, I did hear the riotous sounds coming from the dining room and, within seconds, found the book near "dead center" of the dining room floor. Please note: there is an open entranceway between my living room and the dining room. I was sitting approximately thirty feet from all the commotion as it happened.

Interpretation of the event. The book, *How to Fix Damn Near Everything*, offers a direct and logical solution to my lifelong mechanical problem. Because this event occurred no more than 10 seconds after I posed my meditation question, and because it provided a sound and logical solution to my problem, and also because the force experiment findings were highly significant (i.e., basically *zero chance* involved), I submit that this event was no accident.

My belief is that this phenomenon was orchestrated in a purposeful manner by an underlying intelligence – providing the forethought, the precise utilization of energy, and the necessary and sufficient force – to cause the most meaningful book to shoot from my bookcase and land with a strident boom. Due to the rowdy nature of the machinations, I took immediate note of the situation and found the *Damn* book – *the classic textbook answer to my meditation question* – parked in the center of my dining room floor.

Supernatural addendum. Who caused this mind-blowing phenomenon? Was it God? An angel? An ascended master? A saint? A poltergeist? A principality? A spirit guide? Max?

Just whom I do not know, and I won't hazard a guess. Yet, since this episode happened in my home, I have learned from a number of readings (to paraphrase):

> In addition to humans and ghosts, **vestiges of life**[57] or ghosts that have not yet left the **astral plane**,[58] the entities who come 'round to greet and assist us are coming from one source, *The Source, Spirit.*

---

[57] **A residual haunt** is a **vestige of life**, a strong imprint left on our reality. A well-known example of a residual haunt concerns those who have recently "seen" soldiers fighting at the Battle of Gettysburg. Over time, quite a few visitors of this renowned site have had sightings of ghost soldiers. Records show that some have even witnessed full battle array in motion.

[58] **An intelligent haunt** involves ghosts residing in the **astral plane** of existence. Intelligent haunts are associated with a strong presence, physical interaction with the environment, or an apparition. Some haunts involve multiple channels or means of manifestation.

Some folks say, "May the Force be with you."[59] I like that. But I will tell you that since this extraordinary event happened to me, I find myself saying, "May The Source be with you," if only under my breath.

Max used to say, "Magic abounds everywhere!" At times, I reacted to his beautiful and unwavering belief in a rather cynical way. How I wish I hadn't been so impervious, so unyielding.

"Hey guy, I believe you now, you know?"

---

[59] *Star Wars*. Dir. George Lucas. Perf. James Earl Jones, Mark Hamill, and Harrison Ford. Fox, 1977. Film.

Journal Entry 29

Thursday, 05/13/2004
Time unknown

A Friend and Neighbor
Dies Unexpectedly

Heard Cat Stevens' heartfelt song, "Trouble," tonight...[60]

I cannot comprehend that there has been another death. Fritz, our dear next-door neighbor, died yesterday due to complications from routine surgery.

I am in an awful way. I just can't believe he's gone.

You see, Fritz had retired about a year ago from his career as a pharmacist. He was a good friend to Max and me. He went to see Max at the hospital almost every day, sometimes staying with him for hours on end. He did this especially when my job required me to be in Phoenix on special assignment, like when my supervisor, the director of a State department, requested I present statistical analyses of complex research studies to the management and staff. You can imagine my state of mind, attempting to explain abstruse formulas and multifarious figures to a listless audience when my thoughts were focused on one thing and one thing only: being with Max.

Regardless of this conundrum, I was so grateful for Fritz, Tessie, and others as well, who were willing and able to stay with Max on the days my boss called me to the office which was an hour drive from the hospital. *Cognitive dissonance* rears its ugly head again. Basically, one wants to be relied upon to perform her job duties with excellence. At

---

[60] Stevens, Cat. "Trouble." *Mona Bone Jakon*. A&M, 1970. LP.

the same time, she also wants and needs to be with her husband in his last days on this planet. Of course, nobody had any idea how long Max would live, or would even want to live given his terminal condition. Six days? Six months? The doctors were clueless. Yet, we hoped to be there for him during his time of greatest need.

I just happened to be one of the lucky ones. Lucky to be with Max on his last night, as were Tessie and my mom.

Now, I can't comprehend that Fritz's last days have come and gone too. He was a kind person who gave us support and a real sense of comfort. Now I'm distraught because I wasn't there for him. Unfortunately, I didn't know he had to have surgery. At the same time, I'm feeling sad for his family. His death was so sudden. Yesterday afternoon, JC called to tell me his father had been in the hospital and had lapsed into a coma, just hours after his surgical procedure was done.

And then, he died.

🐾 🐾 🐾

On some level, I know that action is the only way. I have to stop sitting here feeling awful and go get some flowers for Fritz's family. Now.

Saturday, 05/27-05/30/2004
Memorial Day Weekend
First quarter moon

Holiday Weekend in Las Vegas

"I Know You're Out There Somewhere" [61]

Considering all that has happened of late, I decided to spend a long weekend with Mom and John at their home in Las Vegas. It was one of those power-packed weekends including the holiday, my birthday, and my former wedding anniversary. But my ability to predict the roller coaster ride did not make it any the less riotous – a little four-day package filled with love, fun and frustration.

Did I neglect to mention that teeny-weeny slice of guilt and annoyance that come with any visit to the family abode? "Dear, you haven't been going to confession. How come?"

"Oh Mom, it's been years. You know that."

"Father O'Laughlin would keel over in the confessional if he saw you coming!" she said.

"Exactly!"

My mother has no idea how long it has been since I last went to confession. Well, it's been exactly thirty-four years. (I'm not about to tell her this. At her age, we'd have to carry her to the recliner!)

Yet ever since Max appeared to me on New Year's Day, I've been going to church every week of my own accord. Before that, I hadn't gone to Mass since I was twenty-two. (That doesn't count Christmas

---

[61] The Moody Blues. "I Know You're Out There Somewhere." *Sur La Mer.* Polydor, 1979. LP.

Week, of course. I was forced to go to church with my mother over the holidays when she came to see us. She would not accept it any other way, so I tried to please her.)

Since I have returned to some core beliefs (very different from the beliefs I had as a child), I've thought about going back to confession. Now they call it reconciliation. See, everything has changed since those days. Regardless, I'm not ready to reconcile or to even commit to one church. I'm still looking at other forms of belief. For instance, why isn't prayer alone in the woods just as valid as prayer in church? I believe it is. How can it not be?

I don't talk to Mom much about my newfound beliefs or how they might differ from hers, just as I didn't talk to her much about my lack of belief all those years. You see, whenever we got going on the subject, we'd end up in a shooting match. I certainly do not want that to happen again. You see, my mother is a very devout Catholic. She just sees her faith and her beliefs. Her way is the only way. Well, that is wonderful for her. I am very happy for her, and I mean that sincerely.

Now I, too, am going to church and liking this experience. I would describe the encounters as childlike. Nevertheless, I have a new and different kind of relationship with God, Nature and All of Existence than I experienced as a child – because of all that I have experienced since the first day of January. I would definitely call my beliefs newfound. They don't compare in any way to my beliefs as a child.

I am thankful for everything I have experienced, the good, the bad, and the ugly. For without life's challenges, no matter how bad or ugly they may appear to be, what would we learn?

❧ ❧ ❧

On to lighter moments….

Las Vegas, that roller coaster ride. How could I have forgotten the hyperactivity and sleep deprivation that comes along with any trip to a town full of one-arm bandits bustling like bee hives… and the busy bees swarming around them. Even the airport has slot machines. Nevertheless, the strip has taken on a more sophisticated air, of late, what with the high rise buildings and the grand opening of a casino almost every time I go. It's beginning to look more like little New York.

Thankfully I bought myself a day to recuperate. When I got home, I rolled myself onto the sofa to bask in the beauty of my lovely ladies (the cats), while watching videos and eating bon bons. Can't even recall the videos. Nevertheless, these fortifying essentials were there for me. But because of the fun time engaged in next to nothing, the holiday weekend has since become a blur.

So, what did we do?

Hmmm, let's see….

I remember exchanging gifts with Mom and John, always a hoot with tea, coffee, cakes, fruits, and John's latest craze, dark chocolates. "Mandy, it's a health food now, you know?" he said in lip-smacking delight. (One would never suspect John is eighty-nine years of age.) As Mom and I sampled what was left of the goodies, we opened our gifts and got caught up on all the talk. Then we decided it was high time to play a little Scrabble. But we don't follow all the instructions because we usually don't keep score.

In our house, the person who wins a game of Scrabble is the one who has the "best" word of the game. It may be the longest word or the strangest word, but for each game, we subjectively determine whose word is the best. Oddly, we've never had an argument about it. The best word just shows up on the board and we agree that's it. For example, one of John's best words was "roadrunner". He created the word by adding his own Scrabble tiles which spelled "runner" to the word "road" that was already on the board. (By the way, roadrunner is the state bird of New Mexico and John's favorite bird.) One of Mom's best words of the day was "archangel". One of mine was "behemoth" which was formed by adding my "behe" tiles to the board word, "moth". Oddly, we prefer to play Scrabble this way and have lots of laughs at it. By the way, kids, if you play the game long enough, it does seem to improve your spelling.

So, after John won his first game, he announced that his children would be coming over to spend the night with him. Thoughtfully, he said this would give Mom and me a chance to spend some time together. Due to his religious affiliation and the poor condition of his legs, he tends to avoid the Las Vegas strip whenever possible. Of course, given his age, we'd been concerned that he would soon need someone to watch him. Now knowing that his children would be coming, Mom and I agreed it would be the best time to celebrate my birthday, a la girl's night out.

We talked about going to a restaurant near the strip. That way, we would be close to one of the new casinos; maybe we'd take a tour. I use the term "new" loosely. What is new to Mom and me may not be new to others. We're undoubtedly behind the eight ball when it comes to the Las Vegas scene. Though Mom and John live just twenty miles from the strip, we seldom go, yet alone pay to see lavish shows. In fact, many of the locals dodge the strip altogether unless their frolicking friends and relatives happen to coax them along for the ride. Surprisingly, people of different religious persuasions sometimes move to Sin City to proselytize those obsessed with its folly – one of the true dichotomies of Las Vegas life.

❧ ❧ ❧

Tucking John into his easy chair, we said so-long to him, his lovely daughter and granddaughter. Then I backed the van out of the drive and we headed in the general direction of the Strip. Nevertheless, I soon realized we couldn't go any further because we hadn't decided on a restaurant.

I slowed the van down to a crawl as Mom and I quibbled over food. "So, what shall it be, Italian? American?"

"Oh, how about Indian? I love chicken masala with basmati rice and poppadoms."

"Yeah, but it's Friday," Mom said. "So, let's go to Friday's. I'm in the mood for breaded shrimp, and I mean the crispy kind!"

"Okay," I said, eyes crossed from the profusion of prospects flashing along the highway – the signs, that is.

"Sounds good. Parking should be a cinch. We won't be on the Strip."

"Great, let's go!" Mom said, giving me her cute little smirk.

We had a nice meal – a couple of drinks, two colossal shrimp dinners and a little light banter to round off the evening. But as I felt the blood flow from head to tummy area, I could only come to one conclusion. *Man, I need eye picks. I'm gonna crash.* Propping my elbow up on the table, I managed to catch my bobbin' head just in time. Luckily, Mom didn't notice. She was furtively preoccupied with a hand mirror… a dab of cheeky pink here, a flick of fuchsia lip gloss there…

… and a bombshell of a party smile!

Oops, I was thinking we might just go home.

At this point, I could think of only two things to do: boost myself up and beg for more service. "Hey guy, thanks for coming back. Let's have a decaf mocha latte for Mom and an iced cappuccino for me. Tall, please."

It didn't take long. And as I tossed down the last of the froth, I started feeling pretty perky. Soon, I was sitting up straight as a post.

Wow, feelin' cool, yet alert…

"Well doll, are you ready to roll?"

Mom nodded with pink lips pursing a straw, sipping the dregs of mocha madness.

♪ ♪ ♪

You can't miss the Luxor with its blue-white light beaming high into the midnight sky from the center of a dusky bronze building – the only pyramidal-shaped hotel casino in the world. As we drew close to the creature, I admit, I began to feel something akin to awe, remembering the wonderfully whimsical night Max and I had there just a few years ago. Mom hadn't seen the Luxor yet, but I figured if this doesn't turn her on, nothing will. Besides, I'd been summoned by Osiris himself. Sure I was into it, or maybe it was the jolt of java. Didn't matter, we were out for fun!

As we entered the lot, I turned up the tunes and turned the van around. *No parking lot is good enough for my mom.*

It's Valet or nothing. So I steered the van back to the valet line, just in time to catch a flash of strangeness sprinting in our direction.

Squinting, at last I made out a mouth moving faster than a chipmunk's. But it didn't have that happy tilt. So I turned down the radio and rolled down the window to find out what this grey valet was grousing about.

"Sorry Miss," he said, shaking his head, "no valet parking."

"What?"

"We're full up."

"But, pooh! I mean…." Glancing up at chunky cheeks, I decided a smile wouldn't hurt our situation any.

"Sir," I said, "how far is open parking from here?"

"Ma'am," he said while he scanned the interior of the van and stopped at my mother's age. "It's quite a ways to walk from there, but if

131

you'd like to try, you might still find a space. Unfortunately, our guys are booked for the next, oh, forty-five minutes."

I checked my watch. *Eleven thirty-five.*

He shrugged and said, "Sorry, Memorial Day weekend."

"Oh, how could I have forgotten?"

At last, Mom chimed in. "Honey, I can't walk that far. Wish I could."

"I know, sweetie."

Valet or nothing.... I was about ready to carry my mother from the far reaches of Hades to the Luxor, or to any casino for that matter. Unfortunately, my mind began to focus on the old sciatic nerve condition. The doc told me I could still lift about fifteen pounds. "If you do it properly, but no more," he warned.

I turned to my mother and took her hand. "Darling," I said, "wish I could carry you there myself. I mean that."

"Thank you, dear."

"But hey, honey the night is young!" *Blessed stimulant.* "So c'mon, let's go cruise the Strip." I turned up the tunes and whipped the van past the cheery chipmunk.

"Okay, honey," Mom replied. She never did yell, like, "Hey, turn down that radio, will ya?" I glanced at her sweet profile and found her head bobbing up and down – but not from old age – from the music.

I could have kissed her.

"We're having some fun now!" I smiled and gave her a wink, maybe feeling a bit like Steve Martin. "Hey, throw me my 3-D shades, will ya?"

Well, that really got her to laughing.

♪ ♪ ♪

132

We ended up in Paris that night. Paris of Las Vegas, a charming hotel casino in the heart of the Strip. Maybe I wanted to take Mom there because it was the last casino Max and I had ever seen before he left our crazy planet. I suppose going to Paris was a risky move on my part. Yet, on some level, I was up for the challenge.

Now, as we stroll through the ornate doors, fond memories flood my mind and heart. And as we take in the fine fragrances of Parisian-style cuisine, Mom says she's actually getting hungry again. "Me too," I say. Soon, we join the crowd ambling slowly toward the casino proper. I look up to see the blue sky and billowy clouds painted on the central dome. Now I understand the risk first-hand. I'm starting to sense that softness again, sounds from another world. Soon, the incredibly vibrant tones begin to drown out the casino pipes and even the brashest of bells. I feel his mouth brushing up against my cheek and I get misty-eyed.

But I must tend to my mother.

With nothing less than Trojan effort, I try to brush aside his mind-blowing murmurs and the sweet sensations that surround my very being. Trusting he can hear me now, I send him a silent message, one that I truly do not want to send.

So long for now, dear one. I must carry on tonight – if not for myself then for my mother.

See you in my dreams?

Hope so....

Sighing deeply, I nod and try to smile as I watch Mom dart with single-minded purpose into the gaming area. Chuckling, I see that she has finally found the slot machine of her choice. She sits down and puts her purse between her legs, searching for cash or a casino card. Soon, she's tugging on the arm of the big bad bandit.

I drift off for awhile, then try to focus again.

Feeling more with it now, I see my mother has won several games in a row. Prompted by success but mostly because of Mom's amiable nature, I sit down beside her and play a few rounds. I'd already decided to forego blackjack in favor of spending time with Mom. And hey, we really did have some fun there in Paris, whooping it up with a couple of highballs, playing half the machines in the room... and as our evening (morning?) came to its natural conclusion, we strolled arm in arm through the doors of Paris with two double lattes for the road.

Heading northeast, I survey the vastness of a star-studded sky. Then glancing over at Mom, I happen to catch the time on the dashboard. *Wow, two ten in the morning... my God, it's May 29th.*

Now I know why you were here!

Lifting the visor, I spot a dazzling slice of moon high up in the heavens. *Happy Anniversary, Darling!* I say, as if it's Max. *You know, this would have been our eleventh.*

Yet, it's really our seventeenth because we were together almost every day from the start. I stifle a gulp. Though I'd heard his voice not long after midnight, I find myself missing him again. When will that ever change?

I know it sounds strange, but I feel lucky to be alive.

Why would this be?

Maybe because so many of our loved ones are not...

... or maybe because I'm star-gazing, enjoying the brilliance and beauty of the early-morning sky. It's shimmering so softly as we wend our way home.

♫ ♫ ♫

The next morning (er noon?) I roused languidly from sleep as I remembered a vivid dream I had about Max. He said he had come to reveal some phenomenal secrets about his "new realm". What's more, this dream was gift wrapped in signs and symbols.

But did I write it all down? Well, not exactly. I did jot down a few sentences hoping to jog my memory, or so I thought. Now I am sorry to say I don't recall much of anything, not even one of the symbols! I could guess and might even be right, but that wouldn't get at the meaning which was lost by the time I got up out of bed. Each sign and symbol had its own connotation. Now, all I can see is Max's face in my mind's eye and remember how happy I felt as I stirred from a deep, satisfying sleep.

If I should ever have another awesome dream, I will try to be more diligent and write down every word as soon as I wake up. Dreams like that come along only once in a purple moon; doubtful ever a blue one.

Journal Entry 31

Thursday, 06/03/2004
Full moon
Around 7:30 p.m.

Max and The Ethereal Eye

The words to the magical song, "Only You,"
came to mind as I felt Max touch my hand today [62]

After an inane day at the office, I tossed my purse on the living room floor and collapsed on the couch.

Though I hadn't planned to meditate, I soon find myself slipping into a meditative state of mind. Then from nowhere, a figure begins to form to my right. Out of the blue, I feel a gentle pressure on my hand, as if Max would have a corporeal hand to offer me.

"Max," I smile and say, "you seem to be doing well." On some level, I know he's in good hands, now that he's so beyond mine.

Closing my eyes, I catch the eye now starting to form in my field of view, just as it had before (reference Journal Entry 20). It is vivid, large and pixel-like. I do not know where this eye comes from or what is causing it to appear, but I call it my "ethereal eye", my window into uncharted territory.

The eye blinks ceaselessly. I look on in awe. Then without warning, poof it evaporates! Light trails of pixel powder shimmer and scatter like particles of dust into a burgundy night.

---

[62] The Platters. "Only You." *The Platters.* King, 1956. LP.

Post Script

I have been wondering what is causing this eye to show up. Sometimes I think it's Max winking at me. After all, tonight he made his appearance just before the eye materialized. I don't mean to sound facetious. Of course, it is possible that something in my mind or brain may be triggering this visualization. Nevertheless, I need to find out more about the eye and what is causing it to appear when my eyes are closed. Is this a mental image or is it a physical phenomenon, set off somehow by the neurons of the brain? Or is it something else entirely? If it is mental, am I receiving the image through some kind of telepathic signal (by means of electrical input frequencies) or is my mind manifesting the whole scenario? Also, what causes the perceived movement of the eye?

I haven't even talked about the full moon. It is common knowledge that the moon and various planetary conditions affect the tides in measured ways. Some studies have even found a correlation between lunar phasing and the number of visits to emergency rooms, for example. However, this research tends to be inconclusive. In the general sense, then, the moon may affect behavior, wellness or illness in some way that has not been fully examined.

In light of the fact that today's event happened on the full moon, what can of worms would this open up?

It's obvious I have more questions than answers about the ethereal eye. The possibilities appear to be endless. I plan to do some research on this matter as soon as I figure out where to begin.

JOURNAL ENTRY 32
Tuesday, 06/15/2004
Afternoon

Sudden Death of My Girlfriend's Husband

"Shadow of the Day" [63]

"You look young for your age," people used to say. Of course, when I was eighteen, it took me a while to find a job. I mean, I looked twelve. But even at the mature age of thirty, I still got carded. Drawing on such good fortune, I thought why not start using it to my advantage. So, by the time I reached thirty-one, I finally figured out how to get my youthful appearance to work in my favor. And the better jobs began to roll in.

Despite those happy, carefree days, I realize I'm starting to feel older than my fifty-odd years – and odd they are. It is hard to fathom that yet another of our dear friends has slipped beyond the boundaries of this earthly existence. Dennis, my girlfriend's husband who had not been ill in any visible way, was even younger than Max.

Is it truly possible that he is gone too?

***

I met Dennis through Nikki Stamatin with whom I had spent many a relaxing weekend on the shores of the Connecticut coastline. Back then, I was living with my parents again because my first husband had

---

[63] Linkin Park. "Shadow of the Day." *Minutes to Midnight*. Warner Brothers. 2007. CD.

to serve a whopping year-long tour of duty in the Philippines. Ugh! What a time. It's a good thing Nikki and Katie Lee were there to help me wait out the seemingly endless months before he returned home.

Soon Katie Lee and I were spending many an evening at Nikki's house, sometimes weekends too. After all, she was the creative one – stuff always happening at her place, you know. She'd have a gang over and we'd draw, paint, play board games or just shoot the breeze for hours on end. It got to the point where people would walk in unannounced, sit down and make themselves at home. Reminds me of that hippie folk song, "Walk Right In."[64] Yet, the never-ending invasion didn't seem to bother Nikki. As a matter of fact, I think she liked it that way. We did too. Even doing dishes was fun at Nikki's place.

Now for over thirty years, Nikki, Katie Lee and I have somehow managed to keep in touch. I also had a chance to get together with Nikki and her husband a while back when they traveled out to The Wild Wild West. As luck would have it, the day before they arrived, Max's employer requested he fly to California to conduct an urgent meeting with a client. Alas, he would never have an opportunity to meet Dennis or Nikki. We were both disappointed. I so wanted the two to meet Max and I knew he was looking forward to meeting them.

Nevertheless, Katie and I decided we must get together with the pair so we joined them on a day trip to Sedona. On the way, we met a few of their friends who lived in a lovely canyon area just south of town. What a wonderful time we had, touring Bell Rock and other scenic spots, complete with meandering drives along colorful canyon roads. We had nothing short of a beautiful day! And as I snapped their pictures, I will never forget how happy Nikki looked in the arms of her loving husband.

---

[64] The Rooftop Singers. "Walk Right In." *Walk Right In!* Vanguard, 1963. LP.

On April twenty-eighth, Nikki found Dennis dead of a heart attack in their Florida home. She had no warning. You see, Dennis had fallen asleep while watching television on their bed. Nikki said she could hear him snoring all along. Then, perhaps an hour later, as she was walking down the hall toward the open door of the bedroom, she said, "Hey, let's go out to dinner!"

Hearing nothing, she looked in and to her utter shock, she found him unresponsive. Quickly, she shook him and checked for a pulse, but there was none.

He was dead on the bed.

Nikki later found out that this snoring sound is called "the death rattle." Such a heartbreaking blow, and to not know about this sound and the medical implications beforehand – just as I did not know until Nikki told me. I am feeling so sorry for her in the loss of her husband and beloved companion of twenty-three years. Dennis's death came as a terrible shock to Katie and me, but all the more to our dear friend, Nikki.

Post Script

How do we prepare when death comes so unexpectedly? Must we always be on guard? Even if we are, sometimes it is to no avail as Nikki learned so sadly.

On the other hand, I am sure that living in fear is not the way. We must get beyond troubling thoughts, more than ever during the rough seasons and tides that rise without warning from time to time.

Yet, I realize I'm beginning to feel a bit sorry for myself as well. I don't like giving in to it, believe me, but why do I suddenly feel like all the people around me are falling off the face of the earth? I am not old, and I don't feel old. So how and why are all these things happening so soon in my life? When will it ever end?

My friends at work tell me I must move on, get over my husband's death. I know I must, and I do try. But how do I not think about death when these things keep happening? How do I not think about Max and Dennis and all our loved ones who have died? I can't forget about them, and furthermore, why would I want to forget about all the incredible people I have known in my life? And many of them have passed away recently. Is this some kind of a cruel joke?

JOURNAL ENTRY 33

Wednesday, 06/23/2004
Around 5:00 p.m.

Meditation – Charlemagne and Max

*I'm ready to go anywhere I'm ready for to fade
Into my own parade cast your dancing spell my
way I promise to go under it...* [65]

In light of all the rare and heartrending events that have taken place this year, it occurred to me that I ought to be meditating more. So, as daylight turned to dusk, I settled down for the night and put on one of Sylvia Browne's discs, similar to the one I played back when.

♪ ♪ ♪

As I become engrossed in the meditative process, my patio chimes start to ring. Yet, they are not so much ringing as clanging now. *Is it the wind?* It would seem so, but I don't bother to check because I'm already immersed in deep breathing. Then several minutes into my meditation as I follow along with Sylvia's instructions, I hear not only the chimes but an amazing communication as well. The words seem to be coming from Charlemagne, my spirit guide. I can hear him very well. Not only that, but I am also able to see his pronouncements in my mind's eye, like so:

Cloud pole

Smart spirit

Thanks for coming to help!

---

[65] Dylan, *op. cit.*

I have no context for these words, except for the phrase "smart spirit". Sounds like an entity who thinks quite well of himself. Or is he, perhaps, referring to the spirit in me? In any case, I am so in awe of his visit that I prefer to think it's the former.

So, I say:

Hello Charlemagne

Thank you for coming!

I wonder if you can tell me how Max is doing

Spirit response:

Echo

Bravo

Charlie

The reference to "Charlie" is interesting in light of Charlemagne's name. Nevertheless, these words sound more like something Max would say. Because of his military training, he often used the **NATO phonetic alphabet**[66] especially when talking on the phone. For example, if the other party seemed unable to decipher his words, he'd usually resort to code: "Alpha" stands for the letter "A", "Bravo" for "B", and so on, with a unique code word signifying each letter of the alphabet.

---

[66] **The NATO phonetic alphabet** is formally called the international radiotelephony spelling alphabet. It is the most widely used spelling alphabet for the intelligibility of voice signals by radio or telephone. "Phonetic Alphabet." *Communication Specialists Limited.* Communication Specialists Limited, Ltd. N.d. Web. 29 Aug. 2011.

Well then, Spirit sent me the words "Echo, Bravo, Charlie." If we resort to the NATO phonetic alphabet, these words stand for the letters E, B, and C. And although these three letters are just one letter away from Max's old employer's name, they are not exactly right. So, at this point, I am unable to determine the meaning of this message. Yet, I would like to think that Spirit is saying Max is doing great!

Then, before ending my meditation, I ask my guide the following question:

Charlemagne, what is my purpose here?

No more than a moment later, I receive the following transmission:

Letter

Sunshine

Write

Now this is starting to make more sense to me. I enjoy writing letters and stories, and I hope that my writing will bring sunshine and a sense of hope to others. My first book, a memoir and family scrapbook, contains a few of the letters Max and I had sent each other, along with our poetry and prose (reference Journal Entry 5). Though I published that first manuscript not long after Max died, the first several sections contain some (hopefully) comical elements. Perhaps our humor in this my third book, will bring a sense of joy and hope as well to readers all over the world.

This was my first effort at interpreting today's transmissions. Perhaps these messages have other meanings too. For example, I live in sunny Arizona. Is "sunshine" a reference to my locale? With respect to the phrase, "thanks for coming to help," I wonder how I might possibly be helping; through my writing? With this means of expression, we are potentially able to reach millions. Yet, maybe I'm helping in other ways, too. I have come to understand that time, as we know it, has no meaning in the spirit world. Perhaps my "coming to help" resides in some future set of circumstances. In any event, I have recorded and will retain all the communications I have received, and might as yet receive, in hopes that these connections will come to have even greater meaning over time. Regardless, the value I have already derived from these mind-blowing encounters truly surpasses all experience!

Post Script 1

No doubt someone will set forth a plausible question like this: are you just hearing your own thoughts?

At times, it is difficult to decipher the words that arise from Spirit versus those I bring to consciousness of my own volition. However, I find that Spirit words have a distinct murmur and often arrive with a spectacular visual flash. Most of the time, such words are transmitted in a strident voice permitting me to determine the source at once. At other times, the prominent words, numbers and symbols arrive in motion, as if emerging from a great distance. With eyes closed, these objects increase in size as they fly to the forefront of my visual field. When this happens, I am generally able to determine the words because the text and background tend to appear in contrasting colors, i.e., red text with a yellow background, dark blue against pink, and so forth.

Yet I have more difficulty discerning what I call pure thought transmissions. These are not visual, nor prominent, nor do I perceive any word movement. However, the thought transmissions I do receive tend to have a murmuring quality which facilitates discernment. As a rule, I am able to ascertain that a thought has been transmitted from an *external* source if it is uncommon, eccentric, or even fantastic – a thought I would probably not have entertained – not even in a most bizarre dream.

I feel especially confident that Spirit is sending me a pure thought transmission if some corroborating evidence arrives contiguous in time with the communication, i.e., if something synchronous happens when the transmission occurs. My journal entry of January 1st offers the ultimate instance of this idea. My dear husband's spirit hollered at me, "Pull your socks up, mate!" In a flash, I knew he had come to console me in his own inimitable way. And after several attempts at grasping his words, I actually did receive his entire communication. However, despite Max's characteristically persistent posture during his first appearance, I'd been unable to comprehend the exact meaning of his words. This is because my mind would never have constructed this strange sentence – an alien concept to me. Nevertheless, in time I came to learn and understand the true meaning and value of his paternal greeting!

Along with Max's heartfelt words on that phenomenal New Year's Day, came the most astounding thing – his ethereal image that appeared like a hologram in my field of view. Given my newfound ability to discern, his words had no visual impact. But his ghostly reflection came just after I heard him say, "Pull your socks up, mate!" That is, Max's image arrived <u>contiguous in time</u> to his words. This **synchronicity**, the vivid vision of Max along with my mind-blowing auditory experience, solidified the whole encounter forever in my mind, and in my being. No matter what others might think or say, you reach a point where you just know, and the knowing becomes the cornerstone of your existence.

Post Script 2

Concerning the phrase, "cloud pole", I realized while editing this entry that my spirit guide might have been referring to the ramada on my back porch. The sturdy beams of the ramada hold the wind chimes that rang wildly as I received his communication in time and space. The ramada columns serve as upright supports; albeit posts rather than round poles, but the idea is similar. When I think of my home and the cloud pole concept, I think of a ramada beam. On the other hand, Charlemagne may have been referring to something else. I encourage spirit sleuths to come up with their own interpretations.

In retrospect, I think that the movement words differ from simple thought transmissions in the intensity of the delivery. That is, the words I see in my mind's eye seem to be sent with greater force. As a result, I am able to see them clearly. Then again, perhaps the deeper I go into meditation, the more I am capable of receiving thought transmissions and seeing words and numbers in motion. So, is it the sender or the receiver? Perhaps it is both.

Sunday, 07/04/2004
Waning gibbous moon
Independence Day
Evening

Independence Day and the Theory of Everything

"Haunted" by the Moody Blues [67]

Saturday I went to the cemetery and left a simple bouquet of red, white and blues. (Max doesn't spend much time there, though I know he can see me as I place the flowers by his headstone. Spirits possess the ability to see us anywhere, any time.) I like decorating Max's grave before the holiday. You see, if I am going to express my grief, I want to do it in a private way. Besides, when all is hushed at his beautiful site, the gentle wind speaks to me.

Sometimes after these visits I find it difficult to write. There are just no words. So this time I decided to give myself more time. Well, a day anyway.

Earlier today, I phoned my mom and some friends to wish them a happy Fourth. Then it was time to switch gears. I find it mind-clearing to do things that are radically different, like on holidays. So I spent the day reading some articles I found online concerning a science program I'd seen on television. Amazingly, I'm finding connections between the theories discussed on this show and some metaphysical subjects I have been studying, along with key aspects of my journal experiences.

---

[67] The Moody Blues. "Haunted." *Strange Times.* Universal Records, 1999. CD.

(Readers not interested in relationships between scientific theories and metaphysics, please skip to Post Script 1, section entitled **The Source**).

A Theory of Everything. Some of the world's greatest thinkers have been attempting to develop a physical theory of everything. As I delved further into this subject, I found some mind-boggling material on two models of the universe: String Theory and M-Theory. Both fall under the rubric of TOE, the "Theory of Everything," a grand model of physics which when complete, would allegedly explain and connect all physical phenomena. (For interested readers, my definitions of theory, model, and so on, are provided in Post Script 3.) A grand theory of everything would unify all the fundamental forces of nature: gravitation, strong and weak nuclear forces, and electromagnetism.[68] With a comprehensive model like this, scientists would, in essence, be able to predict the outcome of any experiment. (Please note: since first writing, the references have been updated to reflect more recent information on TOE, and other models, as discussed.) The Theory of Everything has been under development for years, but has not yet provided the desired unification of all natural phenomena. Would it truly be possible?

String Theory. I turned on and tuned in[69] (literally and figuratively) to TOE and something called String Theory while watching *The Universe*[70] and shows of its kind. Earlier in Journal Entry 13, I touched upon the concepts of multi-verses and parallel dimensions which also link to string theory. This model presupposes that the smallest

---

[68] "Theory of Everything." *University of Oregon.* N.p. N.d. Web. 18 Aug. 2011.

[69] From the counterculture phrase, "turn on, tune in, drop out," coined by Timothy Leary; excerpt from a speech Leary delivered at the opening of a press conference in New York City on September 19, 1966. Staton, Scott. "Turn On, Tune In, Drop by the Archives: Timothy Leary at the N.Y.P.L." *The New Yorker.* Condé Nast., 16 Jun. 2011. Web. 25 Aug. 2011.

[70] *The Universe.* Narr. Erik Thompson. History Channel. 2007. Television.

substances of the universe are made of one-dimensional strings.[71] One of the most interesting and bizarre characteristics of a string is that it possesses the dimension of *length only.* That is, the string's height and width are so infinitesimally small that any conceivable measurement of a string would approach zero! In fact, strings cannot be observed by the naked eye, nor can they be measured. However, if one were able to observe a string, it would probably look like a fine hair. String theorists maintain that the strings of our universe vibrate. They can be seen in our three-dimensional world as light (energy), matter and gravity.

Cosmologists, mathematicians, physicists and other scientists who champion string theory, suggest that the universe is comprised of **multiple dimensions** – as many as ten or eleven, or more depending on the theory.[72] Unfortunately, their higher dimensional equations have thus far resulted in a **singularity**, i.e., the equations break down typically after ten dimensions (as in **Type I superstring theory**). A singularity means that something is not right.

As is often the case in science, many versions of string theory equations came to the fore. Eventually, the "five best" superstring theories validated the concept of a ten-dimensional universe. There was just one problem: each of the five theories appeared to be correct! How could scientists possibly resolve this problem?

M-Theory. In the mid-90s, a theoretical physicist by the name of Edward Witten proposed that the main string theories (i.e., the five consistent superstring theories) all described the same cosmological phenomenon. Eventually, he and a number of other researchers developed

---

[71] Güijosa, Alberto. "What is String Theory?" *Princeton University.* N.p., 9 Sept. 2009. Web. 25 Aug. 2011.

[72] **Type I superstring theorists** purport a total of 10 dimensions, 9 spatial and 1 temporal (representing the dimension of time). Other string theorists, past and present, have conceived of as many as 26 dimensions.

something called M-Theory, organizing the five string theories.[73] Finally, Witten and his colleagues proposed a brainchild, claiming that the strings are, in fact, one-dimensional slices of a 2-dimensional membrane (often called a brane) vibrating in 11-dimensional space.

The structure of M-Theory mathematics has been subjected to numerous tests, and it passed them all. M-theory agrees with scientific observations and the top string theories. There is just one problem. *How can scientists test M-theory predictions in a laboratory when they are unable to observe any dimensions beyond 3 + 1?* [74] Simply put: because of the constraints of our natural world, we are physically unable to observe more than three dimensions, plus time if we count it as an "observable" phenomenon. This little snag renders M-theory incomplete as of this writing.

Post Script 1

My notes on these theories with respect to The Source, Parallel Dimensions and "things that go bump in the night."

The incompleteness of M-Theory. There is cause for hope. Theoretical physicist, Dr. Michio Kaku and other scientists believe that M-Theory may eventually present us with a Theory of Everything so elegant and succinct that the main formula would fit on a t-shirt.[75]

String Theory Developments. More recently, Dr. Kaku reported that the string theory equations, though precise and well-designed, are hard to work with. Yet, despite the calculation problem caused by the sheer number of dimensions, scientists made a leap forward in 2008:

---

[73] "M-Theory, the Theory Formerly Known as Strings." *Cambridge Relativity and Cosmology.* University of Cambridge, N.d. Web. 25 Aug. 2011.

[74] The three spatial dimensions plus the temporal dimension.

[75] Kaku, Michio. "M-Theory: The Mother of all SuperStrings." *Welcome to Explorations in Science with Dr. Michio Kaku.* N.p., 2009. Web. 17 Jan. 2009.

Last year, a significant breakthrough was announced. Several groups of physicists independently announced that string theory can completely solve the problem of a quantum black hole. (However, the calculation was so fiendishly difficult it could only be performed in two, not 10, dimensions.) So that's where we stand today. Many physicists now feel that it's only a matter of time before some enterprising physicist completely cracks this ticklish problem. The equations, although difficult, are well-defined. So until then, it's still a bit premature to buy tickets to the nearest wormhole to visit the next galaxy or hunt dinosaurs! (para. 7)[76]

Multiple Dimensions. We may be bound by the limitations of the latest and greatest equations, which generally have to be modified almost as fast as thoughts create them. Given such a soup, is stability and universal description ever possible? Hopefully soon our mathematics will catch up with our ruminations, revealing the riches that surround us, along with the treasures that lie within us as divine creatures of the cosmos.

Despite the hitch of solving equations in ten or more dimensions, I find these n-dimensional theories very relevant in light of the mind-bending incidents and accidents we encountered when Max passed on. You see, my experiences did not end simply because my journal had ended in December of '04; not by any stretch. Soon I began bumping into more phenomena. In 2004 and '05, many of the events I experienced had a synchronistic quality.[77] (More tomes to consecrate based on hundreds of notes taken soon after the happenings.) I have

---

[76] Kaku, Michio. "Blackholes, Wormholes and the Tenth Dimension." *Welcome to Explorations in Science with Dr. Michio Kaku.* N.p., 2009. Web. 17 Jan. 2009.

[77] **Synchronicity** and **synchronous events** were first defined and discussed in Journal Entry 5.

kept my notes in calendars by month and year and, more recently, in bound books and journals. I must transcribe them soon or seek a bigger storage space!

Infinite Number of Dimensions? As a statistician and layperson relatively new to the incredible worlds of String and M-Theory, I wonder: what are the odds that more than ten or eleven dimensions exist? After reading some recent articles on these topics, it is feasible that the universe might be comprised of more dimensions. Yet why would we stop at ten or eleven, or even twenty-six? *Perhaps the universe contains an infinite number of dimensions.* But the word contain is itself imperfect. *What could possibly contain the infinite?*

The Source. Digressing a bit, but still related to these concepts is the idea that perhaps *the Infinite (with a capital "I") might contain the infinite,* if one could ponder such a thought. It doesn't matter whether we call the Infinite God, the Source, the Center of the Universe, the Zero Point Energy Field, Allah, El, Yahweh, Jehovah, I Am, the Alpha and the Omega, Elohim, Yeshua, Divinity, A Higher Power, the Architect of the Matrix[78] (not being facetious here), or simply Consciousness. To my knowledge, there is no mathematical proof of the existence of God. *Yet, how could there be if God is Infinite – beyond our methods of observation, control, measurement and calculation?* Perhaps someone will prove me wrong and come up with a mathematical proof that God exists.

Yet the proof of God's existence might never be found, directly that is. However, a great deal of indirect evidence comes to mind – rare events, miraculous happenings, synchronicities, signs, and wonders. Does the tiny ant recognize a human hand as it scurries all over it? The creature seems to be oblivious to our very existence. Would we recognize

---

[78] *The Matrix.* Dir. Andy Wachowski and Lana Wachowski. Perf. Keanu Reeves, Laurence Fishburne, and Carrie-Anne Moss. Warner Bros., 1999. Film.

the hand of God if it were offered? If God carried us figuratively, or perhaps even literally, would we be aware of His presence, yet alone able to acknowledge it?

With respect to indirect evidence, we have boundless reams of data and information based on tomes written over the centuries. The Bible is at once a work of art, experience, and knowledge. From my experience, God's existence is not something I believe in. It is something I have come to know through the awesome events I have documented herein. Before 2004, I had not picked up The Bible in over thirty years, because I was agnostic. Now as I mull over the pages, I find numerous scriptures that speak to me, especially given these recent experiences. Yet The Book, if I had deigned to read it years ago, would not have made any sense to me. As a child, I did not understand one whit of it. True knowledge, or at least a better understanding of a subject, comes with experience – and perhaps as in my case, with a little divine intervention.

Delving further into the realm of Belief, I see that for over thirty years, I must have resembled Thomas, the doubting apostle. As Jesus once said, "Blessed are those who have not seen and yet believe" (John 20:29). For me, it took seeing in ways I never thought possible. No, I did not see God nor Jesus directly – not in 2004. However, in that one year alone, I saw enough to know. Now, since the mind-blowing adventures of these journal pages, I have witnessed miraculous events, yet to be revealed. I am currently discussing these beautiful happenings in confidence with a theologian and with my mother who is still cogent and cogitating at 94 years of age. Bless her!

Parallel Dimensions and *The Secret*.[79] What is the basis of our reality? Did our external world exist before our internal world, or vice versa? What comes first, the chicken or the egg? Is there, indeed, an

---

[79] Byrne, Rhonda. *The Secret*. New York: Atria, 2006. Print.

external world or is it just the figment of the ever-changing imagination? As a species we are not bound in thought. Yet based on certain levels of *awareness*, we are bound (or so it seems) by the physical conditions of our world. However, if we delve into concepts of New Thought like those suggested by the authors of *The Secret* (further discussed in Journal Entry 49), the Law of Attraction says something very different. The concepts contained in The Secret video, the book, and CDs can be summed up with a slogan. Whenever I get off-track, that famous quote by Dr. Norman Vincent Peale comes to mind:

Change your thoughts and you change your world.

After years of serious testing, I have found this to be true. *The Secret* authors suggest that what we create (with our thoughts, feelings, beliefs and attitudes) is paramount to manifesting what we would like to have, be, do and see in our world. These notions are detailed in many books, such as a meticulous treatise by Charles Haanel,[80] which I have found to be especially helpful in my quest for knowledge and understanding. For the initiate or for those who are just too busy to digest and absorb Haanel's work, I believe *The Secret* video and CDs are probably best for gaining a good understanding of the concepts and methods. These books and materials have all worked well for me in practice.

The Law of Attraction connects in interesting ways to the parallel dimensions (or universes) model of science. One theory purports that we may enter and leave a parallel dimension without ever having had any conscious awareness of the change that has been introduced into our reality. "Parallel" scientists tell us this is so because one or more characteristics of the environment (scenery, persons, possessions, or less

---

[80] Haanel, Charles. *The Master Key System*. St Louis, MO: Inland Printing, USA, 1919. Print.

obvious features of our physical reality) change as we enter a parallel dimension. Otherwise, it may look the same as the dimension we just left. Think about that the next time you lose an article, like your wallet, only to find it days later in a place you were sure you had checked two or three times. Or think about it the next time an unexpected friend pays you a visit. Was he really so unexpected? Perhaps you had been thinking about him for hours or even days before he arrived. Was it simply a coincidence that he showed up at your door? From day to day, what is your focus? How is that focus affecting your reality? Change your thoughts, change your world! The notion of parallel universes is depicted clearly in the novel, *Parallelities,* as discussed in my Journal Entry 13. These are just a few ideas that connect *The Secret* to concepts in parallel dimensions. Of course there are more, but that is not the intent of this section. That might take an entire chapter to discuss.

Parallel Dimensions, Max and Energy Vibration. According to the Many Worlds Theory (Level 3) of parallel dimensions, people are in contact with other worlds (dimensions, universes).[81] All possibilities exist. Then, as you make one decision over another, the universe splits. According to this theory, each of the parallel dimensions is as real as any other. As you enter another dimension, you are probably not aware of the change in state, i.e., not consciously. The change may (or may not) be subtle, but it is natural, of course. One feature or many features of the universe may change. There may be a change in the weather or something might drop out of your universe entirely, signaling that you have entered a parallel dimension. For instance, you might misplace your keys or start talking to somebody you just met. You might never see this person again. On the other hand, you may

---

[81] "The Many Worlds Theory Today." *Nova.* WGBH, 21 Oct. 2008. Web. 26 Mar. 2012.

end up in a relationship with him (another decision point) and that just might change your life – as Max changed mine when he was alive, *and after he died.* There are many ways to conceive of parallel dimensions. I like to think of them as alternate realities where like-minded spirits (living and deceased) meet and carry on.

Thoughts to ponder on a rainy day: did I enter a parallel dimension when I first encountered Max's spirit? Or did his spirit cross over some (mental/physical/spiritual) threshold, entering my universe? Perhaps Max moved on to another dimension, later returning to see his loved ones – like Tessie, who became aware of his spirit presence, as well as those who remained unaware. Maybe when Max died he did not leave our world at all, at least not for awhile. Then on that awe-inspiring day in my dining room (January 1, 2004), his being and mine reconvened in one dimension, reminding me of the fateful night we met in a bar in Tempe, Arizona.

Parallel dimension and law of attraction concepts link to the principle in quantum physics that energy vibrates[82] at specified frequencies. As we have seen according to string theory, the strings that make up our world of gravity, matter and energy, have different frequencies. That is, strings vibrate with varying levels of energy depending on the form of matter in question. Of course, everything in our universe is made of energy. This truth is evident in Einstein's seminal equation, $E=Mc^2$. Though mass and energy reflect different properties of the same physical system, they are *equivalent*. (The letter "c" in the equation represents the speed of light – a constant which, as such, never changes.) In

---

[82] A vibration is a wave rather than a solid particle. Subatomic particles, like light, exhibit the properties of a wave or a solid particle interchangeably. For an interesting law of attraction treatment on wave versus particle, refer to: Ray, James Arthur, and Sivertsen, Linda. *Harmonic Wealth: The Secret of Attracting the Life You Want.* New York: Hyperion, USA, 2008. Print.

effect, if you multiply the constant by the mass (of any object in our physical system) you will obtain the amount of producible energy, i.e., the object's *frequency of vibration.*

Water, trees, rocks, and yes, even money (!) possess the properties of mass and energy. Think about that the next time you wonder where your next dollar will come from. Are you creating your financial future *energetically,* i.e., through your thoughts, beliefs, attitudes and actions? Your feelings and beliefs about money are as important as your actions.

As part of all matter and energy in our universe, different substances vibrate at different frequencies. For example, the vibrational frequency of a rock varies depending on the type of rock. Quartz crystals are manufactured for frequencies from a few tens of kilohertz to tens of megahertz.[83] Sadly, the water we drink is becoming more and more de-energized, having lower (unhealthier) vibrational frequencies than in previous years.[84] Our bodies are made of seventy to seventy-five percent water – one of the reasons the purity of our water is of great consequence – not only for us, but for all living creatures on our still-breathing planet. The vibration of a rock can be higher or lower than the vibration of a human being. Visit the sacred red rocks of Sedona, Arizona. Absorb the powerful energy of the awesome vibrational structures. Beautiful high frequency locations can be found all over the globe.

We vibrate twenty-four seven. As carbon-based creatures, we are the living, breathing quintessence of *all matter and energy* that ever existed. We are truly the stuff of stars!

---

[83] "Technical Information: Pezoelectric Frequency Control." *Advanced Crystal Technology.* Advanced Crystal Technology, N.d. Web. 1 Mar. 2012.

[84] Suddath, Ralph. "Vibration, Energy & Water." *Shifting Frequencies.* Shifting Frequencies, 2011. Web. 1 Mar. 2012.

Our vibration may be high or low at any given point in time. In terms of consciousness, our variable levels of energy depend greatly on our thoughts, feelings, beliefs and attitudes. These, in turn, affect the body, mind and spirit. Dr. David Hawkins' Map of Consciousness (converted to a logarithmic scale) is a method of charting (potentially raising?) the vibration of human consciousness. The map is based on Hawkins' studies in kinesiology. Using a large world-wide sample, Dr. Hawkins found that the vibrational frequency of love is 525 on the consciousness scale, regardless of where in the world the measurements were taken. Shame and misery hardly vibrate at all, gauged below 50 on the scale. The highest level of attainment, 1000, is beyond the common realm of humanity, i.e., at the level of Christ, or Buddha, or Infinity, "the source of reality manifest as divinity."[85]

There are numerous ways to increase your energy vibration, such as through frequent exercise, meditation, reciting (and believing) positive affirmations, prayer, by cleansing toxins from the body, or just by being a caring, compassionate person. Journal writing is another wonderful way to raise your vibration. It is one of my favorite ways. On the other hand, you can probably think of activities that tend to lower your energy. What about watching negative movies and television shows? The use of illicit drugs? Taking excessive prescription drugs or even OTCs? Drinking alcohol frequently and excessively? Arguing to no purpose, i.e., outside of the debate arena or classroom? Compulsive shopping? Perhaps the need for more material goods reflects a core need, unexpressed. Like many addictions, extreme shopping may seem to raise your energy initially – only to cause it to plummet when the shopping must be abruptly removed from your agenda, due to a subsequent budget drain. Perhaps even the credit cards are maxed out.

---

[85] Hawkins, David R. *Power vs. Force*. Sedona, AZ: Veritas, 1995. Print.

What about the strain on your mind, body, spirit? What other activities tend to lower your vibes?

Proponents of the Law of Attraction tell us that like attracts like. This means that like thoughts attract like thoughts. So like thoughts, feelings, and beliefs attract like actions – and like results. Your thoughts create patterns or frequency vibrations, i.e., the frequency at which you are vibrating from moment to moment. Different frequencies attract different kinds of matter and energy. We receive results that vary based on our thoughts, feelings, beliefs and actions. More and more I realize that, whether living or deceased, Max and I were often vibrating at a similar level. We were tuned to the same virtual radio station for a long time, even after he died.

Yet no matter how highly (or lowly) our energy vibrates, consciousness is consciousness. It does not matter whether we are living or deceased. At death, your energy is simply *transformed*. Einstein reminded us of this truth when he said that energy cannot be created nor destroyed. Energy simply is. Spirit never dies. Consciousness lives on, forever. If we are truly aware, we can tap into that consciousness any time. All it takes is some learning and practice. Initially, without any awareness, I was learning and practicing while I meditated; still do whenever possible. However, just after Max died, all I was attempting to do was to get some sleep. Little did I know what would happen next!

People sometimes say, "If I was 'alive' before I was born, why don't I remember?" You see, we have forgotten that we lived before we were born into this life. Before coming into this world, all or at least most of our memory was removed as a form of protection. In this way, we are able to live our lives completely. We have little or no prior knowledge to depend on, thus it will not interfere with our lives. We came into this world our minds a blank slate. We carry no crutches. How else can we learn from the life we are now living?

Nevertheless, there are people who do remember having lived before. Many incredible cases can be found on the Internet or in your local library. Some have solid, truly amazing physical evidence (going well beyond coincidence) to back up their stories. They are here to teach us something of value. God created randomness (like the randomness we received at birth, i.e., such as access to past memories or no access to them at all). He created these things and all the laws of probability to make our world possible and rich beyond our wildest dreams; to assist us and the other divine creatures of the universe. In all of His wisdom, He knew that if everything in life were totally *certain*, we would probably not want to stick around. And if everything in life were absolutely *uncertain*, we would probably not want to stick around. But between the monotony of certainty and the chaos of uncertainty *flows an endless stream of potential called infinite possibility.*[86] Think of all the incredible possibilities accessible to each of us every day, if we but tap into The Source of all creativity!

Now go, and create your life!

Post Script 2

Months after writing Post Script 1, I received another answer to the question, *"What 'thing' would contain the infinite?"* The answer tends to parallel (no pun intended) my thoughts as set forth in "The Source" section of this journal entry. The reality came in a blaze as I read Gregg Braden's book, *The Divine Matrix,* concerning the experiments that changed everything. Based, in part, on the works of Max Planck and

---

[86] I highly recommend this motivating and insightful book, beautifully written by the author: Dooley, Mike. *Infinite Possibilities: the Art of Living Your Dreams.* New York, NY: Atria, 2009. Print.

on Braden's metaphysical discussion, he describes the characteristics of the energy field he calls the Divine Matrix:

> Of the many ways we could define the Divine Matrix, perhaps the simplest is to think of it as being three basic things: (1) the container for the universe to exist within; (2) the bridge between our inner and outer worlds; and (3) the mirror that reflects our everyday thoughts, feelings, emotions, and beliefs.
>
> There are three more attributes that set the Divine Matrix apart from any other energy of its kind. First, it can be described as being everywhere all the time... it already exists.... Second, ... this field originated when creation did – with the big bang or ... the "beginning".... The third characteristic ... is that it appears to have "intelligence." In other words, the field *responds* to the power of human emotion. In the language of another time, ancient traditions did their best to share this great secret with us.... It's only now ... that the language of science has rediscovered the very same relationship between our world and us....
>
> Beyond any reasonable doubt, the experiments and discussion... [in Braden's chapter] show us that Planck's matrix exists. Regardless of what we choose to call it or which laws of physics it may or may not conform to, the field that connects everything in creation is real. It's here this very instant – it exists as you and me. It's the universe inside of us as well as the one that surrounds us, the quantum bridge between all that's possible in our minds and what becomes real in the world....
>
> **But our connection to the Matrix of all matter doesn't stop there... it continues into the things**

that we can't see [my bold]. The Divine Matrix is everywhere and everything.[87]

"What 'thing' would contain the infinite?" I asked. Though Braden approached the subject from a different angle, his answer is not so different from mine. If we think of the universe as infinite, as most scientists do, the Divine Matrix is "the container for the universe [the infinite] to exist within." Then, might we not call the Divine Matrix God or The Source of all that is? We might call Him anything we want. But it is this Energy – this ceaseless stream of Consciousness – as It connects with our lifelong thoughts and feelings (and we with It) that is most meaningful and relevant to our lives, and life beyond this world.

Post Script 3 - Definitions

As a research scientist, my definition of a **theory** is a formal cluster of beliefs (called hypotheses) concerning a phenomenon or a system, such as our universe. A theory is often called a **model**. The model embodies the phenomena under study, the environmental conditions necessary for the existence of the system, and its functional operation over time.

The model or theory may be deemed relevant for any given period. However, it may eventually be branded as weak, unsuitable, or even obsolete by the scientific community. As experts receive new information about a phenomenon, they tend to develop new theories that may unseat or partially supplant any existing theory. If the process involves significant changes in a model or cluster of theories, the

---

[87] Braden, Gregg. *The Divine Matrix: Bridging Time, Space, Miracles, and Belief.* Carlsbad, CA: Hay House, 2007. Print.

resulting transformation is generally referred to as a **paradigm shift.**[88] The subsequent swing of scientific focus and technical thought, as well as varying attitudes of scientists, tend to result in theoretical change and occasionally even a scientific revolution!

Much of this journal entry was added to and further revised long after my experiences in 2004. At that time, I was not aware of the Law of Attraction (as in *The Secret)* nor some of the quantum theories as discussed. Bearing this in mind, let's return to my journey and the awesome happenings I experienced in July of 2004.

Selected References:

Kaku, Michio. *Parallel Worlds: The Science of Alternative Universes and Our Future in the Cosmos.* London: Allen Lane, 2004. Print.

Musser, George. *The Complete Idiot's Guide to String Theory.* Indianapolis: Alpha, 2008. Print.

Schwarz, Patricia. "The 'Official String Theory Web Site'." *Superstringtheory.com.* N.p., May 2009. Web. (Excellent references on string theory and M-theory for the layperson and the expert.)

The Elegant Universe. Dir. Julia Cort and Joseph McMaster. Perf. Michael Duff, Michael B. Green, and Brian Green. Nova. 2003. Television.

---

[88] Kuhn, Thomas. *The Structure of Scientific Revolutions.* 2nd ed. Chicago: U of Chicago Press, 1970. Print.

Journal Entry 35

Tuesday, 07/20/2004
Around 6:45 a.m.

The Hair Dryer Affair

My friends wonder what is wrong with me
Well I'm in a daze from your love you see....[89]

Standing in the bathroom getting ready for work, I'm talking to Max as I sometimes do. Yet, who is there to listen besides my little ladies? Perched in the hall are my two lovely cats, ears flicking with each inflection. Now they're gawking at me as I natter on while brushing some blush on my cheeks. Then I dry my hair and when I'm done, I turn off the hair dryer and set it down on the counter as one would normally do. But even as I start to brush my hair, straight away I hear the word *Beautiful!* as full-bodied as it can be. At once, I turn and say, "Who's there?"

Taking a step back, I glance down at the hall carpet. Why, of course, it's the cats, Allie and Tiggi sitting up, wide eyes tracking my every move.

Nothing more, nothing less.

But when Max was around, the word "beautiful" had become a standing joke between us. Sometimes when we were getting ready to go out for the evening, he would lean up against the bathroom door and watch me fix my hair. Then, when I was done, he'd say, "Beautiful!"

"Max," I'd say, smiling. Then we'd smooch or something.

At other times, I'd hear him say "Beautiful!" in passing. I'd peer out into the hall, and say, "Oh, you're just saying that to hurry me along," as in, hey you look fine, but let's get going, lady.

---

[89] Caldwell, *op. cit.*

165

Still, he seemed sincere. Sweet moments held forever in my heart....

Now I'm standing in the bathroom glancing in the mirror, brushing the same spot, over and over. And again, from nowhere comes that vibrant sound, *Beautiful!* like an echo in time. I'm brooding now as I stare at the mystified woman who's scratching her forehead, staring back at me. *Is this just another memory, a fond recollection of a time gone by?*

Or am I "hearing" his thoughts?

So I set my brush down and stand very still, close my eyes and breathe as I do when I go into a meditative state.

Deeper now, I breathe and say, "Max, are you here?"

No response.

Then, out of the blue, an idea pops into my head. With utmost concentration, I say, "Darling, if you're here, would you give me a sign?"

Feeling calm and relaxed from the breathing exercise, I continue to get ready and put on my lipstick. While doing so, I recall something that happened when Max was alive. Chuckling, I say, "Hey guy, remember the time...."

But even before my sentence is finished, whoosh, the hair dryer starts to blow! *That's weird, I never touched it.* I'm aghast because it doesn't fall – it's gyrating all over the counter! Suddenly, I'm hot, like my skin is crawling with ants. I jump back and away – and let out a blood-curdling scream – as if this thing is a Giant Ant Eater about to devour me!

By this time, the cats have vacated the premises.

I side-step into the hall as the Ant Eater rages on.

What to do? I know it makes no sense, but I can't go back in there....

Then, as astoundingly as it started, the machine stops.

Slowly, I tiptoe into the bathroom, afraid of who-knows-what. But it's just the hair dryer setting on the counter. The machine had turned itself OFF. (Well, at least that is how it appeared.) The hair dryer is not running. How it got that way, I do not know.

Obviously, a machine that contains no programmable devices cannot turn off like a preprogrammed water timer, for example. My hair dryer is definitely not a programmable machine, and I promise you, I never touched the darned thing!

Stunned, I sat down on the toilet seat and tried to comprehend what had just happened.

Post Script 1

Since Max died, my hair dryer has turned ON approximately four times without my intervention, i.e., without my making any move toward the contraption whatsoever. That is strange in itself. Nothing like this ever happened before Max died. Not once. What's even more incredible is that the hair dryer had never turned off without my first clicking the switch to the OFF position. Not until today, that is.

Of course, I must be sure my hair dryer is working properly. So, while I continue to get ready for my proverbial job (if, indeed, I still have one) I proceed to test the contraption.

First, I turn the switch ON. No hesitation there, the dryer powers up just as swiftly and forcefully as ever. Then I flip the switch to the OFF position. No problem, the dryer stops as it should. Then, to be sure, I flip the switch several times in succession to find that my dryer is working just fine. No problems were encountered during the test.

Yes, my hair dryer had turned ON without human intervention several times in the past. Yes, this time it stopped (turned OFF) without my ever touching it – certainly something new and out-of-the-ordinary there. *Regardless, I'm overlooking something. What is the missing link? Hmmm….* I need a cup of coffee but I'm too engrossed to bother going to the kitchen. So I return to my focal point (the toilet seat) to collect my thoughts and pull at caked-on mascara. Then, as I pull and breathe, synapses spark the answer to my weary brain:

Bingo! I don't believe it. The hair dryer came ON soon after I made my request: "Darling, <u>would you give me a sign</u>?" Seconds later, the Ant Eater went Whoosh!

Pattern: Stimulus – Response
Contiguous in time

Post Script 2

Was this hair dryer affair just another fluke, another coincidence within an inordinately large series of coincidences and bizarre happenstances? I don't think so. In light of the fact that I have tested my hair dryer and find that it works properly: *the ON signal that arrived seconds after my verbal request, and the hair dryer clicking OFF without any human intervention – both phenomena, occurring contiguous in time, <u>point to the involvement of a higher intelligence</u>.*

There comes a time when one must concede there is more going on than meets the eye.

Saturday, 07/24/2004
First quarter moon
Time unknown

Max's Guardian Suffers a Stroke

I'm on your side, when times get rough...[90]

Last December Max's guardians, James and Wilma, had flown from England to see Max in the Oncology Ward before his chemotherapy treatments were to begin. They stayed with their daughter, Paulette, in Sonoita, Arizona, and had a full itinerary of plans to visit friends and relatives. All the way around, they'd had a trying year; now this trip on top of it.

After making the difficult but so appreciated journey to the states, James and Wilma flew home to get some much needed rest. But alas, both of them took down ill; then James got worse. I just received word from their daughters that their father has suffered a stroke. I'm so sad and disappointed to hear this. I had been hoping that they were doing a lot better.

It distresses me even more to say that I am not very surprised because of James' age and the hardships he and Wilma have endured in recent years. It is my hope that they will soon be on the healing road to recovery. They are in my thoughts and prayers.

---

[90] Simon & Garfunkel. "Bridge Over Troubled Water." *Bridge Over Troubled Water.* Sony, 1970. LP.

JOURNAL ENTRY 37

Sunday, 07/25/2004
First quarter moon
Around 5 p.m.

The Crazy Treadmill

Reminds me of the light-hearted song
"Stairway to Heaven" by Neil Sedaka [91]

With all the recent news, I had to get to the gym to ease my stress. Today seemed like as good a day as any to get back into the routine of things. I mean, if you can't get to the gym on your day off, when can you?

In the course of a typical workout, I often start with the treadmill, like today. I usually run, then walk, intermittently, for about twenty or thirty minutes.

So, I step up on the machine and start running. Then, after a few minutes, I push and hold the heart rate bar and the LED light displays "138". This is a normal heart rate reading for me after my first run, so I stop touching the bar. Then, sticking with my usual run-walk sequence, I select "random climb" and begin to walk with my arms moving. I haven't pressed down on the heart rate bar, so the LED does not light up. Makes sense.

So it would seem.

After several seconds of walking, the LED light comes on. But it shouldn't light up because my hands are nowhere near the heart rate bar. Nevertheless, I continue to walk and, *geez*, the light is flashing

---

[91] Sedaka, Neil. "Stairway to Heaven." *Neil Sedaka Sings Little Devil and His Other Hits.* RCA, 1961. LP.

the numbers "162... 163... 164... 165... 166..." rapidly, and in succession. Why is the machine displaying any numbers? My arms are moving but my hands are nowhere near the heart rate bar.

Furthermore, why numbers in the 160s? Strange. Maybe I don't run very fast, but I've never had heart rate numbers that high. The highest number the machine ever recorded for me was a 152 while running. If I use my run-walk progression, like today, the numbers seldom go as high as 145.

Despite growing skepticism, I plod along, careful to keep my hands away from the heart rate bar. Then, I check the LED light – it's blazing a whopping 166! *Not possible, I'm not even running.* And, in a flash, the numbers move up and down in a seemingly random manner like the lights on a bouncing pinball machine. However, in fact, neither machine displays true randomness. In the case of the pinball machine, the pinball player manipulates the machine, so the resulting flashes are not random. In the case of the treadmill, the numbers aren't random because they're based on physical conditions, such as the runner's heart rate, or so it would seem. Now, in the case of this treadmill, the red light returns to the magical number, 166. *Hardly random.* Then, the lights flash on and on, up and down, always in the same weird number sequence and always returning to 166. Always! I've seen strange things happen with treadmills, but nothing like this. So I slow down and finally stop the machine.

What's going on? My hands never touched the bar, so why did the numbers light up? And what's with 166? I never get that high. (Well, not without alcohol – which doesn't sound like a bad idea right now.)

So I hop off. *Take five....*

A banana daiquiri without the "daiq"? Still sounds good.

.٭. .٭. .٭.

After sufficient irrigation, I feel energized. In fact, I've built up enough pluck *(foolhardiness?)* to return to the same machine. However, this time I have a new idea. I'm going to test the blasted thing with the "same subject" – moi. My test question: will this machine "behave" the same way over time?

ℒ ℒ ℒ

I give it a decent run, say ten minutes. Now amazingly, my regular numbers show up only when I press the heart rate bar, i.e., the way it should be. This time, nothing weird happens even though I'm using the same treadmill that just went nuts a little while ago. The machine and monitor appear to be functioning normally and my heart rate numbers are ranging from 100 to 145.

Now, no matter how long or how fast I run, I am unable to re-create ~ or even approach ~ the magical number 166.

So, what just happened here?

Post Script

Was this just another dysfunctional piece of equipment? I don't think so. The second time I used the treadmill, my heart rate readings fell within my normal range of scores, i.e., the ones I've had since time began. (Geez, I suppose that doesn't say much for my progress at the gym!) Regardless, the second time I used the treadmill, it worked without fail. This fact alone tells me that the machine and the heart rate system were, in all likelihood, in working order when I first set foot on the contraption.

Then, what about the magical number 166? What does it mean? Was this just another one of those quirks defying explanation – like the significant book that flew four feet from the bottom shelf while

I was meditating on the question, "What should I be doing with my life?" Or the hair dryer that turned on full blast within seconds of my saying, "Would you give me a sign?" Or the same dryer that stopped, i.e., switch "moved" to the OFF position, without my ever touching it?

Just how many wacky incidents have happened since December?

How many more will there be?

Journal Entry 38

Friday, 07/30/2004
Full moon

Survivor Max

Thinking of the song "The Lights Go Down"
by ELO [92]

A few weeks ago, I installed a new three-way bulb in my reading lamp. Well, the bulb worked three ways (50-100-150) for about a week. Then a few days ago, I turned it on to find the 50 watt capacity fully engaged, and the higher wattages gone – fried out.

I'm certainly not implying that Max caused the bulb to lose power. Light bulbs sometimes drift into defect mode or burn out within a shorter timeframe than is generally expected, or desired. Then again, Max was the one who loathed the excessive use of electricity, or the excessive use of anything for that matter. His "wary light" turned on whenever I switched my lamp to full power (due to my vision, of course, and only while reading). Whenever possible, Magoo does try to be environmentally aware. Barring close work, I keep a low consumption profile at all costs – er, at lower costs.

Survivor Max, he's another story. If we hadn't lived together, his consumption profile would have hovered somewhere near the zero mark. Regardless of his stalwart nature, I would soon learned that our married life was going to be charmingly predictable. Like, whenever I got up from my reading chair to grab a snack or something, I returned to find that Max had (rather stealthily) turned my reading lamp down

---

[92] Electric Light Orchestra. "The Lights Go Down." *Time.* Jet, 1981. LP.

to 50 watts. How sweet of him to remember our electric bill! And if I stayed in the kitchen any longer than that, I'd often return to the living room to gaze into the splendor of night.

"Max, how thoughtful of you to turn off the lights. What, and the TV too? I must say, you had your thinking cap on there."

"Hey Max…."

"Where are you?" *Trip… stumble… wobble… thud….*

"MAX!"

Sunday, 08/01/2004
Full moon
Evening

The Director Blows

*This little anecdote calls to mind
another tune by ELO – "Starlight"*[93]

I installed a brand new Director bulb above the kitchen sink. Well, literally about five minutes later, it blew! *Maybe it's the socket,* I thought, *but I want to test the bulb first.* So I tried another socket.

Nope, no light… my Director bulb is "toast".

Peeved, but with the thought of illumination still burning my brain, I remembered the old "50-watter" in the living room lamp. Rummaging through the pantry, I searched for a new three-way. As luck would have it, I found one hidden on the bottom shelf. So I swapped it with the 50-watter and powered the lamp up to 150. *Yay, now I can actually read!*

Hope this one lasts.

---

[93] Electric Light Orchestra. "Starlight." *Out of the Blue.* Jet, 1977. LP.

JOURNAL ENTRY 40

Friday, 08/06/2004
Third quarter moon
Around 6:30 a.m.

Solid State

"I'm Your Angel"...[94]

This morning on awakening, I hear a loud whirring sound in my right ear. The humming gradually softens, as if descending... then turns strident, ascending... and softens again (decrescendo... crescendo... decrescendo....). This reverberating hum lasts about a minute, if not hours. Now in a synchronous state of mind, I close my eyes and merge with the boundless stream of consciousness.

---

[94] Dion, Celine and R. Kelly. "I'm Your Angel." *These are Special Times.* Sony Music Entertainment, 1998. CD.

Journal Entry 41

Sunday, 08/08/2004
Third quarter moon
Around 6:30 a.m.

Awe-Inspiring Winged Creature

I'm like a bird, I only fly away
I don't know where my soul is...[95]

In a twilight sleep, I found myself weaving in and out of the dream state as Allie purred and curled up in the crook of my arm.

♪ ♪ ♪

Out of the blue, my eyelids start to blink and quiver. I try to hold them but soon give up because I'm unable to control this curious movement. Then, at once, I find myself staring at two silvery-blue balloons that look like butterfly wings, or perhaps the wings of a bird, yet way overblown. Suddenly, the being plummets from a white ceiling fan that is, in reality, nowhere in the room. Abruptly, he freezes, a tightwire artist in midair! Radiant light shines a spotlight on the creature as he descends in slow motion. Now I hear the whirring sounds again (as in Journal Entry 40). His enormous wings flap and swoop down as if he's coming to raise me up, a collaborator in his dazzling aerial show. Strangely, I'm not afraid. I am bowled over by a stunning array of silvers and cobalt blues – this incandescent peacock flitting right before me.

---

[95] Furtado, Nelly. "I'm Like a Bird." *Whoa, Nelly!* Dreamworks, 2000. CD.

Then the awesome being flaps his wings, working them into a deafening thunder, and at last, he begins his ascent. I shout, "Yes, you are here!" But truly I'm thinking, *please don't go! Take me up there with you!*

Still sensing traces of his vibration, I'm feeling very much at peace as I slip into a comatose kind of sleep.

Post Script

I am blown away by the beauty and wonder of the visions and dreams I've been having of late. This morning's vision was clear, lending a compelling sense of realism to an otherwise unfathomable exhibition. Were my eyes open when the being appeared? I don't know for sure, but I do believe they were, though they were quivering at first. The room looked the same except for the presence of the ceiling fan, the bright light, and the phenomenal creature, whether bird, butterfly, or spirit being.

Monday, 08/09/2004
Around 6:00 a.m.

Max the Astronaut

I think my spaceship knows which way to go
Tell my wife I love her very much.... She knows...[96]

I had a dream that Max was an astronaut. Before his scheduled blast-off, I had been anxiously trying to reach him. Alas, I learned he was being held in isolation in preparation for this record voyage. Eventually NASA relayed a message to me, saying Max was following the pre-programmed protocol, required for an unprecedented spacewalk. He and his fellow astronauts would be performing the walk soon after their arrival on Mars; or was it Jupiter?

How could I have forgotten already?

Of course, if a space expedition of this magnitude were truly going to take place, Mars would be the most likely planet for it. Someday anyway....

Post Script

This is all I have been able to get down on paper since about six o'clock this morning. I'm assuming the dream happened around three or four o'clock. And yet, like so much we seek to capture consciously, it is starting to fade away.

---

[96] Bowie, David. "Space Oddity." *Space Oddity.* Virgin, 1969. LP.

JOURNAL ENTRY 43

Sunday, 08/15/2004
Around 5:00 p.m.

Baffling Warning at the Gym

She stayed with me just long enough to rescue me....[97]

Getting ready to do the next set of workouts, I waited next to one of the weight machines. Nevertheless, I was unaware how closely I was standing to the metal bars. Fixated on the latest in gym shoes, I had no idea the fate that was about to befall me – or would have – if I had not responded to an ensuing telepathic racket and the awesome words: *"Move now!"*

Almost involuntarily, I hopped to my left and, in less than a split second, a load of weights comes crashing to the floor! Sheer luck does not even come close to describing my fortune. The bars barely graze the hair on my down-turned head. If my crown had taken a direct hit, no doubt I would have suffered a concussion or I might have been killed. Stunned, I roll onto a nearby mat and whisper, "Thank you, whoever you are." Choking back the tears, I silently say, *I am so grateful!*

Toweling-off, I sprawl out on the mat while trying to gain some sense of composure. Soon, from the periphery, I catch a bunch of people running in my direction.

Who me? I'm thinking.

"Hey, what happened?" says the first, a broad-shouldered fellow. "Are you okay?"

---

[97] Hendrix, Jimi. "Angel." *The Cry of Love.* Reprise, 1971. LP.

Attempting to work up a smile, I say, "Yes, I'm fine, thanks. Just a little stunned, that's all."

The nice man nods and a couple of them behind him break into smiles. Others remain more reserved as if heeding caution.

I give them a wink and say, "Thanks for checkin' on me."

"Sure," they say, almost in unison, and skip off to do their workouts.

Not wanting to be the center of attention, I pick up my stuff and move to the far corner of the gym; planning to take five and finish my routine. But as I bend down to tie my shoelaces, I soon realize my hands and legs are still shaking like the streamers on a gift box. *Time to clean up, I suppose.* Slowly, I make my way to the locker room.

In awe of the baffling warning that saved me from such a dreadful fate, I lug my gym bag and wobbly self to the car. Fumbling for the key, at last I toss my junk in the trunk and head home. Originally, I'd planned to have dinner out and do a little reading. It's funny how quickly things change.

Peering through the windshield, I'm a turtle looking up at the fearsome sky – scoping out the cosmic possibility that somebody up there likes me. "Thank you for being there, whoever you are! There are just no words!" And I brush a tear from my eye.

Wednesday, 08/25/2004
Waxing gibbous moon
Morning

Elisabeth Kübler-Ross Passes On

I regret to have learned that Elisabeth Kübler-Ross passed away at her home in Scottsdale, Arizona. I did not even know she lived near me.

Along with being a wonderful doctor, Elisabeth was a resolute research investigator who wrote, in part, about the near death experiences (NDEs) of her patients and research subjects. What an articulate author and incredible individual.

My recent writing gained momentum, in part, because of my fascination with her studies on death, NDEs, and the growing body of research suggesting that death is not the end of life. For example, see Kübler-Ross' book, *On Life After Death*.⁹⁸

I am sure that dear Elisabeth would have even more to tell us now. Wouldn't she?

---

⁹⁸ Kübler-Ross, Elisabeth. *On Life After Death*. Berkeley, CA: Celestial Arts, 1991. Print.

Thursday, 08/26/2004
Waxing gibbous moon
Around 11:00 a.m.

Toe Mishap On a Sunny Day

"I Only Have Eyes for You" [99]

This morning I was running around the backyard for no reason. "No reason" is the key phrase here. Yeah, it was fun for awhile, but I wasn't watching where I was going and slammed my foot into a rock. Or was it a boulder? Regardless, I managed to wedge my poor footsie beneath it, and in a wicked forward shift, found my body catapulting like a shuttlecock high into the air!

As luck would have it, I landed rather unceremoniously on a thick patch of grass.

Sure glad of that! But then around twelve-thirty, my big toe started to swell into something resembling pork sausage. *Yeow!*

Been soaking my foot for hours. Now, as I try to elevate it, I'm getting even more perturbed because the thing's throbbing so. And because I see that I'll be taking my vacation with my new lumbering sidekick, about an eighth-pound of blue-black sausage. The thought of shuffling around Piccadilly Circus in meat wraps and clodhoppers is anything but pretty.

---

[99] The Flamingos. "I Only Have Eyes for You." *Flamingo Serenade.* Collectables, 1959. LP.

PART III
THE KNOWING

Sunday, 08/29/2004
Full moon
Mid afternoon

A Shining Piece of Silver

Remembering the song
"Book of Love" by Peter Gabriel [100]

Today I began to rummage through some jewelry bins and boxes to prepare for my first trip abroad. I still had plenty of time to pack, so I decided to start by polishing some rings, earrings and bracelets to take with me on my vacation. *Moving at this leisurely pace might help heal my toe,* I thought. So I hobbled to the kitchen and made up a tray of tea and cookies. Then, after setting the tray on the coffee table, I sat back, raised my bandaged foot and set it on the far end of the table. "Ouch… there. Once it's steady, it's fine."

🌙 🌙 🌙

Soon my attention turns to an antique basket of rings and I begin to poke through it. As I set each piece on a tea towel, the gold, silver, and variegated stones remind me of days gone by. I brush back a tear, feeling around the bin until my thumb and forefinger touch bottom. But there's something chunky and out of place. Pulling it up, I smile.

---

[100] Gabriel, Peter. "Book of Love." *Shall We Dance Soundtrack.* Casablanca. 2004. CD.

"Wow, it's yours," I say to my alter ego as I put it on my thumb. "You used to call it your Turkish wedding ring."[101] *Thought it was in my velvet pouch. So many memories....* I study the interlocking chain and spin it around.

Suddenly, I can no longer contain the water so I let it flow.

"This band is sure oxidized; time for a buff," I sniff, and reach for the silver polish and a soft cloth. It's a stubborn one, but little by little, the tarnish starts wearing away. *Nice.* I'm beginning to see the natural gleam of silver, so I add some more polish and rub even harder.

Nevertheless, as I continue to buff the ring, something is bugging me. *Why do I have two of your rings? I don't need more than one.*

Besides, most widows get rid of their husband's things soon after they die. Some of them even do it right away. But I can't seem to...

I just can't... sighing, I try to alleviate this discomfort by reiterating what my friends keep telling me, "Well, maybe you just need a little more time, dear." Nevertheless, one thought leads to another. Soon I'm remembering the rose I bought for him, and my wedding ring with the interlocking band that matched his own. On hearing our friends and loved ones as they enter the funeral parlor, I quickly placed my ring in his keepsake chest. "Take this with you, darling." And smelling the sweetness of the solitary rose, I placed it gently beside the ring.

Now I look up at my living room ceiling, as if my dearest friend and husband might still be hiding there like an enchanting caracal. I cry out in sadness, yet with the greatest joy, "Max!"

"Honey, I'm going to England!"

"Going to see your sisters and the family first. Then, guess what, I'm going to take the train to Wellington. You know, the headmaster's

---

[101] Max owned two Turkish wedding rings, each one fashioned a bit differently. The ring with the thicker band, I call The Greater. (See Journal Entry 13 for the story behind it.) The thin-banded ring, The Lesser, is the one I found in the basket today. Both are striking when polished.

taking me on a tour of your school. How cool is that baby?" The room is getting warmer as evaporation tickles my cheeks. I scratch my face, yet nothing can stop the babbling stream. "Guess what else, I'm going to Windsor to see your cousin Nate, and… and…" then in a flash, comes the roar of an engine, gaining in speed and might. I whip around, as if I might suddenly find myself stuck on the frightful railroad tracks of yesteryear. Tiggi darts down the hall, stopping short by the living room just as the clamor rises. I watch in disbelief as her eyes practically pop out of their sockets. An ungodly sound is emanating from her mouth.

That's the first time I have ever heard a cat snarl like a salivating pit bull! She's ogling something at the east end. Fear crawls like thorny branches up the back of my neck. "My God, it's in the dining room, whatever it is!"

Never mind my ailing toe, I couldn't budge if I tried. A crackling sound, an electric pop and a crash… "What's happening?" I scream. Despite the mallets now beating at my chest cavity and a deep-seated desire for self-preservation, alas, curiosity conquers all good sense. I get up and hobble to the dining room entranceway, only to watch in horror as books, candles, flowers, and my purple vase hurl themselves off the table and onto the floor! That's how it looked!

I make a lunge for my purple pot. Too late though, as I'm no match for the velocity of this mighty projectile. I can only look on in indignation as my prettiest vase smashes on ceramic tile… slivers fly everywhere in slow motion.

"My God, this can't be happening!" I scream.

And, as my little darlings stop spinning and settle in place, numbness covers my body like a sheath, dampening down my brain. *This is not real.* No sound. No movement. Nothing. I'm sitting in a crumpled ball on the futon, staring at bits of glass. My ears ring as an eerie calm descends upon the room. Tiggi mews disconsolately as she tries to coil her trembling body around my arm. I would like to stroke her but my hands feel like fossils, petrified. Before long my brain lapses into a chill like I've never known.

♫ ♫ ♫

After who-knows-how-long and the shadows that skulk like trolls along the dining room wall, I come to the dim realization that I had lost consciousness. After viewing what I thought was impossible – a manifestation made for moviegoers – I literally collapsed. Now, in an effort to get my bearings, I finally come to the vast conclusion that I must do something. After all, the clutter is not going to rise up off the floor and set itself back on the table. *Well, what are the odds?* Zero, I used to think. Not anymore.

I doubt I'll ever be surprised by anything weird again.

Nevertheless, I'm gratified to note that nothing more has moved. *Well, that's a start!* Hearing the heartening mews of one courageous cat, I pull her up and give her the bear hug she so deserves. "I'll make it up to you, Tiggi. I promise."

Soon I turn on the high beams and, like an inspector, conduct a sweep... from the bare table to the unlikely mess on the floor. All the while, I'm shaking my head. It is incomprehensible that all of the things cluttering my table for about a week, are now strewn about the floor. Under normal circumstances (hmmm, like when would that be?), I keep stuff on the table to take with me on the way out the door. *Maybe I'll read a chapter at lunch,* I say while grabbing a book and the car keys.

Now I'm staring at the whole daunting mess. *What to do? What to do?*

In due course, this (all too familiar) state of bewilderment begins to wear off. Perhaps more brain cells are forming again. And with a renewed sense of purpose, I focus my attention on the shards and pieces amassed at the west end.

"Wait a minute, my tablecloth!" The lace had come to a perfect point on the floor as if draped by a master decorator. "How strange, it

190

appears to be pointing to the plant." Soon, like a jolt from a super-sized espresso, I'm stiffly alert, scrutinizing the shattered glass and remnants around the tablecloth.

"No, the tablecloth is not pointing directly to the plant. It's pointing to..."

"What?" I ask, quizzing any shadowy imp who'd like to play. I bend down to take a closer look as Tiggi wriggles around like a bunny on the futon. Soon, she's making sounds like a wookie. Then she jumps down and sniffs the shiny object near the tip of the tablecloth.

I pick it up. "Hey, it's a coin!" I say, tossing it up in the air. Tiggi rears back on her hind legs, ready to go for it. Sometimes I don't think she's a cat; more like a cross between a dog and a rabbit. A dabbit? But of course, I'm taller so I catch it. The poor thing mews disconsolately. I'll have to give her a special treat tonight. "Good girl for trying," I say, brushing through her coat with my fingertips.

Now I must have a closer look, so I take off my glasses and set them down. Oddly, I can see things better when I bring them up to my face. Stooping, I examine my find. *So, where did this coin come from, hmmm?* Tiggi zeroes in like Watson nosing the prize, as if she can determine its value with a couple of sniffs.

"These markings are different." I sit down. "That's odd, no date." I check both sides of the coin. "Strange, no currency value on either side."

A few days ago, I had dusted all the knickknacks and sundries on the dining room table and I knew there were no coins on it. I'm puzzled. Where did this coin come from? One thing is clear, it's not a quarter – it would never spend. I've never seen anything like it! So I tap the coin on the table and put it safely in my purse.

Then, as if a certain someone might still be around, I look up and say, *Hey Max, what just happened here?*

Post Script 1

The day I left for England, I received the answer to my question. But because of what Max used to do when he was alive, I see that I should have solved this mystery much sooner. The answer is contained in my poem, "A Shining Piece of Silver," as published in our first book, *For the Time Being*, penned under my married name (AuthorHouse, 2007). I shaped these verses in a style reminiscent of the Victorian Era, a favorite period of mine:

A Shining Piece of Silver

Gath'ring up my courage with my clothing
For a voyage I knew that I must take
All purpose had died along with you, dear,
Oh Lord, it was a time I couldn't shake.

Packing jewelry, thinking and rememb'ring
My wedding ring you carried to your grave,
When before me, a quaking at the table
And the tablecloth flew off with a wave!

Before I knew it, clutter crashed on ceramic ~
Books and orchids, my lovely purple vase.
"This can't be happ'ning!" I said in sheer amazement,
Then sat and stared at the remnants, in a daze.

Befuddled, I picked up all the pieces,
And the tablecloth that was so elegant,
Lay pointing to a shining piece of silver
Hidden shyly beneath a blooming plant.

Perplexed, I sat down with the silver
Not knowing from where the coin had come.

I studied that shining piece of silver
Most certain it wasn't from that room!

So simple, it looked just like a quarter,
But it wasn't ~ the coin was something else!
I shook my head, returning to my business,
And slipped the piece safely in my purse.

The day arrived when I'd venture on my journey
And a thunderbolt hit me through and through ~
I locked the door, keys landing on the silver,
And remembered something that you used to do.

"You're trav'ling, my sweetheart," you would tell me,
"And to ensure that there is no blasted curse,
Take this coin along with you on your journey
And keep it tucked away inside your purse."

"And when you're weary and your trip is over,
Fly back to me and I will see you through,
But don't leave behind this little piece of silver;
It will guarantee that I'll be seeing you."

'Though we're parted and you're so far away now,
I keep your silver coin tucked away inside
To remind me, again, we will be meeting
When my journey takes me to the Other Side.

Post Script 2

Since August 29, 2004, I have found no earthly nor scientific explanation for the phenomenal event that happened on that beautiful day. My poem provides the best explanation I have to offer – from a supernatural standpoint – based on the tradition Max had set in stone.

For all the years of our marriage, he never failed to give me a coin with a hug and a kiss whenever I had to travel far from him and our happy home. Likewise, I started giving Max a coin or my lucky bug to take with him whenever his employer required him to fly. Max so disliked flying, I always hoped it helped. Somehow, I think it did.

Months after the first writing, as I edit this entry, I glance up from my work to catch a television commercial in progress. What is the announcer talking about? Why, vintage coins, of course. No, I'm not joshing you! Another synchronous moment in time.

Max and me near an old mine in Jerome, Arizona. Circa 1992.

Saturday, 09/04/2004
Waning gibbous moon
London, England
Evening

Char in London

Through the door, there came familiar laughter
I saw your face and heard you call my name....[102]

Max's sister, Char, met me in London. My first trip abroad and oh, what a trip! She told me they'd had nothing but rain and cold weather for weeks on end, but the day I arrived the sky was clear, the air balmy, and temperatures were climbing high into the seventies. Char said I must have brought the desert heat with me. I chuckled because the air seemed a tad brisk to me. In any event, these delightful conditions certainly satisfied both of us.

What a great landing. It took me less than an hour to fall in love with London: people promenading in the streets and that catchy tune, "England Swings Like a Pendulum Do" reverberating in my brain. It was an ice cream, popcorn and beer kind of night. After all those years, I was finally learning first-hand what the hullaballoo was all about.

Despite that residual case of balloon toe, I silently applauded myself for keeping up with Char. I'm sure she thought differently, because every so often she'd turn around and holler, "C'mon, let's go!" We had to run-limp to get to the theatre on time to see *The Mousetrap*, an incredible play that has been performed for over fifty years. Not fifteen – fifty! Things like that just don't happen in the States. We

---

[102] Hopkin, Mary. "Those Were the Days." *Post Card*. Apple, 1969. LP.

are all too ready to throw out the historic hubs of yesteryear in favor of a couple of catchy sound bites and the must-have toys of today, all of which lose their luster as soon as we've had our flimsy fun with them. But England doesn't strike me that way. Most people seem rather unassuming and perhaps a bit more appreciative of what they have. Was it World War II and the bombing of London that had such a strong and lasting effect? Or maybe it's the form of government. On the other hand, England's hefty tax structure would probably cause any inhabitant to be more appreciative of possessions, material or otherwise.

Amazingly, we arrived on time, and what a great show – enigmatic, funny, and powerful performances. I could have watched the whole show if my eyelids hadn't kept drooping – thanks to the all-nighter I pulled while crossing the Atlantic. The ill-fated seating arrangement placed me next to a mother and her newborn baby who cried all the way to England. I caught perhaps a couple of nods, but it didn't matter. I certainly couldn't stay mad at the little darling, stuck up there on the plane like me. I mean, we had a lot in common. I was just about ready to bawl too. Let's face it, we were all in the same boat – er ship – er contraption that attempts to fly in the air.

Thank goodness, it did!

For these reasons, my descent into oblivion began not long after the curtain ascended – as I settled back into my seat. Yes, Char did her best and gave me a couple of nudges… or more. Lucky for me, she wasn't hardnosed about it. And yes, I did try to straighten up, but my body had other ideas. I'd sit up straight as a post and soon find myself drifting off… again.

During the intermission, I begged Char to pour vast quantities of coffee down my throat. "Oh, their espresso should work just fine," I said.

She just smiled dubiously.

Well, the stuff did help, for about ten minutes or so. Never mind if I hadn't been punch-drunk, I'd have been mortified by my own behavior.

After the final curtain and copious rounds of applause, Char was finally able to slip into the powder room and tend to herself for a change. I hoped she wasn't too annoyed with me, but I decided it best to wait outside.

Maybe the brisk night air will clear out this brain fog.

Ah, taking in a vibrant range of city smells, I thought, *where's all the soot they kept telling me about?* Smiling, I savored the richness of the extraordinary evening. Yet, as I watched the passersby, I was beginning to feel like a kid at the zoo. *Something strange is going on,* I thought. *Maybe it has happened already... a dash of déjà vu... or as Max would say, déjà went.* Had the play made me giddy? Perhaps it was the coffee, or just a lack of REM, or maybe it was the narrow buildings, pitched at an angle (like me) as if they might topple over at any moment. No matter, I just stood there, enthralled by the sights and sounds of London.

♪ ♪ ♪

Then, without warning, a blast of cigarette smoke sears my nostrils. "What the *hack hack...* heck?" I rasp. Sensing the perpetrator to my right, I turn wanting to say, "You ridiculous fool, how dare you blow smoke in my face!"

I look hard, expecting to find the joker doing his dirty deed. But, oddly, not a *soul* is there.

Perhaps I've stymied the very word. For my eyelids start to flicker and no sooner than you can say "magical mystery tour",[103] a hologram-like figure takes shape before the leaning towers... no more than a

---

[103] The Beatles. "Magical Mystery Tour." *Magical Mystery Tour.* Capitol Records, 1967. LP.

few feet from my nose. I can almost make out the image, translucent yet diffuse in color... then, a maroon jacket emblazoned with a crazy Rupert the Bear insignia...

...the one so dear to me. "It's you!" I gasp even as I think, *So you're the culprit I've been looking for.* And I watch him glide around London in that juvenile jacket of his, incongruously smoking one of his favorites... flowing toward me like the cloud of smoke he's exhaling.

A design within a design – Chaos modeling at its finest.

"Max," I smile and say, "you're like a Lorenz attractor, but wavier."

Swept up on the wings of a profound sense of awe, I try to gather what's left of my earth-bound self – if only for the benefit of the lingering few who might think I've lost it, talking to the air and such. Then, going deep, I step back into the shadows and breathe in the spicy scent of a wayward city: London, the cacophony, the ultimate harmony. And, in the stillness of the deep, a trace of sandalwood and a smile... he comes rippling through. *Max....* home, at last, I merge with the heart of him. For here, time has no measure. Here, we turn together in silence, marveling at the mind-boggling slopes in the sky. Here, my sight softens into the sliver of a moon and a star. And in this singular moment, I know the meaning of forever.

JOURNAL ENTRY 48

Wednesday, 09/08/2004
Oxford, England
Time unknown

Oxford and the Hedgehog

"Willow Weep for Me" [104]

I met up with Char in London again and she drove us on to Oxford, her home. Because there was still so much to see, she decided to take more time off. This gave us the opportunity to tour Christ Church, Warwick Castle and some quaint shops in dreamy Oxford, not necessarily in that order. Knowing our time was short, we tried to cover as much territory as possible – that is, considering my marshmallow toe.

First, we stopped by Char's house so I could spend some time with her parents, James and Wilma, and drop off my luggage. I hadn't seen them since they had flown back to the states to visit Max and their daughter, Paulette, in Sonoita. Char said her folks weren't well, but they were doing a little better than they had been for quite some time. I was glad to hear that they were improving, at least. I so hope their progress continues this way.

Amazingly, as we pulled up to her home, on another one of those sweet sunlit days, Char spotted something wiggling in the bushes. "Look, I think it's a hedgehog!" she said, jumping from her car seat.

"Oh, where?" I said, hobbling around the other side. One time Max told me that when he was a lad, he had found a hedgehog somewhere in the brush. He said he tried with persistence to make a household pet out of the little fellow.

---

[104] Chad & Jeremy. "Willow Weep for Me." *The Very Best of Chad & Jeremy.* Varese, 2000. CD.

Char zeroed in as I trailed behind. "Char, I don't see him at all."

"Shush, over here!" she whispered, pointing and tiptoeing through the brush by the house. Before long, I actually spotted the brown-barbed creature, quivering and darting about. "How cute he is!" But, alas, he scampered away, tunneling under the leaves and loam.

"Oops, maybe not so happy to see us," Char said.

"I've never seen a pint-sized porcupine before. Let me have at him!" I said, lunging forward, forgetting that to touch the prickly animal would no doubt prove to be painful.

"Watch out, he might get you!" Char said. Leaves scattered as the miniscule hedgehog burrowed even further underground. Probably thought he'd be lunchmeat if he stuck around too long.

"Okay," she smiled, "he's buried."

"Hey, come back, little guy! Darn," I said.

"You'll never find him now," she said, shaking her head.

Nevertheless, our little hedgehog encounter couldn't have been a more auspicious way of welcoming me to the lovely home where Max had once lived with his guardians "…and my sisters!" as he used to say. Though James and Wilma adopted Max sans records, he always called their daughters his sisters. I liked that.

One time when Max was talking about his pint-sized playmate, he told me the hedgehog was the only pet he'd ever had as a child. And so, with a lump in my throat, I followed Char to the ivy-lined house where her parents stood waving and opening the screen door, ready to welcome us inside. On the way, I couldn't help but think we were somehow playing a part in the delightful tale, *The Wind in the Willows*,[105] with the hedgehog, Mr. Badger, Toady and the whole gang.

Of course I believe The Toad was there with us that day – not in corporeal form, but surely in spirit.

---

[105] Grahame, *op. cit.*

The Horses and On to Surrey

Bit by bit, I've realized
That he was here with me...[106]

The London and Oxford tours were conducted by my personal guide, Char. How lucky could I get? Then, Thursday we enjoyed a tasty Middle Eastern dinner with Char's sister, Alicia and her daughter, Sandy. The next day, Char carted me off to the pastures for a mixer with Alicia, Sandy, and their beautiful horses grazing in a field greener than anything I'd seen since the Amish country. Just before sundown, we snapped a few shots, "manely" of the horses, of course. (Sorry, couldn't resist!)

In the morning, we moved on to Hensley for lunch with Max's cousin, Nate. After a few laughs, some who-do-you-knows, and an authentic shepherd's pie, I unhappily said so-long to Char, in hopes we'd meet again soon. Then Nate took over and drove us on to Surrey where he and his wife, Chloe, live with their lovely daughters, Carmella and Rianna.

On Saturday, the five of us motored to Windsor for a tour of the Queen's Castle. The knowledgeable staff provided us with an in-depth look at the royal family – the allure, the joys, the responsibilities, and the sorrows that they had endured. Some would say, what about the wealth? We don't have what they have. Yet, I came away with the

---

[106] Clapton, *op. cit.*

feeling that the old adage, *money can't buy happiness*, holds true for this family as well. (My upcoming postscript highlights the subject of wealth, ponderings written years later.).

After our tour of the awesome castle, we hiked over to the gift shop to engage in blatant browsing. In the end, I did purchase a few things. You see, I just had to get some Windsor silver, four ornate towels, five boxes of fragrant soaps (they were small, really) and several calendar collectibles – gifts for Mom and a few of our friends. Then, being the record-keeping fool that I am, I bought and kept a Buckingham Palace calendar for my office.

Thoughts before leaving: *how will this stuff ever fit in my suitcase?*

We returned to Thorpe before dark, a little bushed yet ready for dinner. Chloe's spaghetti had the wonderful effect of reviving my spirits. Then after her delicious meal, we revved up some more with high tea and conversation. What a time we had, remembering the love, joy and humor our dear ones, Clyde and Max, had brought to our lives. Nate's father, Clyde passed away in March, not long after Max. This terrible time happened just months before my trip to England. I shared with Nate and the family how much I had been looking forward to meeting Clyde – even more because Max and I had been corresponding with him for so long. Though my travel plans had been in the making for months, regrettably, I was too late.

Nate, Chloe and the girls had so many amazing stories to tell me that they made it easy to paint a picture of their father and grandfather in my mind's eye. He was a family man, a caring man – truly a *gentle man*. Somehow, on this extraordinary night of Saturday, 9-11, I had the feeling that Clyde and Max were there with us. I can't help but believe Nate and Chloe felt that way too as we shared an evening of joyful memories and lots of love. I do not exaggerate when I say we had a night I will never forget. It will be fixed in my heart forever.

Post Script

Concerning the royal family and the subject of wealth, I have since learned that no matter how much money we may amass (or not), happiness is truly a state of mind. As Rhonda Byrne, Mike Dooley and the inspiring authors of *The Secret*[107] say, "Thoughts become things. Think the good ones." Isn't this where wealth – the wealth of a full and meaningful life – begins? We would do well to focus on the power of our thoughts. From birth to death, regardless of any outside forces that seem to impinge upon our lives, every thought we have is ours, and every choice we make is our own.

The Secret and the Law of Attraction tell us that we manifest or materialize all things (positive and negative) because of the *kind of energy* we create with our thoughts, words, beliefs, feelings, and actions. As a result, according to law, we are the masters of our lives. Concepts from *The Secret* link ancient metaphysical notions with the scriptures and, most incredibly, with energy theories of quantum physics. This is where science, metaphysics, and spiritualism join forces.

By the power of our minds, we possess the tools necessary to design whatever we would like, i.e., using a "mental" pencil, pen, paper, crayons, brush, paint, and easel. But what are the *internal tools* needed to see our desires come to fruition? Amazingly, these are simply our thoughts, feelings, beliefs and the inspiration required to paint the pictures we wish to see: that is, whatever we would like to do in life, the people we would like to meet, and whatever way we would like to live. As a result, we need *nothing outside ourselves* to bring into material existence the things we wish to have, do or be. Stated differently, using our thoughts, beliefs and *energy vibration,* we attract certain kinds of people, places and things into our lives. These things form the fabric, "the stuff" of our lives.

---

[107] Byrne, *op. cit.*

If you think about it long and hard, would you really want it any other way? The Infinite provides for us in ways that many of us have never even dared to dream possible. Yet, it is possible, and *indeed probable* if we but choose to harness this knowledge – and practice, practice, practice.

The Secret arrived at my door in 2006, like a dynamic force in my life! From the video and audio teachings, I have since been applying these concepts to attract amazing people, places, events – and yes – even written checks, rings, and material things that have enhanced my life in so many wonderful ways. Of course, I'm always creating more, as are you! It's easy because, like gravity, the Law of Attraction is always in operation – whether we choose to think with intent and use our energy effectively or not. In the last analysis, it's a matter of learning how to apply the Law of Attraction proficiently to create the results we wish to achieve. Yet, it's not so much the *quantity* as the *quality* of the outcome that most appeals to me. I certainly don't need another wardrobe of clothing right now. I have already manifested that very well. However, a summer home would be nice. The hundred-degree temperatures in Arizona have tested my faculties quite enough. I'm using the Law of Attraction now to visualize my lovely home – up in the pines!

An abundant life truly comes in different packages for different people. Thank the universe for that. And thank yourself for thinking about it!

Monday, 09/13/2004
Somerset, England
Around 9:30 a.m.

Wellington School and The Willows

My love is wider, wider than Victoria Lake...
Is it a crime that I still want you? [108]

On to amazing Stonehenge; then to Taunton and Wellington School. I was delighted and privileged to be on the agenda for tea with the Headmaster, Alan Rogers, and his lovely wife Sheila who taught at the school. Both were heavily involved in campus affairs and activities at all levels. Following introductions, we traded some interesting off the cuff information about Max. And I was proud to present them with a selection of our poems, then being prepared for publication in our book, *For the Time Being* (as in Journal Entry 46).

After mid-morning tea, Alan gave me an awesome tour of their beautiful campus. We then headed to the school cafeteria for lasagna with Sheila (how much better than the macaroni and stewed tomatoes Max used to grumble about, back when? He had talked about that antediluvian dish from the time we met until the year he flew off into the New World!). Now I am here to tell you that student life at Wellington has improved by leaps and bounds, because the cafeteria lasagna was simply delicious.

After the wonderful repast, the Rogers spirited me away to their home for coffee and a lovely chat. We must have talked about Max the

---

[108] Sade. "Is It a Crime?" *Promise*. Epic, 1985. LP.

most. This seemed to have the effect of connecting us in a heartfelt way, as if we'd already known each other back in the day. Then I glanced up and saw an amazing throng of butterflies on the wall – Alan's own collection from his travels in Africa. These stunning specimens, along with Alan's discussion of their natural habitats, reminded me of something else close to my heart – Max's birthplace in Victoria Falls, Livingstone, once called Rhodesia. (Livingstone is now the capital of the Southern Province of Zambia.) Just as suddenly, Max's wild stories about his childhood in Khartoum came to mind – his exposure to the elements and the little lads who possessed amazing skills with some serious tools. I could see how these extraordinary experiences had shaped Max's life, helping him to grow, both physically and mentally. Then as the subject of sports came up, I simply had to mention Max's accomplishments in track and judo. Of course, I dared not forget his school record in the javelin throw (reference Journal Entry 14).

As I got to know Alan and Sheila more, I made a risky decision. I decided to let slip the uncanny incident that had happened in my dining room a week or so before leaving for England. That is, the incredible object-flying phenomenon and the tablecloth that seemed to point to the undated coin.[109] I had brought the coin with me so I took it out of my little velvet pouch and rolled it across the table. I knew I was crossing into uncharted territory, but the couple was paying attention. And they shook their heads in disbelief as I told my story. Alan then examined the coin, turning it over and over in his hands, as if searching for a plausible explanation for this mysterious episode of mine. Yet, there was no normal or natural explanation that we could readily deduce from this rather shocking happenstance.

---

[109] "A Shining Piece of Silver" as described in Journal Entry 46.

One time I'd heard that people of the British Isles tend to be fairly tolerant, and perhaps as a group, more accepting of talk about the supernatural and the phenomenological in general. Was I trying to test this assertion? Perhaps. Or maybe it was simply my need to test the limits, so I gave it a roll, just to see what would come about. Luckily, I found the Rogers to be gracious and supportive, as they listened to my rather fantastic story. Until that time, I hadn't been able to bring myself to share my mind-boggling account with more than a few friends, and my dear mother, of course. These were the people I felt wouldn't rush to judgment. Indeed, I include the Rogers in this rare and thoughtful group.

♪ ♪ ♪

Later that day, the three of us took a stroll along the main street by the campus. Then Alan turned and quickly snapped my picture as I stood in front of Max's old dormitory hall, The Willows. Funnily enough, I had the strongest feeling I'd been there before, because I (Magoo) had spotted his dorm long before seeing the sign in front of it. Wellington has many dormitories, of course, and although Max had talked about The Willows a lot, he had never shown me a picture of it. I doubt he had any. You see, he always liked to share his old scrapbooks and photos with me, but The Willows wasn't among them.

Nevertheless, as I zoned in on the building's ambiance, I thought, *this must be The Willows*. Just then, Alan said, "And here is The Willows!"

I can hear Max now. "Luv, it's another staggering case of 'déjà went'!"

Tuesday, 09/14/2004
Wellington, England
Around 9:00 a.m.

Max's School Chum

Just as kindness knows no shame, know through all your joy and pain
That I'll be loving you always....[110]

At last, I had an opportunity to catch some of the Zs I'd been missing. Around nine o'clock – late in the morning for me – I found myself wrapped in down, courtesy of the B and B. Despite my lassitude, made more pronounced by the cozy coverlet, a teapot beckoned me. So, pushing off with a grunt, I made the grueling journey to the other side of the room.

The sweet cakes and tea are well worth the effort on such a blustery day, the wind whistling through the eaves. Sinking my teeth into a mouth-watering tart, I'm toting a cup of Earl Grey to the windowsill. Then, drawing the blinds, I plop down on the ledge as tea spills all over the place. It doesn't matter. I'm captured by the view just across the road: an English countryside lined with trees and acres of hills about as green as Easter grass. Well, on a sunny day they would be that green, but now they're darkened by a cloudbank, causing them to look more and more like what they are, the Black Hills.

What a way to wake up! And I don't even have to go out... not yet.
Think I'll watch the BBC and press whatever clean clothes remain in that
fright of a suitcase.

---

[110] Wonder, *op. cit.*

"Maybe the clouds will be gone by then," I say to no one there.

After ironing the stuff in my case, it's time for some dawdling – watching TV and stuffing my face with too many cakes for my own good. Then, a banging sound and another trip to the window…. I fling open the blinds. "What, hailstones?" The sky is as black as onyx. Certainly not what I'd planned, but why am I surprised? I should know England by now.

Still, I think, *it's beautiful in an ominous sort of way.* Whipping around, I take a real look at the room – white on white, small but full of life – not claustrophobic at all. Just the same, I'm in a slump. "Hadn't planned to order in for the day. There's so much to see."

Guess I'll have to brave the weather or hang out at the B and B all day.

No, I don't want to do that. At last, I sigh and force myself to do something, anything. "Okay, where's the umbrella?" I say while rummaging through piles of junk.

"Oh, it's here!" Somehow, I'd managed to mash it into my tawdry duffel. *How boringly prepared.* Sniggering, I recall the time Max said I'd never make the Sierra Club backpacking team. "Sweetie, your entire wardrobe stuffed into a sixty-pound backpack? Whoa, you'd break your ego if not your spine!" *Hoot hoot… holler holler….*

"Cute, Max." Pointless to argue, I knew he was right. I might even try to squeeze my umbrella into the pack. "Honey, I must have it! What if it rains on our hike up Sterling Pass?"

"Besides," I add, "aren't you the one who always says, 'Semper Paratus?' Well, that's me baby, always prepared!"

"Cute, Mandy."

"So, what now, darlin'?" I say, jerking the umbrella from the duffle. "Should I stay in or go out?"

Well, no point in sitting here all day. Go ahead, brave it! You never know what the day might bring.

I stop short and look up at the ceiling, as if Max's spirit might be pasted to it. "Max?" I ask, trying to stay still. "Is that you?" I close my eyes, take a few deep breaths, and wait to hear more.

But no other sounds spring forth, at least none I am able to detect. Before long, I release my breath, whoosh… long and slow.

"Anyway guy, you're right. No point in sitting here all day." And with this daring decision comes the long awaited something. A sense of focus? So I turn off the blasted boob tube, take a shower, blow dry my hair, and don my woolies: a sweater, jeans, coat jacket, high boots and a long scarf. AND I grab my camera, shoulder bag, the umbrella and some shades – just in case the sun should show his fickle face.

Turning, I do a double take and spot my briefcase in the corner. *My journal!* Rather than lugging a computer to England, I had printed some pages of my journal and brought a notepad with me. I remember the old adage, "*I must write today!*" Tomorrow exists only as a notion in the mind. Something to prepare for, never to embrace. If I choose to write tomorrow, not a word will reach the page.

So I grab my briefcase and make a beeline for the door. On the way, I tsk at the mirror like the baggage is its fault.

Must you always look like the terminal tourist?

Man, that amazing sound! Looking up, I say, "I hear ya, Max, as clear as the chimes on my porch!" Chuckling, I add, "No matter where I am, you make me feel right at home."

⁂

On time to the minute, a buggy-shaped taxi pulled up to the B and B and whisked me away to downtown Wellington. Stepping from the cab, I handed the driver the full tab, a tip, and another six quid. "Sir, I wonder if you'd be heading back this way tonight, say, around six?" He nodded and gave me the high sign. "No trouble, ma'am. I'll be back to pick you up promptly at six." There was no doubt in my mind he would. Pleased the day was turning out as it should, I thanked him and moved along with briefcase, purse and paraphernalia in hand. Dashing between the raindrops, I glanced uptown and down-, and soon spied a cute little cafe near the corner phone booth.

Strange, I never did open my umbrella.

The coffee arrived in no time. I savored a cup, then asked for a refill. Caffeine sometimes has the reverse effect of slowing down my mind. Sitting back, I smiled at the nice server who brought me a salad and a basic hamburger. Turned out a tad overcooked, but that didn't matter. I drowned the thing in condiments and ate it anyway. Nothing could possibly dissatisfy me now that my thoughts had turned to Wellington and my journal. As the hours soared by, I actually wrote two journal entries and addressed some overdue post cards.

Bleary-eyed but feeling great, I glanced up to find an awesome sight. The rain clouds had drifted away from the sun at last, transforming an already charming Wellington into an amber-colored scene, like from old world France. The dazzling rays bounced off the storefront windows straight into kaleidoscopic eyes. "I'm in love," I said as I donned my shades. *Quickly now, I must pack up to go.*

Toting the dry umbrella *and stuff,* I strolled up and down the streets of Wellington. How I admired the optimistic people and their quaint little shops. Then, after snapping a ton of photos, I ended up at a little jewelry store on the main drag. Browsing from case to case with my mother in mind, I took my good old time.

As a Navy man, my father had been stationed in the South Seas. Perhaps because of his (mis)adventures as a pharmacist's mate aboard the Carrier WASP, my mom had taken a liking to coral jewelry. On the other hand, I couldn't dismiss the thought that maybe she preferred these gems of the deep because her husband liked to buy them for her.

Either way, I reasoned that the coral necklace I'd been turning over in my hands would be a good bet for Mom. Yet even as I paid the relieved clerk and stashed the gift-wrapped box in my bag, I looked out the window to find the amber colors of midday dissolving into the blues and grays of late afternoon. With all the walking and picture taking, I realized I'd worked up an appetite too soon. So I slipped into a nearby deli to order a *take away* for the B and B. Little did I know what – er who – would be waiting for me there.

I was certain I had never met the man. All the same, I sensed that in some vague way, I already knew the all-too-jovial fellow who stood behind the counter. Then, from the irregular movement of his shoulders, it dawned on me that he had to be limping. But to his credit, he paid his handicap no mind. He took my order in a cordial way and as he fixed my sandwich, we struck up a conversation.

He, whom I will call Mick, had been swift to conclude that I had just arrived from the states (*hmmm, do I look that "touristy"?*). I relayed that I'd come to Wellington for the grand tour and to visit my deceased husband's relatives in two other counties. Well, in the process of conversing with this cheery guy, I discovered he knew Max very well, though not necessarily in a pleasant way. They had been schoolmates at Wellington, same level and years of attendance, but alas, one day during their first term, Max punched Mick in the face for no apparent reason – and knocked him out, cold!

My throat felt like a knife was gouging it out. *What made me come to this place?* Little did I know, I was about to find out. On some preconscious level, I suddenly realized that despite Miss Paratus' daily planning, she would never have been able to prepare for this.

Mick began to tell me his story in a blunt sort of way. *And to my sheer amazement I heard Max cut in,* as if he needed to tell me his own inimitable version of the same account. Even so, Max's words and feeling-tone came across soft and comforting. His compassion came through even more than it had so many years before, when he first told me the story.

⁕ ⁕ ⁕

One sunny September day not long after we met, Max sat me down and told me about a terrible fight he'd had during his freshman year at Wellington. He admitted the brawl had been one-sided – he had caused it. Nevertheless, he wanted me to know how much he had changed since his early teen years.

The altercation happened in the mid-sixties not long after Max's parents had separated. Sadly, they never told him they were planning to get a divorce and when he found out, he was not just upset – he was filled with rage. You see, the news arrived not only late but second-hand. His guardians apprised him of the divorce some time later. To add even greater difficulty to the initial deception, this all happened while Max was preparing for his first term at Wellington. Originally, he thought his parents had sent him to his guardians' home to facilitate his attendance at this independent day and boarding school. Later, he learned the reason they shipped him off was due to the divorce – at least, that's what Max said and how he felt.

Why Max's parents tried to hide the divorce from their son, I do not know. But regardless of their intentions, Max felt betrayed, and not just by one person. I understood how he must have felt. He was angry at his parents for their deceitfulness. He was also upset with his guardians for initially attempting to keep this information from him. But, right or wrong, I believe they were just trying to abide by his parent's wishes. Knowing them as I did, I did not think they wanted to be in the middle of such an untenable situation.

Max and I talked at length that beautiful fall day. He felt that his parents' covert divorce was, on some subconscious level, one of the reasons he rebelled so strongly his first term. But he also said that, as he learned and understood more during his first year at Wellington, he began to accept full responsibility for the incorrigible things he had done. He said he started changing even more after getting involved in sports and other school activities. As a result of his total immersion in Wellington's programs, a number of positive changes began to take place. His judo instructor may have had the greatest influence of all, teaching Max how to gain control, to meditate and put his spirit into the sport... to achieve a sense of balance... and, at last, a sense of peace in his life.

Max had always been a quick study, this I knew. I was amazed at how much he retained over the span of his life, not only in quantity but in value.

♪ ♪ ♪

Out of the blue, my mind flips back to the moment. I'm studying Mick as he puts peppers on my sandwich. But why is he still carrying on about the schoolyard scene? Somehow, I thought we had gotten beyond that. Am I being insensitive? Perhaps I'm just cranky for food.

And why is this sandwich taking so long? *Be patient, Mandy, he's almost done.*

Mick's topping my baguette with onions and brightly colored vegetables as he continues to cover the clash like the Friday night fights. Then, out of nowhere, he zooms in for a punch, slapping the meat with a red pepper – the blood. (I wince as Figaro comes to mind.[111] How

---

[111] Papi, Gennaro, cond. *The Barber of Seville*. By Gioacchino Rossini. Libretto by Cesare Sterbini. Chorus and Orchestra of the Metropolitan Opera. CD. Guild, 1941.

strange!) Then he whacks it with a green – his ailing face. And he pounds it with another red... and another.

Shock follows chaos. I open my mouth but words won't come... I'm bone-parched. Then, at once, I hear Max's spirit resound like the static between radio stations. Soon the random noise subsides and I hear his resonance as if it is being superimposed onto Mick's... like they're talking simultaneously... telling the same story yet with different words and expressions... confusing my thoughts and the signals I'm trying to snatch like fastballs whizzing by my head.

Mick rants on and pounds some more. I hold my head. My face is wet. "Stop!" I shriek. But he doesn't seem to notice that I'm still in the room.

In a blur, I turn away from the window not wanting the bystanders to see such a glum face. Wiping the water with my sleeve, another dreadful thought takes form.

Oh no, is this why the man limps? I thought.

"Oh geez, I don't want to know..."

Did I say that? I thought.

"No, it was I!"

My God...

"Max?" I whimpered softly.

The knife hits the board... *thwack...* but no other sounds come through.

MAX? I scream in silence.

♪ ♪ ♪

I was tapped out, unable to hear more. Wobbling, I closed my eyes and tried to get my bearings... to focus on the man nattering behind the counter. I knew, of course, that Mick could not hear Max. In fact, he could hardly hear me. He didn't seem to notice I was carrying on a conversation with a *being* who wasn't even *there*... not in the natural sense, that is.

Gaining my composure, I turned to face the man still wearing the crackpot smile. I watched as he topped my sorry sandwich with bread. Then he cut it in half... *thump*... ending the bloody opus in one fell swoop.

A concerto it was not.

Overwhelmed, I couldn't speak, though I knew I must say something. I owed the man that much.

But did I owe him, or did Max? No matter. I knew that I must speak for him.

"Oh Mick," I said, feeling inept. "I am sorry to hear what you went through. It sounded terrible." I truly meant it, but as hungry as I was, I doubt my words came across. Floundering around, I finally said, "I just hope that, I just...."

How can I do this?

"I hope you are able to forgive Max for what he did. Somehow?

Looking quite cross, Mick gawped at me. Boy, was I in trouble. Nevertheless, I knew I must go on.

"I can tell you, Mick that as Max progressed through his teen years, he began to develop a better attitude about life and people. I mean, he changed a lot, I can sure tell you that! By the time I met him, he was just a great guy, and a caring person too. He used to go out of his way to help people, friends and strangers alike. I mean, it didn't matter who they were. That's one of the things that impressed me most about him," I smiled. "One of the reasons I married him."

No response. *What now?*

"I certainly... hope you... can forgive him?" Then, at once, the parallel buzzing in my head and a shimmering light to my right, *wow....*

But I must maintain somehow. *Keep straight.*

"I mean, he uh, Max uh… he wants you to know he is sorry." I turned to my right with the buzz… *Yes, yes, I know…. I will tell him!*

I turned again to face Mick. "He isn't just sorry, man. It goes deeper than that. This is at a soul-felt level." My hand covers my chest, eyes running now. "My husband feels awful he ever did anything to harm you in any way."

From nowhere, from outer space, the thoughts and words keep rushing toward me, nonstop. "And he… he needs you to forgive him, Mick. For you, for him, for his pro…

… pro?… okay, I get it…for his *progression.*"

"And for your progression too!"

But Mick didn't say a word. He looked puzzled as he clutched a white paper bag, the remains of my baguette. Worriment ruled the moment, but not with regard to the sandwich. That was already hacked.

It didn't matter.

I continued. "Max wants to set things straight, you see? For the record. For the past… for the future…"

"For all time." I exhaled, coughing. My hands began to tremble, yet as sick as I felt, I could not allow myself to keel over now.

Bear up, Mandy.

Mick looked bewildered and shook his head. "Oh, no ma'am."

Okay, now I'm in deep doo-doo.

"No?" I peeped.

"No, not necessary, ma'am. Not at all," he said with a wave of the hand. "I just told you the infamous story," he shrugged. "That's all. I wanted you to know how I knew Max. I mean, how well I knew your husband." He seemed so proud of this accomplishment that I felt happy and sad all at once.

"Ma'am, there's no ill will, none 'atall'," he continued. "We were school chums, ya know? Hey, back then stuff happened!" he chortled and his smile grew as big as a puppy's.

Despite the riotous sandwich scene, perhaps a remnant of past angst, it was obvious he had forgiven Max a long time ago. And the content of his words began to sink in. Yet why did I feel as if a boulder had been lifted off my back, like I had been forgiven for doing the very deed?

I had never felt more relieved. "Thanks, Mick," I said. "You're really – you're a good guy!"

We shook hands and I thanked him again, taking his hand in both of mine.

"On that note ma'am, don't forget to take your dinner," he said, and with a grin, he handed me the white bag.

So I put on a plastic smile, for him at least, and took my *take away*. "Nice of you," I said.

"I'm closing shop," he said. "C'mon, I'll walk you out."

As Mick grabbed his keys, I glanced down at the crumpled bag and my tummy did a flip; wondering if I'd ever get up enough gumption to open it. *On second thought, maybe I'll just pick up a snack at the B and B.*

The deli man locked the door behind us and we breezed on into an otherworldly twilight. By this time, he was already telling me about another incident, a terrible motorcycle crash. He said the motorcycle had crushed his leg, resulting in sudden and unwanted retirement from the teaching job he loved. I told him how sorry I was to hear of his misfortune, and I meant it. Nevertheless, I exhaled into my scarf, burying my relief in the knowledge that Max had absolutely nothing to do with Mick's ill-fated limp.

Looking up, I searched the sky and found Max's star. *Did I tell you just how much this makes my day?* I asked him silently.

And mine! I heard him hum as a swift, delightful impression took shape – to watch him dance and whirl from star to star? How I embraced this whimsical image. It's there now and will be forever in my mind's eye.

I sashayed down the street, as blithe as the twinklers above us, while Mick advanced a pace or two ahead. Suddenly, he whipped around and said, "Despite any past misfortunes, ma'am, I'm in training to become a horologist... a watchmaker. Now I'll be able to sit all day and do my work." I told him how awesome that sounded, offering him a few words of encouragement in his new endeavor. In fact, I was beginning to feel like a big sister to my newfound friend. All the same, we arrived at the corner way too soon. I turned to face him. "Hey, I know you're going to do well in your new career. You have certainly picked the right one for you!" And there, with a handshake and a smile, we said our good-byes.

At day's end, with no more than a trace of melancholia, I crossed the street and began the trek back to the phone booth of yesteryear. *How long ago it seemed....* As an afterthought, I turned around to find a bobbing silhouette heading north in the dusky street. "Hey guy," I hollered, "keep up the good work!" He made a half turn and brandished a wave about as big as his smile.

And that was pretty big.

"Take care," I said under my breath to the fellow I came to know in one awe-inspiring afternoon. *No, that's not true. I've known him longer. Much longer....*

Twisting 'round, I saw stars – the ones in my head as I tripped on a park bench – bags flying all over the place. *Good thing nobody's around.* Somehow, I managed to shore up what was left of my sang-froid. Then, turning 'round, I nonchalantly proceeded to pick the stuff up off the street. Regardless, it didn't take me long to give it up again, but it wasn't from the fall nor from any pain or grief – no, not at all.

It was for joy, to be sure, that I plopped down, dropped my stuff on the ground and started to ball my eyes out. For I had finally grasped the reason – the mind-blowing reason I'd made the journey all the way to Wellington, England – as clear as that beautiful September day so long ago.

Friday, 09/17-09/18/2004
Chandler, Arizona

The Taillights Are On

Lighting the spark of love that fills me
With dreams untold....[112]

Following my whirlwind trip, I burrowed in like a groundhog. Of
course, I'd planned it that way. I arrived at Sky Harbor Thursday
night which meant that I had a three-day weekend to play catch up and
lounge around the house. This also meant that I wouldn't be traipsing
into work cockeyed due to some raucous arrival the night before.

Regardless, I forced myself to get up around ten and do the
laundry, practically barking for my attention in the corner. Then, after
a bowl of soup and Scrabble with the cats, I returned to my calcified
spot, lifting only the remote and the hand required to operate it. *Ah,
this is great. No matter where you go, no hotel could possibly outclass the
comforts of home.*

By noon Saturday, some form of sentience had returned, at last.
So I paid the bills, straightened up the house and even felt energetic
enough to get Max's truck washed and waxed. Then, on the way home,
I bought some groceries to replenish my all-but-bare pantry. But as the
sun started to sink into the haze, I realized I'd spent more time browsing
through stores than buying.

Oh well, I shrugged, *dusk is fast approaching.* Quickly, I tossed the
groceries in the truck in hopes of getting home before dark (it's a Magoo

---

[112] The Platters. "Twilight Time." *Encore of Golden Hits.* Mercury, 1960. LP.

kind of thing). Hey, I remembered to turn the lights on before exiting the parking lot. *Really something there.*

Lately, I've been parking Max's truck in the driveway. You see, the left side of the garage is filled with boxes, all awaiting review and impending disposal. Not unlike impending doom. So I parked the truck in the driveway and hopped over to pick up the mail. It's a good thing I didn't wait till morning because, while glancing at the junk mail, I looked up to find the taillights burning a bright crimson. *Oops....*

♪ ♪ ♪

I dash to the truck and jump in. But despite several tries, I am unable to turn off the tail lights. Oddly, the headlights are off, no problem. *So, what's with the tail lights? Let's see...* I start the engine and let it run. Then I turn the light switch on and off a few times and turn off the ignition. Sure of success, I hurry back to the rear of the truck.

The taillights are blazing a fire engine red! *What the hay?*

Darkness looms as I enter that state of Magoo Madness where any ambition I had of playing fixit has long since vanished. *How do I test the lights when I can't even see my own shoes?* I fumble around for the flashlight, but it's off the radar screen.

Sigh... okay, time to call Stan. Luckily, my cell still has some juice left. But after asking for his help, I hang up and say to the truck or anyone who would deign to listen, "Boy, he must think I'm a crank. Why would the headlights be off and the taillights on?"

Did I detect a snicker at the other end?

Well, at this point, it doesn't matter. All I can think of is the wear and tear on the battery. Soon, I'm relieved as Stan whips his truck into the drive just minutes after my call.

Despite all, we're both surprised. After numerous manipulations, Stan is unable to turn off the taillights. "Mandy, looks like you have an electrical problem. I'll pull the fuse and disable the lights in the interim. I'm sorry, but you'll need to take 'er in. I'm sure your favorite repair shop will have all the equipment necessary to test your truck and fix the problem."

I thanked him for coming in a pinch and said reluctantly, "Okay, I'll take it in Monday after work." Regardless, my brain is still searching for other options. *Let's see, it's Saturday night. No garages are open now or on Sunday. So the truck won't be fixed before I go back to work... darn. How often do cars break down on the weekend? Hmmm, in my case, it seems like all the time.* Nevertheless, there's consolation in the fact that, as dawn approaches Monday, I'll be driving my car, the one with working lights.

🐾 🐾 🐾

Yawning, I lift the garage door to find Allie patiently awaiting my return. "Hey baby!" As I pick her up, I wiggle her tiny paws.

"Isn't it strange how many electrical problems we've had lately?" I say, half to her, half to myself. *Wiggle wiggle...* "Hardly ever had them before Max left town. I mean, if he were around, I know he'd fix things in a jiffy, wouldn't he? *Wiggle wiggle...* yep, in a jiffy, babe." Allie's purring and looking up at me in that cat-knowing way.

Yes, electrical was one of his specialties. He knew it well, and loved it.

Journal Entry 53

Sunday, 09/19/2004
Around 2:30 a.m.

Earring and Post-Holder Travel into Ear

I'll come around to see you once in a while
Or if I ever need a reason to smile...[113]

Having slept on my back, I am awakened by a persistent buzz in my right ear. The sound reminds me of a cell phone on vibrate yet louder. Simultaneously, I feel a load in my ear and weird movement. Startled, I jump up and cry, "There's a giant bug in my ear!" and I shake my head fiercely to get it out.

To my amazement, two objects fall in my hand: my right earring and the earring post holder. I am so relieved it's not a bug! Still, I am perplexed. How could these two objects have traveled from my earlobe *up* into my ear as I slept?

Indeed, I have outlined the following questions for anyone who would like to analyze this:

1. How does an earring travel from the pierced part of the earlobe into the ear above it, rather than below it? Is it possible for an earring to move or "float" into one's ear while one is asleep? I suppose it is possible but highly unlikely. The force of gravity ought to enter into play here.

2. A post holder secures a pierced earring in place. Of course, the holder itself is secured behind the earlobe. Tell me then, how is

---

[113] Rundgren, Todd. "Hello, It's Me." *Something/Anything?* Bearsville/Rhino, 1972. LP.

it possible for a post holder to travel from the back of the earlobe to the front, and then "float" vertically into the ear above it while one sleeps? Shouldn't gravity cause the post holder to descend and drop directly onto the pillow or bed?

Yet, in this case, the post holder shifted with a semi-circular motion and ascended before landing in my ear. This is not simply bizarre. It is contrary to natural law.

3. What may have triggered the long, loud buzzing noise? It felt as if this sound and the corresponding sensation (of an energy charge or a pulsing electrical current) had caused both of these objects to float or otherwise travel into my ear.

Though stunned by this off-the-wall event, I lie down and try to get some rest. Soon, I drift off to sleep again.

🌛 🌛 🌛

Around 4:00 a.m.

As I glance at the clock, my heart is doing flip-flops in my throat because the phone is ringing.

"Who would be calling at this ungodly hour?" I say as I sit up and rub my face. "Could be an emergency. Better get it."

Still half asleep, I stumble across the room and fumble around for the receiver.

"Hullo," I say, not trying to stifle a yawn.

But no sound is coming through.

"Hello!" I growl, cranky as Kong.

Still no response....

So I wait... and wait... hoping to hear something, anything.

Alas, a click. "They hung up," I say in frustration as I put the receiver down and rub the goose bumps on my arms. "Must be the night air."

Resigned, I plop down on the bed and hug my comforter. Soon, my mind begins to replay the tape of all that transpired in one wee morning. Sighing, I just shake my head. Too full of stuff!

With all this tomfoolery, I'm wide-awake now. So I get up, about as frozen as a popsicle, grab my robe and turn on the heat. *Why bother going back to bed?* Then, before long, big slippers stomp off in the inevitable direction of the kitchen.

"It's a darn good thing I like coffee!"

Saturday, 09/25/2004
Waxing gibbous moon
Evening

Blown Down Bulb

Whatever gets you to the light 'salright, 'salright
Out of the blue or out of sight 'salright, 'salright...[114]

The three-way light in my reading lamp has "blown down" to a one-way. If memory serves me correctly, I replaced the bulb around the end of July. The month before I left for England, my work and home life had become rather hectic, so I seldom had time to sit and read or even use the lamp. Then, before leaving for England in September, I left one light on in the kitchen – the reading lamp was off the whole time.

Strange. Is this just another case of bad bulbs?

---

[114] Lennon, *op. cit.*

Saturday, 10/02/2004
Waning gibbous moon
Afternoon

Stan's Taillights Are On

On this delightful day
I couldn't help but recall
the song, "Magic" by Pilot [115]

Today I went over to see my neighbor, Kate, the mother of Stan who has been doing my repairs. I don't recall much of our conversation except for something she said that caused tingles to go up and down my spine. She said that *Stan has to have the electrical system fixed on his truck because, after many tries, he has been unable to turn off the tail lights* (reference Journal Entry 52 and Stan coming to help with the taillights on Max's truck).

Here we have two trucks, one parked almost perpendicular to the other, each having the same electrical problem. How often does a tail light problem *occur*, let alone happen at about the same time, and in the same manner as another tail light problem... on two trucks parked in the same vicinity? Shall we say, and truly believe, that this is just another coincidence?

What about you, Max, my electrical wizard? What have you been doing on weekends, hmmm?

---

[115] Pilot. "Magic." *Pilot (From the Album of the Same Name)*. EMI, 1974. LP.

Sunday, 10/03/2004
Waning gibbous moon
Around noon

Electric Light Show

"All Day and All of the Night" [116]

I was standing at the kitchen sink doing dishes. Suddenly, the floodlight blazed and I felt an unmistakable pinch at the waist. "Yeow!" I shrieked and jumped back.

Still the pops and flashes rage on like a blitzkrieg, gaining in power and might! I'm quaking like a wide-eyed cat staring straight into the headlights of a semi. At last, the electric light show sputters and spits to an eerily ineffectual conclusion. Yet, just as amazing as the light show is the fact that the bulb never did burn out!

Well Berlin, you ought to know by now. What makes you think logic would ever enter into this situation?

It never did before – not this year anyway. I glance down to find my hands and legs still shaking like the lime jello in a Christmas tree mold. "Looks like the dishes will have to wait," I say as I swivel my way to the living room. "Maybe I'll just catch a comedy show for the day." Yet, even as I crawl into the sweet softness of the sofa, I'm out like a veritable light bulb.

Soon I awaken as thoughts of the blitz and a golden elixir come to mind. With one eye on the clock, I try squinting. *Just one thirty? I've never been one to sport scotch-on-the-rocks before six.*

---

[116] The Kinks. "All Day and All of the Night." *Kinks-Size.* Earmark, 1965. LP.

"Well, perhaps a change of pace is in order," I say as I lean into the bar like an old friend. Raising my glass to the light, I toast to the powers that be – the enigmatic ones who have finally gotten the better of me. "Cheers!"

Down the hatch....

"Smooth, I must say!"

Post Script

Was the 10/3 event caused by an electrical charge or was it something else altogether?

How many weird and wacky events must I witness before I really get it?

Journal Entry 57

Friday, 10/22/2004
Waxing gibbous moon
Around 6:00 a.m.

Vision of Max

Since you're gone I been lost without a trace
I dream at night I can only see your face...[117]

I had a dream this morning, but because of the clarity and the incredible colors, I believe it was truly an epic dream. Max had broken through the front door of our home. All dressed in grey, he frantically called out my name.

"Mandy, where are you? I don't see you!"

Awestruck by his wild eyes and tousled hair, I attempt to call out to him. But I seem to have lost all ability to speak as I try to spit out words that will not come. Max is in a frenzy, a smoky panther pacing around in a loft that is really our foyer. Then without warning, he roars from the rafters, "Mandy, I need you! Where are you? I must have you!"

I open my mouth to call his name, but I cannot, for I am still mute. I want to be there for him, to hold him even for a little while. And with that thought, at last some raspy sounds emanate from my vocal cords, and I shout, "Max, I'm here!"

"Over here!" Excitement turns to delirium as I run to welcome him home, as if he had only been away on a hunting trip. Suddenly, the panther springs forth and raises me up to his incredible energy as he shape-shifts into the living, breathing being of...

---

[117] The Police. "Every Breath You Take." *Synchronicity.* Interscope, 1983. LP.

"Max!" I scream. Our eyes lock in a boundless moment as we meet in joy and desperation, hanging on as if that one moment might be taken away. "Mandy, I'm sorry," Max blurts out, a sad look in his eyes. "I won't ever leave you again. Promise!"

"Max," I sigh, relieved and happy just to put my head on his shoulder and hear his resonant voice. Yet because I fear that he might drift off again, I cannot – will not – loosen my vice grip on his arm. *He left me once, in death.* Even though I know it was not his want to leave our beautiful home, I am certainly not about to let it happen again.

In the indescribable stillness of the moment, I am amazed because I can read his thoughts and sense his feelings. I know he must be sensing mine. And as I hold him near, I gaze in awe as the water from my eyes bathes his aching heart, soothing his restless soul. Now I understand. All these months, he has been as weary as I – two lost souls, both in search of the light. But it doesn't matter now, because I know that together we will find peace and wholeness once more... even in a dream.

Hand in hand, like children, we are carried on a breeze to a beautiful land of sea green gardens, cascades and clear running streams where every winsome wish becomes manifest. A thrilling sense of delight washes over my body, mind and being. Released from the worrisome past, we rocket through to a mind-blowing state of joy and tranquility. At last, I loosen my grip on my darling's arm. I do not have to hold him so tight, for my consciousness flows naturally with his. And as we cross the threshold and soar into the light, we merge into a state of harmony – a synchronous state of divinity – where we carry on as one with the cascades, the green gardens and the dear ones who envelope us, welcoming us home.

Post Script

Waking up was a real bummer.

It was rough, at first, but ultimately I realize it does not matter. All that matters is the vision, more real than life itself. This vision will be made clear to everyone who lives when it is "time to go" – to make that breathtaking journey to the Other Side. Death is an illusion, yet a fundamental transformation. Then there is life, once again.

Journal Entry 58

Saturday, 10/23/2004
Waxing gibbous moon
Around 6:45 a.m.

Blinking Ethereal Eye

*Once upon a time, once when you were mine
I remember skies mirrored in your eyes...*[118]

I woke up this morning to discover the ethereal eye in the center of my visual field. When I first saw it, my eyes were closed. Nevertheless, I have seen this eye before, as recorded in Journal Entry 31, for example. Sometimes the eye pops up while I'm meditating or as I awaken from sleep.

I find the ethereal eye to be mystifying and even entertaining. Sometimes it blinks and moves around in my visual field, but most of the time it remains centered while my eyes are closed. I find it baffling and often wonder what is causing it to appear. What does it all mean? I do not know. Prior to 2004, I had never experienced anything of the sort.

Post Script 1

Searching for an answer to the eye phenomenon, I again broke silence and shared my experience with a few close friends. I even mentioned it to my work partner. For several years now, Fred and I have been consulting together on government projects requiring statistical expertise and technical manuscript writing. Along with trusty Steve,

---

[118] The Moody Blues. "Your Wildest Dreams." *The Other Side of Life.* Polydor, 1986. LP.

our data warehouse guy, we often present our research results to the directors of various government offices.

Fred and Steve are both affable, work-oriented fellows. As a matter of fact, when we aren't busy blasting out statistical reports, Fred sometimes likes to sit back and talk about non-technical matters. Along with being a friend I trust, Fred has become a great source of information for me. He seems to know a lot about many things. For these reasons, I didn't think it unusual to talk to him about the recent eye activities I experienced. So, after telling him, he nodded like a seasoned doctor – as if he already knew what had happened to me. He turned and said without any compunction, "I believe you're experiences are related to *the third eye.*"

"Wow," was all I could get out, because something caught in my throat and the room began to spin. Years ago, I had seen something about this on television. It was creepy. So I just shook my head and quickly changed the subject.

(I see now that Fred's suggestion was probably more than I could deal with at the time.)

Later, I talked to another trusted friend of mine concerning an angle that had been whirling around in my head. I caught Marcy on her way to lunch and tried to tell her about the eye phenomenon without sounding wacky, a real feat. "Well, what do you think?" I asked. "Maybe Max is sending me signals in the form of an eye. Or maybe I'm receiving images through mental telepathy, thought forms or pictures from beyond. Do you think he's trying to tell me something? Like, 'Hey, watch out!' or 'Just wait and *see* what happens next!'?"

This time it was Marcy's turn to shake her head. "Nah, too far-fetched," she said as she lit another cigarette. She's been gaining a good reputation for her right-on reports. Still, she is attempting to live down her past with that motorcycle papa she married (really, a nice guy). Regardless, Marcy's nickname is not going away anytime soon. That's because Fred keeps teasing her with it. "Hey, Motorcycle Marcy! How's it going?" Now everybody's calling her that.

Honestly, I doubt she cares.

In spite of it all, I'm beginning to feel a tad uncomfortable about revealing too much, even to Marcy. You see, she told me that when she was watching my cats, something (a dish perhaps?) crashed to the floor. Since then, I have welcomed her into my home, but she has refused to come in. That's not like Marcy. Now I'm hedging even more. If I should tell anyone anything, I follow it with a disclaimer. "Oh well, just thought I'd bounce that doozy off you to see where it lands, ha, ha!"

Time to move on to another subject.

Yes, I have felt somewhat weary of the need to clam up, yet stimulated because so much has happened this year that is incredible, if not unfathomable. Now I'm beginning to believe that there are no limitations in terms of life and death possibilities – or even probabilities. Now it's rare for me to hear about a phenomenon that I think is too far-fetched. As a statistician and research scientist, this is a new and unusual perspective for me, as it would be for most people who have a science background at the doctoral level. Regardless, it is becoming more difficult to keep my own counsel about these unusual happenings, 95% of which never happened before 2004!

Not long after talking with Marcy at work, another strange thought came to mind. Is Max attempting to give me some information about his 1993 eye accident?

Max's accident was a hair-raising experience, bar none. About seven months after our wedding day and approximately two weeks before Christmas, Max injured his eye. Early that morning, he had been designing a fire safety system at his place of business. In the process, he realized he needed some important codes from an engineering notebook, the one in his truck, so he beat feet to the parking lot to retrieve the notebook.

On the way back, he opened the trusty book to search for the required codes. Reading and walking, reading and walking... I am sure Max was just trying to be efficient. I admired how he devised ways of getting his job done before the due date, and with high precision. But for this project, the due date was fast approaching! So Max dashed through the parking lot with open codebook in hand, and as he glanced up, he ran his eye into the corner of the open rear window of a truck.

Max nearly lost it – his eye, that is.

Minutes after the accident, I received word and rushed from my office to his. Quickly but cautiously, I took my husband's hand and lead him to my car; then drove him to the ophthalmologist's office where his staff were waiting anxiously to receive Max. I felt terrible for my husband, in so much pain. I was also worried that he might lose his eye. But amazingly, following the doctor's swift treatment and three long nights of moaning, Max's eye began to heal. In the end, we were both ecstatic because he regained every bit of his sight. From this harrowing experience, Max and I learned that the healing properties of the human eye are nothing short of extraordinary.

When I first caught a glimpse of the ethereal eye in February, it occurred to me that this might be a new way for Max to communicate with me. One thought followed another, and soon I began to wonder if that freak eye accident had somehow caused the cancer that spread so insidiously through Max's body. Is this what he was trying to say, projecting the image of an eye? In 2003, the doctors had found malignant tumors in Max's neck, head and upper torso. *Perhaps,* I thought, *the cancer had first formed in his eye and then spread through his head and into the neck area.* This would be possible if any metal, glass or other window bits had remained in the eye, only to travel to other parts of the body. I know that malignancies often result from toxicity, like from the contaminants of metal and glass.

So is this what Max was trying to tell me? Soon however, Marcy's unassuming words came to mind, and I thought, "Nah, too far-fetched."

Post Script 2

Since those early, probing years, I have come full circle – back to Fred's *third eye* proposal. I must say, it took nearly three years of mind-blowing change for me to begin to accept the third eye, not only as a concept but as a way of life – of seeing and sensing things. My breakthrough gained further support from those in the know, intuitively speaking. After Max died, as discussed previously, I began to meditate to help me relax and sleep. It seems that the frequency and depth of my meditation exercises, in part, had caused me to sort of break free, and I began to connect with Spirit in ways I had never dreamed possible.

When it comes to topics concerning the mind and spirit, measurement becomes a difficult prospect. However, I do not believe it is necessarily impossible. Barring IQ tests and mental questionnaires, I once thought measurement of the mind and particularly the spirit was an absurd idea. But that was back in the so-called Dark Ages.

With my epiphany at full tilt, I have a relatively new stance on measurement. While editing this tome, I stumbled across a wonderful book, a collection of works by science writers concerning a number of well-documented and esoteric topics in research and measurement. I encourage you to get your hands on a copy of *Measuring the Immeasurable*,[119] a veritable "eye" opener. (Couldn't resist!) Aspects of quantum theory and related notions are speeding toward unification with ancient metaphysical beliefs – *synchronicity and expansion like the path of our great universe.*

---

[119] Goleman, Daniel, et al. *Measuring the Immeasurable: The Scientific Case for Spirituality.* Boulder, CO: Sounds True, 2008. Print.

JOURNAL ENTRY 59

Tuesday, 10/26/2004
Full moon
Evening

Third Eye Definitions and Commentary

Am I awake or do I dream,
The strangest pictures I have seen...[120]

I researched a number of definitions and discussions pertaining to the concept of the third eye and discovered that it is associated with clairvoyance (clear vision, a form of ESP) and precognition. In particular, I found Adele Nozedar's treatment to be comprehensive and straightforward, i.e., the third eye characterized as "the seat of the soul".[121]

> The eye represents the "god within," ... as the "third eye" whose position is designated by the small dot called the bindhu above and between the actual eyes.... Here, the eye signifies the higher self, the part of man's consciousness that is ego-free.... this "eye of wisdom" directs its view internally as the... "eye of the heart".... symbolism too (556-557).
>
> The dot is also called the bindhu which means "drop." The bindhu is... believed to be the seat of the soul (3).
>
> The Wisdom Eyes (of Buddha) have a bindhu above and between them at the point of the third eye,

---

[120] Electric Light Orchestra. "Twilight." *Time.* Jet, 1981. LP.
[121] Nozedar, Adele. *The Element Encyclopedia of Secret Signs and Symbols.* London: Harper Element, 2008. Print.

signifying enlightenment. Underneath the eyes is a squiggle that looks a little like a question mark. This is the Sanskrit character for the number 1, and symbolizes the unity of all things (201).

The zero is represented as the bindhu…. (482).

Conceptually, zero is the symbol that stands for "no thing." In Buddhism and Taoism, it represents the Void, which existed before Creation, and in India, the word for… zero was Sunya, the Sanskrit word for void…. (484).

Throughout history people have tried to identify the seat of the soul…. Once, people believed that it was lodged in the heart. The seventeenth-century philosopher René Descartes placed it squarely in the pineal gland… (of) the brain…. In… metaphysical belief the pineal gland is associated with the third eye, a mysterious inner eye that can somehow be awakened, resulting in telepathic communication (575).

Post Script

With respect to the third eye, readers will find a number of articles on the Internet or in almost any local library. I have not attempted to draw any conclusions regarding this intriguing subject as it concerns the soul. At this stage, I seek only to convey these concepts and use them as "food for thought" vis-à-vis my recent experiences and endeavors. Readers may wish to consider how this information relates to the ethereal eye which I have seen while meditating or as I awaken from sleep. More and more, I realize that I have already embarked on the footpath of a new adventure. Into the grove I go….

How can I possibly turn back now?

Wednesday, 10/27-10/28/2004
Full moon

Max's Healing Spirit

I'll find my way through night and day
Cause I know I just can't stay here in heaven...[122]

For months, I have slept on the couch. I find this arrangement satisfactory and in more recent months, even pleasant. On the other hand, I ordered a new sofa and love seat which meant that the old ones had to be hauled away. Oops, too late I realized I'll have to spend a whole night without my sofa. Well, for about ten months now, I've been unable to sleep in the master bedroom. The bed is too large for one such as me, and perhaps too vacant as well.

Then this morning it dawned on me that I have a newly decorated guest room with a twin bed. Well, why not give it a try? I suppose the worst that could happen is that the bed won't work for me. If so, I'll just pull out my sleeping bag and go camping on the living room floor. I've always found my tufty bag to be quite comfortable, thank you.

As night-time approached, I peered into the guest room only to find it strange in some mysterious way. Still, I didn't have much of a choice. I'd have to sleep on the twin bed if I didn't want to conduct a late-night search for the sleeping bag. After Max became ill, we regretfully had stopped camping. Then, over time, I just lost track of the bag.

So around ten-thirty, I resigned myself to this gladly temporary situation and got in under the covers.

---

[122] Clapton, Eric. "Tears in Heaven." *Rush.* Reprise, 1992. CD.

Thursday, around 3:00 a.m.

After some preliminary tossing and two trips to the kitchen, I downed a glass of warm milk and ambled my way back to this strange room. Before long, I began to wonder what my guests thought of it. *Is it stiff? Perhaps overly decorated? Geez, I hope it's not pretentious...* I yanked the comforter over my head. *When I get my next paycheck, maybe I'll redecorate... take out a few knick knacks... go for a relaxed air....)* At last, the mind-numbing pursuit of removing all cast-offs somehow had the effect of lulling me into a deep, deep sleep.

Soon my mind, spirit and seemingly my body flow... further and further... up and away to another place in time. Vivid colors and amiable voices fill my midnight milieu as I drift along to who-knows-where. Soon I rise high above the building and trees and find myself wandering in and out of rooms made of billowy clouds. I'm lagging behind several multi-hued creatures who appear to be spirits gliding from one room to the next. At last, they transport me to a beautiful and unusual dwelling place....

Max's bedroom, of sorts, is of a grey and white hue. Both he and his room are coming through in those colors, not in a bland way, but in a serene way. It's as if grey and white are the most soothing shades the soul can possibly absorb, as if Max has been resting on tufts of cotton in a space filled with comfort and bliss. The spirits watching over him are also infusing me with information. Max must remain in convalescence for a long, long time.

I look on in awe as these delightful beings – young souls, luminous angels, dazzling fairies and colorful sages – try to satisfy Max's every requirement. The spirits are there to see to it that he receives whatever he needs to be whole once more. They do not allow him to move around much, insisting he let them tend to all of his needs, wants and desires. What a challenge for Max! When he was a child, he mostly had to fend for himself. His father, an airline manager, had to travel for months on end. Then, unfortunately, his mother was bedridden from time to time because of illness. At an early age, Max and his brother learned how to cook, clean and care for their mother. The two boys carried these grown-up habits into adulthood.

When I first met Max, I was surprised to find he possessed a keen sense of responsibility. Unfortunately, because of his absolute reliance on self, I found it difficult to do much for him. You see, he disliked imposing on others, including me. Well, in some sense, this became my challenge. I actually had to convince him to let me wait on him – something I enjoyed doing – maybe even more because he objected to it! Sometimes I gave in to his stubborn ways, but just as often I refused to take no for an answer. When you care for someone, doing things for that person comes naturally. The idea of putting forth effort doesn't even enter into the equation.

So, when I refused to let Max have his self-sufficient way, he would sometimes cave and let me take over... such happy times, serving his dinner in the living room as he watched his favorite show... bringing him a snack while he worked on a computerized design. Our munch time together, along with a joint propensity for verbal jousting, added to the fun. And as his trust in me grew, Max learned how to let go and allow me to do even more. Nevertheless, he still maintained a degree of independence, as did I with respect to our inalienable boundaries. In that sense, we were made for each other. We understood and appreciated one another's changeable needs for socializing and solitude.

❧ ❧ ❧

Now as I gaze at the joyful spirits darting to and fro, I feel a sense of relief and awe to find Max so well cared for and sheltered from harm.

Not wanting to interrupt the vital work of these beautiful creatures, I say nothing. Then, out of the blue, Max turns to me and shouts, "Yes, I am alive! And I am getting well!"

Waves of love, the elixir of life, radiate from his triumphant smile. My arms reach out to him as I scream in joy, "Max!" Nearer to him now, I gasp because the cancerous lump has vanished from his neck.[123] His careworn spirit is free, on the road to recovery!

Post Script

After having this awe-inspiring vision, one which I shall not soon forget, I began to do more research. I don't know how else to say this, so I will do so boldly. Because of this clear vision, I awoke with the sense of knowing that this was not just a fantasy created by the sleeping mind. These interactions and manifestations happened during soul travel.

Eckankar's definition of soul travel is as follows:

> In the simplest terms, Soul Travel is an individual moving closer to the heart of God. This movement takes a variety of forms. One form is the sensation of fast movement of the Soul body through the planes of time and space. In reality, though, is such movement possible? Soul exists on all planes, so what feels like movement, or travel, is simply Soul coming into an agreement with fixed states and conditions that already

---

[123] Many people believe that when the body dies, the soul leaves without cancer, or a scar, or injury of any kind, i.e., without any negative manifestations remaining for the spirit to carry forward. From my vision, however, I have deduced that physical scars or mental distress derived from life on this plane of existence can and often do remain, even as the soul moves on. Such maladies the soul must learn to release of its own accord or through Spirit intervention. Since first writing, I have received corroboration for this line of reasoning as contained in metaphysical and supernatural sources too numerous to detail.

exist in some world of time and space. A contemplative may hear a rushing sound, like a wailing wind in a tunnel, along with a sensation of incredible speed. But as explained, Soul doesn't move; Soul *is*. Time and space adjust to Soul's state of consciousness, and it is this adjustment of time and space that renders an illusion of movement or breathtaking speed.[124]

---

[124] Klemp, Harold. *Past Lives, Dreams and Soul Travel: Soul Travel.* Eckankar Spiritual Center of Minnesota, 2008. Web. 24 Aug. 2011.

Journal Entry 61

Thursday, 11/11/2004
Veteran's Day
Around 1:00 p.m.

"B" is for Bouquet on Veteran's Day

"I'll See You Again" [125]

My mother came to stay before Veteran's Day. She usually arrives a week or two before Christmas, but she came a lot earlier this year. I was certainly glad to have her and made sure the guest room was clean and stacked with extra towels.

In honor of Max and all our veterans, Mom and I visited the cemetery today and placed a bouquet of flowers and a lovely wreathe by his headstone. On the way in, we stopped off at the cemetery computer station. I wanted to give Mom a copy of Max's site map, like mine.

♪ ♪ ♪

As we stroll over to the computer station, I see that the letter "B" is already blinking on the screen. "Hey look, a 'B'!" I say. In fact, the letter started blinking before I even approached the screen to type Max's last name, "B-L-A-U."

"Uncanny," I say as Mom claps her hands in delight. Now, all I have to do is type the remaining letters, "L-A-U" and we're on our way.

We're sure experiencing quite a few coincidences these days, aren't we?

---

[125] Westlife. "I'll See You Again." *Where We Are.* Syco, Sony. 2009. CD.

Journal Entry 62

Saturday, 11/20/2004
Waxing gibbous moon
Around 6:30 a.m.

That Buzzing Sound and Boppin' Sheep

Reminds me of Lamb Chop in the
"Song that Doesn't End" [126]

Awakening from a deep slumber, I sit up straight. It's that buzzing noise again, but now it's by my left ear. I flick at my earlobe with thumb and forefinger.

What is causing this strange phenomenon? Is it simply the remnant of a dream?

I don't think so. The sound is so loud and all encompassing that I think it must be coming from something at my periphery. Flopping to my left, I feel the sheets; then I tap my ear and scour it out with a tissue. *Nothing there, thank you.* I'm relieved it's not an insect. Once as a child, there was a bug in my ear – a hairy experience for any kid!

Finally, the sound subsides, then ceases altogether and I come to the happy conclusion, *it's the weekend. I set my clock for nine a.m., not six-thirty.*

So I lie back on the bed, hoping to catch that longed-for snooze. Nevertheless, as my mind begins to drift, I'm reluctantly replaying the ear episode and the whirring sounds while visualizing books spinning around the table. One by one, these and other bizarre events emerge

---

[126] Lewis, Shari. "Song that Doesn't End." *Lamb Chop's Sing-Along Play-Along Audio.* Universal. 1992. CD.

before my eyes, like boppin' sheep doing a line dance through my life.... Dutifully, I find myself counting them, wishing they'd just go away.

Before long, my riotous recollections and the sheep begin to fade like little clumps of cotton whirling in the wind. The next thing I hear is my alarm clock, about as bristly as the buzz, considering I just dozed off.

"It can't be that time already." Yawning my way to my feet, I hit the alarm button and check the dial. "Yup, it is."

Those boppin' lamb chops did a number on me.

Post Script

Maybe I'll take the truck out to the desert and do some target practice today. This time, I'm going to rustle up a new target.

Disco sheep!

Sunday, 11/21/2004
Waxing gibbous moon
At 6:45 a.m.

Inspiring Words from Max

It's just like heaven being here with you
You're like an angel too good to be true... [127]

In a twilight sleep, I'm hugging a lump of something. Snoozing away, I am inclined to think it's Max. "I'm sorry I lost you," I say as tears stream down my cheeks and dampen downy pillows. A cheery hum fills the room. Soon I come to the cosmic conclusion that the chirp is emanating from a creature of a different sort. Lifting my head no more than an inch, at last, recognition rouses all my senses – I'm sniffing the mane of a black and white cat.

"Oh, Allie!" I snort, wiping angel hair from my mouth.

Soon kitty releases a high-pitched moan as if put off by foul subtext.

So hoping I didn't offend the little darling, I stroke her ears and say, "There, sweet pea, it's alright. I love ya, don't ya know?" Before long, she's hanging loose and I pull her close. "Mmmm, life is good," I say as we lay back and start to doze off.

Not for long. You see, something or someone is trying to disrupt that dreamy state of freedom we so rightly deserve. Groaning, I soon realize I won't get that Sunday snooze after all. It's just impossible to sleep because an incessant murmur is now surrounding my bed like a

---

[127] Rosie & the Originals. "Angel Baby." *Angel Baby.* Highland, 1960. LP.

high-pitched electromagnetic charge. *Where is this strange sound coming from?*

I put an ear up to baby's head and she gives me a sideways glance, like *hey dude, what's happenin'?* She has stopped purring now, but the maddening drone persists!

What can I do?

Nothing.

Well, maybe I'll just close my eyes and focus on my breathing.

Then before long, the solution....

It is coming in more clearly now... that rich, familiar music.

"Max?"

In a blaze, I hear an echo as his thoughts stream to the forefront of my consciousness. I sigh, scooping up the pillows, gathering up the words of my beloved seraphim. Then, turning to the end table, I stumble upon pad and pen. Quickly, before losing this beautiful train of thought, I set his words and sentiments down in writing, beginning with a few of my own:

From the spirit of Max Blau to me
For all posterity to see:

"You haven't lost anything
And you have gained so much more
In Love and Compassion,
In Insight into What Is,
Into All That Is!"

As documented by Mandy Berlin
On November 21, 2004

Toady and the Muppets

*This journal entry is reminiscent of the song
"Wild Thing" by The Troggs...*[128]

Max's brother used to call him Toad. The name had a way of sticking. In fact, one Christmas I bought Max a little light-up toad for his jacket. He even deigned to wear it when he was in the mood. The following year, we ordered Mistletoads labels for our Christmas cards. Toads were becoming a delightful way of celebrating our lives.

Then one night, Max and I were telling each other stories, about all the mischief we'd gotten into as kids. Amazingly, Max learned some lessons about nature at a very young age. I am not surprised. He was always inquisitive and single-minded to a fault. He said that when he was a child, he was never happy unless he saw things for himself. He wondered if his parents and teachers were wrong. So he decided he had to learn firsthand. That way, he would know for sure.

Even back then, he thought like a true engineer.

So, after some prodding on my part, Max finally confessed that one time when he was a tyke, he did something just plain ridiculous. Of course, he did it because his parents told him not to do it – ever. It was a cold winter day and Max was playing in the snow by his house. The time was right. Today would be the day he would test his parents'

---

[128] The Troggs. "Wild Thing." *From Nowhere.* Fontana, 1966. LP.

assumptions. He would make the risky decision to play the game, "I wonder what would happen if...."

And, as if to defy the very laws of nature, Max put his tongue up to an icy pole. Well, it didn't take long for him to find out what would happen. In less than a spine-chilling moment, his tongue stuck to the pole! To make matters worse, Max soon realized that no one was around to help him get his tongue back...

...in one piece! Sticky situation. What could this little boy do?

Well before long, Max noticed that the warmth of his breath began to melt the ice... millimeter by millimeter. And in those daunting moments that must have seemed like hours, at last Max was able to retract his tongue without undue suffering, except perhaps for the indignity of it all. You see, the little lad was so horrified by what he had done that he ran in the house and told his parents.

🎵 🎵 🎵

So today, I'm sipping a mocha coffee, my Thanksgiving dessert, while watching a Muppet movie.[129] And who, or what, should appear on my television screen? Why, it's a tiny toad or frog or other amphibious animal. The poor little guy is crying for Kermit's assistance. Due to the toady's miniscule size, I can barely hear what he says. Perhaps it goes something like this: "Ermie, elp ee! Elp ee, Ermie!" He is moaning, to no avail. Then, as the camera rolls in, at last, I catch a glimpse of the little fellow in full form.

Alas, his tongue is stuck to something.

No, it can't be.

Yes, it is.

---

[129] *It's a Very Merry Muppet Christmas Movie.* Dir. Kirk Thatcher. Perf. The Muppets. Jim Henson Pictures, 2002. Film.

An icy pole! I lose it, coffee shooting out of my nostrils, splattering all over my jeans. Grabbing some napkins, I holler, "Hey, it's like déjà vu!"

Then quicker than you can say *parallel universe,* comes that clear, resolute sound: *Luv, it's like déjà went!*

JOURNAL ENTRY 65

Saturday, 11/27/2004
Full moon
Around 7:00 p.m.

Nativity Scene by the Gift Shop

Seasons change with the scenery
Weaving time in a tapestry...[130]

After Mass, my mother and I took a stroll over to the parish gift shop to buy some cards and curios for the holidays. As is often the case, we ended up purchasing more than we'd set out to acquire.

❧ ❧ ❧

Feeling jovial, even after paying the clerk, we carry our crinkly packages out to the patio and wander around in the brisk night air. Mom sets her gifts down on a bench and buttons up her wool coat. I wrap my shawl around my neck and mouth, covering chapped lips.

"Smells like the white stuff's on its way," Mom says.

"Even if we do live in Arizona," I add in a muffled tone.

"I'd be surprised if it doesn't snow," Mom cries, stomping her feet. "Wish I'd worn my boots."

"Yeah, me too. So, let's get some hot soup," I say, too chilled to elaborate.

Mom turns to me and says, "Okay, where shall we go?"

"Someplace with a hearth."

"Sounds good, let's go," she said. "Mandy?"

---

[130] Simon & Garfunkel. "A Hazy Shade of Winter." *Bookends.* Columbia, 1968. LP.

"Hmmm?" Looking up at the evening sky, I can hardly hear my mother's voice for I'm lost in a dream... low, wintry clouds roll along at a clipper's pace as I step into a clearing dotted with stars. Turning to my left, I am amazed to find the moon half hidden behind the branches of a deciduous tree. Brighter than the evening sun, this perfectly round sphere illuminates a nativity scene perched on a corrugated rooftop.

"What a sight!" I say, as my soul comes to know the bliss of the boundless night.

Post Script

This wonderful evening reminded me that I have not told everything. For, I remember now that I saw Max in the garden south of the church – late in January, I believe. Mom had stayed in church after Mass to talk to Father O'Laughlin.

🐾 🐾 🐾

I'm strolling along the garden path by the church and I stumble across a stone bench. The air is invigorating but not cold. So I stop and sit down, taking in the sweet desert scene and the silence of the evening.

Then, at once, I sense his presence.

Soon I see him clearly. He is wearing that vest with the Rupert the Bear emblem on it. And with that, I smell smoke. Unthinkingly, I almost say, "Luv, you're not smoking, are you? We're at church now." Good thing I bit my tongue. I mean, how can a smoking soul affect anything? Yet, he is affecting me because he seems so real! At last, I say silently, *how are you, Max? You seem... at peace... and I with you.* The essence of his smile envelopes my being and we bask in the joy and wonder of each other's presence.

Then, without warning, I'm smelling my mother's perfume. Slowly, I turn to face the verdict. "Mandy, I've been looking for you! What are you doing all the way over here?"

🐞 🐞 🐞

I jumped up and *poof*, he vanished! Our secret space was gone. Quickly, I tried to brush it off, hoping Mom wouldn't think I might be having a clandestine affair with a dead man, husband though he was!

"Dear, I was just enjoying this beautiful day, that's all," I said rather stiffly. I hadn't told a lie. Yet somehow, I felt about as guilty as a church mouse pilfering a chunk of cheese at the feet of Father O'Laughlin.

"Well, come on!" she said.

"All right," I said, buttoning up my coat and straightening my scarf. Then I took her hand. "Okay, so let's go to breakfast, what do you say?" *Perhaps this will appease her.*

"Okay," was all she said, rather glumly.

Now I see that burying my recollections of this awesome experience caused me to forget all about it. But I must own up. You see, our affair in the garden happened several times again, and I still haven't confessed to Father O.

JOURNAL ENTRY 66
Tuesday, 11/30/2004
Waning gibbous moon
Afternoon

Thought Forms and Automatic Writing
In that small café, the park across the way
The children's carousel, the chestnut tree, the wishing well…[131]

Today I was sitting in one of my favorite cafes where I sometimes grab a bite and do my writing – like this afternoon because the place was almost empty. My work week has been hectic already and concentration is not always the default mode por moi. Still, after a delightful meal, with cup of coffee in hand, I began to feel renewed and ready to write. Music was playing in the background lending a cool, harmonious atmosphere to the place.

♪ ♪ ♪

I am relaxed, at peace.

Though I am not doing any deep breathing or conscious contemplation, the music begins to lull me into a meditative state. Maybe because I'm feeling rather receptive, mental pictures, patterns and sounds begin to emerge. These appear to be thought forms racing toward me without warning. So I set down my cup and fumble through my briefcase for pad and pen as I lightly fall into something I can only describe as a glorious state of reverie. Before long, without any effort, I find my pen moving across the page, recording the flow that comes

---

[131] Crosby, Bing. "I'll Be Seeing You." *Bing: A Musical Autobiography*. Decca, 1954. LP.

seemingly out of nowhere. Because of my doodles and illegible scrawl, I later rewrote these words. However, please note that I did not change or otherwise try to improve upon the words transmitted to me:

> *We are all in and out, coming and going, back and forth, Yin and Yang. God always was, always will be, always stays the same. Like God, our spirit is always there.*
>
> *We simply change form.*
>
> *Change is everything. We are coming and going, Yin and Yang, out and in, around and around, up and down, inside out, outside in.... wheeee!*

As I write what I hear, I feel like a conduit. Images burst forth and flicker in my field of view. I sense a strong presence, an intelligence if you will. Like, I hear the word *"wheee"* and catch an amusingly colorful character doing cartwheels, flips and summersaults in mid-air... so free, *so now*. Is it Max? Perhaps it is, because he was into the now of Buddhism, but I cannot absolutely say that this is his spirit. If it is, then he has changed his normal appearance, like shape-shifting perhaps? In any event, a moment or two before each entity, form, or symbol flies toward me, I hear a voice, like a **vardøger**[132] reminiscent of Spirit's ability to **bilocate**.[133]

---

[132] The **vardøger** or **vardøgr** is a spirit predecessor, from Norwegian folklore. Stories typically include instances that are nearly déjà vu in substance, but in reverse, where a spirit with the subject's footsteps, voice, scent, or appearance and overall demeanor precedes them in a location or activity, resulting in witnesses believing they've seen or heard the actual person, before the person physically arrives.... It has been likened to being a phantom double, or form of bilocation. "Doppelganger." *Haunted America Tours.* Haunted America Tours, N.d. Web. 25 Aug. 2011.

[133] **Bilocation**, or sometimes **multilocation**, is a term used to describe the ability/ instances in which an individual or object is said to be, or appears to be, located in

I feel confident that these images, patterns and expressions are not being created by me. That is, I do not believe I could possibly have witnessed the sights, signs and symbols, nor heard these words – *and* managed to scribble down the lexis in such a cataleptic manner – without having made the connection to Source.

Toward the end of this mind-bending rendezvous, my scrawl trails off into something resembling dots and squiggles. Now as I emerge from this stupor, I find my head bobbing just above the table. *Yikes!* I jerk it back before my nose hits the surface. Dazed, I attempt to focus on my surroundings, and I glance at my watch. *Good thing it's late in the day... nobody around to notice the strange goings-on at my table.* Though not strange to me, I'm sure that to almost any observer, it would seem pretty weird. So I smooth out the wrinkles in my sweater and try to sit up straight before any customers arrive.

Feeling a sense of fatigue after experiencing the incredible connection to All That Is, I call for my waiter who's probably hiding in a back room somewhere. Glad of that, I can only hope he wasn't watching. If he was, he didn't let on because he is now bringing my refreshments and beaming that attractive yet unrevealing server smile.

Well, even if it is an act, he deserves an extra tip, I must say.

A hefty hit of caffeine is my reward for such protracted concentration. Not that any incentive is required. This temporary incapacitation is

---

two distinct places at the same instant in time. The term has been used in a wide range of historical and philosophical systems, including early Greek philosophy..., the paranormal..., spiritualism, [and so on]. Bilocation has been observed in laboratories, albeit on the molecular level.... Several Christian saints and monks are said to have exhibited bilocation. Among the earliest is the apparition of Our Lady of the Pillar in the year 40.... The English occultist Aleister Crowley was reported by acquaintances to have the ability, even though he himself was not conscious of its happening at the time. Rahman, Fasal. "The Quantum Theory of Species." N.p., 10 Aug. 2011. Web. 25 Aug. 2011.

simply the case of human frailty rather than any lack of enthusiasm on my part! Downing the delicious coffee, I turn the page of my calendar to some earlier notes and doodles. And right there, before my bespectacled face, is an anonymous quote set inside a picture of an autumn day with a stream bubbling over brightly colored rocks. I remove my glasses and put the calendar up to my nose to read the ridiculously small script:

> *Change is the law of life. And those who look only to the*
> *past or the present are certain to miss the future.*

Funny I should turn to this obscure quotation after writing down thoughts forms on the subject of change. Synchronous thoughts, synchronous moments in time![134]

Post Script

At the time, I had no name for the remarkable event that transpired on this date. Based on subsequent readings of various books and articles, as well as the intuitive and mediumship classes I have taken since 2005,[135] I have come to know that this was my first experience with automatic writing.

For breadth, I am incorporating two definitions of automatic writing:

---

[134] Later, I learned that the author of this quote was John F. Kennedy, also discussed in Journal Entry 22, under "Max's Notes and an Extraordinary Find."

[135] Courses with renowned and well-established psychic mediums and extensive practice with their CDs, books, videos and other online media since 2005. The mediums include (in alphabetical order): Teresa Brown, Sylvia Browne, Choneye, John Holland, Sunny Dawn Johnston, Gordon Smith, and James Van Praagh.

Automatic writing (spirit writing) as defined by Zerner and Farber [136] is the writing communication that comes through spirit contact. Automatic writing is not always immediately coherent or even readable, but after several sessions it is usually possible to read the instructions or messages sent by the spirits.... **Automatic writing** as defined by Dravenstar is writing without being aware of the contents, as when a medium apparently transcribes written messages from disembodied spirits.

In addition, Dravenstar[137] defines the more general term:

Automatism - Any unconscious and spontaneous muscular movement caused by 'the spirits'. (Automatic writing.)

The reader may recall that prior to this entry, I had received many communications from Source (as in Journal Entry 33 and my documentation of the communications from Charlemagne and Max). Nevertheless, today's mind-blowing trance writing seems to differ in character and kind from my earlier experiences, i.e., hearing and/or seeing discrete words and sentences, then transcribing them one at a time.

---

[136] Zerner, Amy and Monte Farber. *Ghost Writer: Automatic Writing Kit*. New York: Sterling, 2008. Print.

[137] "Paranormal Terminology." *Dravenstar Paranormal Research Team*. N.p., 2010. Web. 25 Aug. 2011.

Thursday, 12/02/2004
Waning gibbous moon
Around 10:30 a.m.

The Metaman Tune

Max, "This One's for You"...[138]

While waiting in the doctor's office for a routine procedure, I was reading a pamphlet when, out of the blue, came "The Metaman Tune!"[139] Straight up I perched, wondering if Max's little ditty had come blazing through to me from some parallel dimension. You see, I never knew how to whistle the tune he created, back when. I mean, I could hardly even remember how it went. Max was the only one who could whistle it as perfectly as I heard it today.

🎵 🎵 🎵

So, what is "Metaman" anyway?

Well, I will tell you. One day about five years ago, Max and I had been lounging on the back patio, talking about the things we'd like to do when we retire. "Hey, I've got an idea!" he said, brushing Tiggi's coat while she lounged on the picnic table. "I'm gonna give the old folks in Sun City a fun time."

"How's that?" I asked, nose buried in a Victorian magazine.

"With popsicles – Metamucil popsicles!"

---

[138] Manilow, Barry. "This One's for You." *This One's for You.* Arista, 1976. LP.
[139] Copyright ©1999 Max Blau

The magazine slipped through my fingers, as my brain lapsed into a stupor. "Whu?"

Having captured my undivided attention, he put down the brush, and said, "Picture this: me driving a white truck, playing a little ditty as I hand out Metamucil ice cream bars in a host of flavors and colors."

"Okay, now I know you're joking."

"Nope, I'm serious as a post. Think of it! It'll be great fun for them, and me too."

I must have been boring a hole through his T-shirt, because he said, "So here's 'Metaman' – dig it!" Suddenly, Max began to whistle a jingle, impromptu, as Tiggi jumped off the picnic table.

Then, as the last lilting note bounced off the table, he sat back beaming a satisfied smile. "Well, what do ya think?"

I just shook my head and cackled, "I have to admit, Metaman, regardless of what Tiggi may think, you've created a catchy little number there. Carefree, light… a popsicle kind of tune!"

And, "The Metaman Tune" was born that very day.

But was Metaman a melody or a man? In retrospect, I think it was a little of both. Like a kid, Max whistled that tune around the house, especially on weekends, and whenever he was able to catch up with the ice cream man to get our Saturday drumsticks. Max had such a gregarious nature, I wouldn't have put it past him to ask the popsicle man what he thought of Metaman – the jingle, that is.

♪ ♪ ♪

So today, as I sit waiting for the doctor, I am preoccupied hearing Max's little ditty for the first time since he died. Its light-hearted tone brings such happy thoughts to mind. Tapping my toes, I turn the page of my medical pamphlet, and there at the bottom, what do I see?

Canisters – brightly colored Metamucil canisters! Max? I holler silently and look up at the ceiling as if I'll find him there at any moment.

Oh, what am I doing? I sigh, stashing the pamphlet in my purse. I certainly don't want anyone to notice the goings-on in my little corner of the room. Besides, it's time to take a trip down the hall before the nurse calls my name. Nevertheless, on the way back to my seat, I'm utterly taken by the voice of Karen Carpenter. Her lovely, melancholic sound resonates through the Musak system:

> *I've just one wish on this Christmas Eve*
> *I wish I were with you...*[140]

Somehow, I manage to keep my sentiments to myself until I reach the car. Then, safe inside, I let go.

---

[140] The Carpenters. "Merry Christmas Darling." *Christmas Portrait.* A&M, 1978. LP.

Monday, 12/06/2004
Around 1:30 p.m.

The Day Before Pearl Harbor Day

I keep holding on to yesterday
I keep holding on enough to say that I'm wrong...[141]

Mom and I carried a wreath of red berries and a white bouquet to Max's gravesite. I have been sad all day. You see, I remembered that one year ago today, he suffered his second stroke.

It happened the day before Pearl Harbor Day, a time of great meaning for Max and me and our loved ones. Max's stroke came on around four in the morning. While the oncology nurses worked hard to revive him, Char and I tried with single-minded purpose to hold down his strong, lean arms so he wouldn't pull the portacath out of his chest. If he had succeeded in his unconscious struggle, he would have succumbed right then and there.

But regardless of the nurses' concerted efforts and our success in holding Max throughout his terrible ordeal, no one could have prevented him from lapsing into the coma that took hold around four-thirty in the morning. Alas, I buckled into the chair at his feet and sat in abject stillness, staring at the white crust of salt on my glasses. Yet through the little holes in my crystalline window, I received some sense of comfort, catching glimpses of my love's sweet face as he lay in quiet slumber.

🙎 🙎 🙎

---

[141] Ambrosia. "Holdin' on to Yesterday." *Ambrosia.* Twentieth Century Fox, 1975. LP.

Though we adorn Max's grave with beautiful garlands and magnificent bouquets, I have come to the realization that some things in life might never be fully reconciled, in one's mind or in one's heart.

Journal Entry 69

Thursday, 12/09/2004
Around 11:00 a.m.

Max Wakes Up!

The song "Morning has Broken"
truly touched my heart on this day...[142]

One year ago today Max came out of his coma.

Early that bright December morning, the ICU nurse and several of our loved ones arrived, wanting to tend to Max's every need. For about a month, Tessie, Fritz and I had been taking turns watching him. Then, whenever possible, we slept in the visitor's area down the hall. I had spent some time with Max that morning and then realized, now that he had a crowd around him, it would be a good time to go home, grab a shower and pick up some things from the store.

When I returned to the hospital, I nearly ran into Max's sisters who were hurrying down the hall of the ICU.

.♪. .♪. .♪.

Char, cheeks flushed, rushes up and gives me a hug. "Hey Mandy, Max just came out of his coma! And when he came to, he was shouting, 'Jubilee, jubilee, jubilee!'"

I could not speak. I was stunned!

"He's sitting up," Paulette fairly hollers, "talking like he never left!"

"Oh God!" I say, at last.

Char chimes in, "Mark is with him now!"

---

[142] Stevens, Cat. "Morning Has Broken." *Teaser and the Firecat.* A&M, 1971. LP.

"Mark?" I ask, still flabbergasted by the news.

"Oh man, he made it!" I say, but silently, I chide myself for not being there when Max regained consciousness. Then, out of the blue, the news flash finally hits me like the detonation of a warehouse full of Christmas candy. "Good God, guys, I have to go!"

"Love you...."

Dashing 'round the bend, I'm crying tears of joy all the way to Max's room.

And there he is perched in bed like a blessed bird, chattering away with his brother, Mark, who has just arrived from Sacramento. I hop on the bed like a jackrabbit, undaunted by the incessant conversation. Then Max turns, beaming a soulful smile as I plant a kiss on his face. Awestruck by the very idea that he is able to speak, I touch his mouth. He takes my arm and draws me near, as he and Mark natter on. *Wow Max,* I silently say, *you're really here.* I marvel at the resonant sound of his voice – and his eyes, all lit up like Christmas candles. It's as if he has been out-of-town on an incredible journey. From the sound of his stories, I believe he has!

Post Script

I will never forget this beautiful day. What's more, I have hopes that these precious memories will replace the sad ones that we tend to remember during the most difficult time of all, the first year after.

JOURNAL ENTRY 70

Sunday, 12/19/2004
First quarter moon
Around 11:00 a.m.

Church and *The Man with Two Brains*

If you like-a-me like I like-a-you
And we like-a-both the same...[143]

I took Mom to church and before the Mass ended, our pastor turned to all of his parishioners and gave us a fatherly directive. Arms spread wide, he said, "And now go forth!"

"Or go fifth and lose the race!" It's Max's voice, out of nowhere.

"Max!" I whisper, trying to choke the chuckle in my craw. *I can't let him give me away – not in church.* Somehow managing to suppress utter glee, I send Max a silent message. *You're trying to crack me up, but I can't do that now. We're in church, man,* I say, as if Metaman doesn't know.

He says, "Hey, hey, Ann Uumellmahaye!" He is telepathically "shouting out" her name. For those who haven't seen the movie, *The Man with Two Brains,* Ann Uumellmahaye (pronounced Uh-mel-ma-hey) is one of the characters who has a rather bizarre relationship of her own with a Doctor Hfurhruhuhr, played by Steve Martin. [144] (But please, don't ask me to pronounce the doctor's name!) Well, for some strange reason – I suppose because the movie is funny and the names are

---

[143] Collins, Arthur. "Under the Bamboo Tree." *Under the Bamboo Tree.* Victor, 1903. LP.

[144] *The Man with Two Brains.* Dir. Carl Reiner. Perf. Steve Martin, Kathleen Turner, and David Warner. Warner Bros., 1983. Film.

269

just ridiculous – it had become the subject of ongoing silliness between Max and me.

Now I realize for the very first time how never-ending a connection can be.

After the priest gives us his blessing, I am struck by the fact that I heard Ann's name about a week ago. Max was the culprit, of course, causing the racket then too. I was having lunch at one of our old haunts – apparently one that he still frequents to this day. But how did this event slip my mind for an entire week? Am I becoming blasé about Max's comings and goings? Still, what happened that day seems so vivid to me now.

At last, the priestly procession reaches the door. Now Max is carrying on even more, with his whoop-de-do blasts from beyond. I just can't take it anymore. Covering my cheery chops, I give Mom the high sign and dash off to the little Ladies.

Somehow, I manage to forestall a belly laugh till I reach the last pew, the one reserved for those requiring assistance.

♪ ♪ ♪

On the way home, Mom and I decide to swing by a cafe. But before we reach our destination, Max is fast resuming his antics, becoming sillier by the second. "Na na na na!" Sounds like Chevy Chase in the movie, *Caddyshack*.[145] The echoes of this fond refrain and Max's eye-catching puppet performance make me lose it again. But at least now, I can belly laugh all I want without fear of reprisal.

---

[145] *Caddyshack*. Dir. Harold Ramis. Perf. Chevy Chase, Rodney Dangerfield, and Bill Murray. Warner Bros., 1980. Film.

Out of the blue, Mom turns to me with that sardonic look in her eye. "You've been hooting and howling all morning. Tell me, what's so funny?"

I shake my head and say, "Sweetie, you wouldn't believe it if I told you."

Of course I'd like to tell her, but what can I say? It's difficult.

Then she gives me a wink, and as we reach our welcome destination, says, "Boy am I hungry." Nothing more, nothing less.

"Me too."

I wonder if she knows.

Thursday, 12/23/2004
Waxing gibbous moon
High noon

The Silver Star and Other
Christmas Mysteries

Here we are as in olden days,
Happy golden days of yore...[146]

It is hard to believe that Max died one year ago today. In some ways, it seems he left just yesterday – like when I see or sense his spirit or witness the phenomenal movement of objects in my home. In other ways, it seems like years since Max passed away because I cannot see him in the flesh, or talk to him in any ordinary way.

Today Mom brought an exquisite white wreath to Silver Star Way where Max was laid to rest. I carried a red rose and placed it solemnly on his gravestone. Together, we carried a beautiful statue of a gilded angel, positioning it and the wreath behind the rose. Yet, no matter what we do or how we try to cope, I realize that difficult days still come, at times. For despite having heard Max just the other day, I could not stop bawling before his shrine as I read Psalm 23, the one so dear to him. Now to me.

♪ ♪ ♪

Perhaps Sylvia Browne said it best. To paraphrase her words: you may be intuitive enough to see or hear your loved one after he dies, but

---

[146] Sinatra, Frank. "Have Yourself a Merry Little Christmas." *A Jolly Christmas from Frank Sinatra.* Capitol, 1957. LP.

it's not like you can take him out to a restaurant and have a cup of coffee with him.[147] Oh, how true that is. I am only beginning to realize what it's all about. We must each accept the torch of grief inherent in loss and embrace ways of surmounting it over time. Isn't that what life is all about – riding the changes we experience because of the gains, losses and break even periods of our lives? Would we truly expect to stay on an even keel from birth to death?

What would be gained from a life without change, if that were even possible? It would probably be monotonous and unenlightening. What would we ever learn?

And so, as I reflect on the day, it seems strange that my behavior should have taken a foul turn so quickly. As we drove past a colorful sea of swags and sprays, I decided it was time to break the less-than-merry news. "Mom, I know you've been waiting for the word, but I've decided I don't want a Christmas tree this year."

"Why, Mandy!" She seemed stunned, but I continued anyway.

"Mom, I can't cope with even the thought of a tree!"

"Well, I was just hoping that…"

"No, absolutely not!" How rude, I wouldn't even allow her to finish her sentence. Water streamed down my cheeks. I looked the other way, appalled by my own outburst.

Soon I began to calm down, feeling awful about my behavior. I finally grasped that all my mother wanted was a little joy and Christmas spirit. How could I deny her that? I certainly could not, and would not. Yet, with the anniversary of my husband's death falling so close to Christmas Day, how could I pretend to be merry or act as if things were peachy?

---

[147] Browne, *op. cit.*

My mind tripped back to the holidays of yesteryear... decorating the tree with Max... a beautiful time for the two of us. Like our May anniversary and my birthday on the first of June, we seldom allowed work to interfere with that wonderful week of ours. Christmas week was the same, a real tradition for us. A few years back, Max fashioned a silver star from cardboard and foil. I remembered his face, beaming like the very star he handed me to place on top of the tree, as I stood on a step ladder.

It was the most beautiful Christmas gift I had ever received.

Rubbing the goose bumps on my arms, I noticed we had just turned off *Silver Star Way.* At last, I understood. This was meant to be my dear one's place of rest. And as we drove past the American flag, blowing freely in the wind, another virtual boulder hit me on the head.

Oh Lord, I don't want a tree because I'm afraid to open the box containing the star.

So that's it. But where is the box?

Well, sigh, *I suppose it's in the garage with a dozen other Christmas boxes.*

So, just ignore the box with the star.

But I don't know which box holds the star!

In quiet desperation, I turned to my mother. How I wanted to talk to her, but the words would not come. How could I possibly tell her about these weird thoughts and fears? I hardly understood them myself.

Then that profile, the inscrutable June Cleaver again. Or was it the Queen of England this time?

No matter. I knew I was lucky to have a caring Mom, energetic and patient more often than not. And as we drove out the cemetery gate, I listened to her suggestion. "Mandy, forget the tree. Maybe we can just set the wooden manger on the mantle along with The Three Kings. We can place them, like guards, all around the manger." The Three Kings is the name I'd given my collection of old world Santas – three ceramic figurines draped in fine cloth. Mom knows I am fond of them too.

"Okay, sweetie," I said. "What do you say we do it after dinner? Maybe I'll be more with it by then." Breathing a sigh of relief, I remembered I had stored the manger and the kings in a closet, not in the garage. They weren't anywhere near the silver star.

"Okay, honey," she replied.

I took her gloved hand. "Mom, I'm sorry. I've had blinders on. I didn't mean to raise my voice or cut off your words." She turned and smiled that disarming, childlike smile of hers and pressed my fingers in her hand, as if to say everything's okay.

How dear she is to me!

Yet, even as we entered the freeway heading south, I knew my biggest fear was yet to come:

How will I ever get through Max's time? Nine p.m., the time of his death. I can't believe it happened one year ago tonight. Oh God, can't we skip this day? Why can't we just fast forward to Friday?

♪ ♪ ♪

I was relieved to get through dinner and the ritual decorating of the manger. We even played two rather upbeat games of Scrabble. But now Mom has returned to her bedroom to put things away... leaving me alone with the television set... leaving me to my own devices....

Leaving me alone with all my fears. Now I see that Christmas will never be the same. How can it be?

All this time to reflect. Why am I pacing now?

Too much time to think.

Finally, I sit down on Max's old hassock and glance up at the mantle. I admit the manger and the three kings look nice up there. No, they look beautiful with a misty kind of serenity. The simplicity of this awe-inspiring scene prompts me to go over to the manger and touch the wooden baby. I stand there in desolation...

... and in exhortation.

"Jesus, why?" I ask, water pouring down my face.

"Why did they leave us so soon, Max and our dear friends and loved ones?"

"I know they are 'there,' but they are not here, in the flesh, and my whole life has changed. Forever."

This woman who, in earlier ruminations, seemed to have accepted and even welcomed the idea of change is balking at the very thought of it.

"I know that I must learn to live without them," I say, softly taking the little icon from His humble bed of hay.

"But Jesus, for the rest of my life? It seems like such a long time. I wish I were there with You, and with them, too."

"But Lord, I know they are in Your hands now. Will You please take care of them for me?" I wipe the water dripping on the loincloth of His likeness and gently place the little statue back in the manger.

"Thanks, Baby Jesus, I know You will."

Returning to the hassock, at last I dry my tears with the recognition that my grief has gone on too long. I thought it had finally stopped. Once again, I am taken by surprise.

What to do now?

Well, maybe some food....

Like that would help, the last thing I need.

"Oh well." I wipe my face on my sleeve, remembering we haven't had dessert yet. So I traipse through the dining room in stocking feet. Shrugging I say, "Just two little pieces of choco...."

"What?" As sweet truffles swim through the recesses of my mind, a clamor rises up on my kitchen counter! I screech, and jump back. "What is this?" Soon my chocolate reverie melts away, and I find myself cowering in the corner like a frightened foal. Or is it fool? For I am unable to make any sense out of the bizarre demonstration happening before me: my mother's Santa tray and teaspoon are spinning wildly on the counter, flying up in the air, and down, then up again. Stupefied, I scream, yet I cannot look away! The energy burgeoning from this *thing* is fantastic! As the tray rotates in mid-air, the spoon spins *upright underneath it.*

"What is happening?" I shout, all the while thinking, *this flies in the face of natural law.* Now the spoon and tray are doing a dance, as if entertaining the cream and sugar bowls beside them. White stuff drifts all over the counter, a dazzling day at Snowbowl. *As if I am not already stunned, the spoon raises the big metal tray high into the air and stands erect like a champion beneath it. The tray starts rotating wildly, buzzing up and down, a spinning top at a three-ring circus. Incredibly, the spoon is still standing upright beneath the tray!* My ears are ringing. "This isn't real." The riotous rumba persists as images from a nursery rhyme come swiftly to mind, "…and the dish ran away with the spoon."[148]

At last, the gyrations begin to decelerate. The spoon topples to the counter, tray collapsing on top of it. Even as my chest retrieves my heart from my throat, I glance at the kitchen clock. "My God, it's almost nine!" *Ten minutes before the time of Max's death, one year ago today.*
"Max!"

♪ ♪ ♪

I rested on the counter barstool just long enough to catch my breath and cool down. Soon I was shaking my head, laughing -- marveling over the whole wacky scene. What about my bizarre fate? *No one will ever believe this.* So I slid a pen and a pad of sticky notes my way and

---

[148] From the "Hey Diddle Diddle" nursery rhyme.

jotted down the time the whole show started -- about 8:45 p.m. Still, there was something else I had to do.

Go, do it now!

I grabbed the note. *This time, I must do it right.*

I dashed to Mom's room; she was sitting there reading a book. "Hey sweetie," I smiled and took her hand. "C'mon, there's something I want to show you!"

"What?" she said.

"You'll see," I said, smiling.

Gently, I pulled her up and out of her chair. This time, she got up and followed me without a grumble. This time, I described the mind-boggling scene that had just taken place in my kitchen. This time, she saw things for herself, marveling over the uncanny mess on the counter.

Then I handed her the sticky note. "Mom, it happened around a quarter to nine, just minutes before Max's time."

She looked at the note, then at the clock. Then she did a double-take and her mouth dropped. "Why, Mandy, I don't believe it!" she whooped.

"But I do!" she continued. "See, I heard some peculiar sounds coming from the kitchen, but I didn't have my hearing aid on to catch it all." Then she chuckled and said, "I wondered what you were up to. Boy, that must have been something, because I could hear clanging sounds even without my earpiece!"

"Wish I'd come sooner," she said in that sweet way of hers. She just shook her head.

"Oh Mom!" I gave her a "smooch" on her pearly face.

Once again, through the Source of all creation, Max had made himself known in a wacky and wonderful way. What's more, Mom believed me this time. We hugged and did a little jig in the kitchen and topped off our miniature champagne glasses with peach brandy the rest of the night. For we had a lot to celebrate. Max had come to greet us on his day and for Christmas too! Once again he reminded us, in his own brilliant way, that he was never late for any important occasion.

Through the years we all will be together, if the fates allow
Hang a shining star upon the highest bow...[149]

Post Script

Well, that was just the beginning.

You know, I'm glad there's no such thing as fast forwarding a date. I mean, who'd want to skip a day like this? No, Christmas will never be the same. It will always be new and bright, a shining silver star to light my way.

---

[149] Sinatra, *op. cit.*

EPILOGUE

September 2011

After reading about a hundred pages of **Death Is Not "The End,"** my mother called to tell me something she said was important – something that had happened in 1968 or 1969. At that time, I was living in Southern California. Mom and Dad were living in their home in Stamford, Connecticut, no more than a block away from the Long Island Sound.

On the night of this occasion, Mom said she awoke from sleep to find Dad sitting up in bed, talking out loud.

How odd! she thought. *He appears to be talking to somebody, but no one else is in the room.*

"Are you dreaming, George?" Mom asked softly.

He replied without hesitation. "No, I'm talking to my mother." Yet, his mom (my dear Grandma Agnes) had died in 1966.

Stunned, Mom said, "Your mother?"

"Yes, I'm talking to my mother."

Mom told me that Dad appeared to be looking into the dresser mirror while he spoke, as if he could see his mother's spirit through the looking glass. Curious, Mom quizzed him. "Well, what are you talking about?"

"She asked me if I'm eating well and if I'm feeling alright."

My mother said, back then, she did not believe he could have possibly been talking to Agnes, or to her soul, or whatever. Then, in an effort to get her husband to come to his senses, she hollered, "George, you're dreaming!"

"No," he said, losing all patience. "I'm not dreaming, Grace, I saw her!"

♪ ♪ ♪

On October 18, 2009, my dear Allie had to be put to sleep due to complications resulting from kidney disease. The front and back covers of my book, and the image on the next page were shaped by a vision I had of Max with Allie perched on his shoulders! They stayed for awhile, then bid me farewell with beams of love, and I watched dumbstruck as Max turned and carried our littlest darling into the light.

Then on December 1, 2012, Tiggi followed with stage IV kidney disease. Bless my little Angel, I am happy and privileged to say that she stayed by my side for nineteen and a half years. Yet, even now I receive sporadic glimpses of our dear ones in heavenly dreams. They want us to know – and to truly bear in mind – that they are all together now, joyously awaiting the day we arrive on the Other Side.

With Love and Gratitude,
Mandy

Max, Allie and the Light at Day's End by Artist Amy Whitehouse
To see more of the colorful artwork created for this endeavor,
go to my website at http://mandyberlin.wordpress.com/

About the Author

Mandy Berlin, MEd, is an author, teacher, counselor, and retired statistician who completed her doctoral examinations in educational psychology at Arizona State University. Berlin loves writing, especially about the supernatural, a subject dear to her heart. She offers workshops and confidential consultations on harnessing the Law of Attraction via orders@mandymax.net.

Front-cover art: Tawny Gamboa
Back-cover art: Amy Whitehouse
Photo of Mandy's Pinned Butterfly: Paula (Cami) Cowan
Author Photo: Edward Buchmann, Edification Studios

INDEX

A

Agnostic
  agnosticism iii, xxviii, 60
Akashic Field
  (A-Field) xviii, xxxi, 28
amoeba 44, 46, 48
astral plane 122
automatic writing 257, 261
Automatism 261

B

bilocate
  bilocation 258
Braden, Gregg 161, 162, 163
brain waves 40
Browne, Sylvia 105, 109, 111, 142,
  260, 272, 273
Brown, Teresa
  (aka Brown-Konell, Teresa) i,
    ix, 260
butterfly 30, 31, 32, 33, 34, 36,
  178, 179
Byrne, Rhonda 154, 203

C

Caddyshack 270
Carroll, Lewis 72
chance ii, 34, 36, 76, 117, 120, 122,
  129, 139
Choneye x, 260
cognition

paranormal 21
cognitive dissonance 124
coincidence 36, 41, 103, 156, 161,
  168, 228
consciousness xxvii, 16, 26, 27, 28, 46,
  57, 145, 159, 160, 177, 190, 232,
  239, 245, 250, 268
cosmos 164
Crowley, Aleister 259
Curie, Marie 59

D

déjà vu 28, 56, 102, 197, 253, 258
  déjà vecu 28
Dooley, Mike 161, 203
Dossey, Larry 64
Dravenstar 261

E

Eckankar 244, 245
Einstein 21
  Einstein, Albert 157, 160
Elegant Universe, The 164
energy xxii, 45, 46, 50, 58, 63, 113,
  122, 150, 157, 158, 159, 160,
  162, 203, 204, 225, 231, 277
event(s)
  phenomenological xi, xxiv, 207
  rare xxi, 23, 153
  supernatural xi, xix, xx, xxi, xxviii,
    7, 16, 24, 26, 54, 193, 207,
    244, 285

synchronistic xxi, xxvi, 152
synchronous 36, 42, 146, 152,
    177, 194, 232, 260
experiment(s)
    blind 120
    least force 117, 119
    main 115, 117, 119, 121, 151
    normal force 116, 117
    preliminary 115, 116, 117, 121
extrasensory perception (ESP) 21

F

factor(s)
    environmental 121
    extraneous 121
Farber, Monte 261
Foster, Alan Dean 63
frequency(ies)
    distribution of 157
    of repetition xxi
    of vibration 157–160, 179, 203
    vibrational 158, 159

G

Ghost xxvi, 39, 41, 42, 261
ghost(s) xxvi, 41, 43, 49, 50, 122
    vestige(s) of life 122
God 5, 15, 18, 19, 30, 41, 45, 46, 85,
    95, 107, 114, 122, 127, 134,
    153, 154, 161, 163, 215, 244,
    258, 267, 268, 275, 277. *See
    also* Spirit, The Source
Goleman, Daniel 238
Grahame, Kenneth 89, 200
gravity 150, 157, 204, 224, 225
Güijosa, Alberto 150

H

Haanel, Charles 155
haunt(s) (ed) 148, 258

haunting(s) 21, 24
    intelligent haunt(s) xx, 122
    residual haunt xx, 122, 195
Hawkins, David
    Hawkins 159
Holland, John 260
holofield xxxi
hologram 19, 27, 28, 40, 146, 197
hypothesis(es)
    null 119
    significant difference 120
    working 119

I

intuition 28
*It's a Very Merry Muppet Christmas
    Movie* 252

J

Johnston, Sunny Dawn x, xxi, xxii,
    37, 260

K

Kaku, Michio 151, 152, 164
Kennedy, John F. 94, 260
Kirkpatrick, Betty 24
Klemp, Harold 245
Kübler-Ross, Elisabeth 183
Kuhn, Thomas 164

L

Laszlo, Ervin xviii, xxxi, 26, 28
Law of Attraction xxii, xxvii, 155, 160,
    164, 203, 204, 285
Leary, Timothy 149
Leave it to Beaver 33

M

magnetic force 45
manifest(ed) 204, 232